THE POWERS
OF
PRESERVATION

THE POWERS
OF
PRESERVATION

NEW LIFE FOR URBAN

HISTORIC PLACES

ARTHUR COTTON MOORE

McGraw-Hill
NEW YORK SAN FRANCISCO WASHINGTON, D.C. AUCKLAND
BAGOTÁ CARACAS LISBON LONDON MADRID MEXICO CITY
MILAN MONTREAL NEW DELHI SAN JUAN
SINGAPORE SYDNEY TOKYO TORONTO

Library of Congress Cataloging-in-Publication Data

Moore, Arthur Cotton,
    The powers of preservation/Arthur Cotton Moore.
      p. cm.
    ISBN 0-07-043394-1
  1. Architecture—Washington (D.C.)—Conservation and restoration.
  2. Buildings—Remodeling for other use—Washington (D.C.)
  3. Architecture—United States—Conservation and restoration.
  4. Buildings—Remodeling for other use—United States. I. Title.
  NA108.W2M66 1998
  720'.28'809753—dc21   98-2784
                                                            CIP

McGraw-Hill

A Division of The McGraw·Hill Companies

1 2 3 4 5 6 7 8 9 0   11MP/11MP   9 0 3 2 1 0 9 8

ISBN 0-07-043394-1

The sponsoring editor for this book was Wendy Lochner, the editing supervisor was Penny Linskey, and the production supervisor was Sherri Souffrance.
Interior design and composition: Monika Keano/Studio 301

Printed and bound by Printvision

McGraw-Hill books are available at special quantity discounts to use as premium and sales promotions, or for use in corporate training programs. For
more information, please write to the Director of Special Sales, McGraw-Hill,
11 West 19th Street, New York, NY 10011. Or contact your local bookstore.

This book is printed on acid-free paper.

TO PATRICIA MOORE, WHO LIKES TO SAY SHE IS MY OLDEST

AND CHEAPEST EMPLOYEE, WHO HAS BEEN MY HELPMATE

IN ALL MY PROJECTS, AND AN ESPECIALLY HARDWORKING

(AND FUSSY) COUNSELOR, EDITOR, AND PRODUCTION

CHIEF IN CREATING THIS VOLUME

CONTENTS

Over a century ago, the Board of Councilmen of Canton, Mississippi, passed the following resolution:

"1. Resolved, by this council, that we build a new jail.

2. Resolved, that the new jail be built out of the materials of the old jail.

3. Resolved, that the old jail be used until the new jail is finished."

One can see by this official proclamation that recycling old buildings is slippery, particularly for public bodies but also for the general public, and for many professionals as well.

This is a book about my personal experiences with the care and handling of both famous and prized and ordinary and neglected old structures. I feel that nothing keeps one's eye on reality more than dealing with old buildings. Nothing grounds one's sense of the ravages of time, be it weather, government actions, foolish fads and fashions, or urban decay, like working with old structures. Nothing reveals our civilization and predicts the future like observing and contending with the old downtowns of our cities.

I have spent thirty-three years crawling through hundreds of marginally safe old buildings and old downtowns, and they collectively have told me about the past and the future, but most of all about reality. Sometimes that reality can literally smack one in the face when the beams or the wooden stair treads aren't as robust as they used to be. Sometimes it can mean being hit on the head after making the wrong turn down the acutely wrong alley in one of the bad parts of our less than charming old downtowns. Along with these physical architectural and planning thumps, I have experienced as a developer or partner in eleven projects the sobering grounding brought by the financial bruises and knocks that are an integral part of gritty remodeling and urban new construction. Singed into my memory are unforgettable scars and wounds inflicted on our old buildings and old cities that acidly articulate the deeper tragedies of our urban landscape.

In this book I have tried to share personal experiences that are sometimes amusing, and sometimes not through a selection of my old building and city projects; my adventures with the quite different new construction portion of my practice awaits another book.

It has always been important to me to say clearly what architectural preservation is not: It is not a response to the anxiety provoked by growth and change, nor is it an antidevelopment, head-in-the-sand form of large-scale antique collection whose proponents hate anything new. Preservation is a carefully considered progrowth attitude that takes the most practical and economical position of working with the equity we already have. It is a point of view that sees the new as a potential beneficial addition to the patrimony of the old. Preservation provides the human-made earthscape out of which the new can freely flower because it sees the new and the old as natural partners in the continuum of history.

On the other side of the coin I don't subscribe to the currently fashionable stance that thinking about history and saving old things have become so obsessive that they are stultifying and crushing contemporary life, a position exaggerated by the current computer-generated professional mania for three-point-perspective zappy fantasies. Instead, I see the balanced logical incorporation of old parts into new compositions as life-and-art affirming and as the basis for a new mature approach to architecture and our cities; one intention of this book is to show precisely that.

All this began for me with a combination of old and new buildings named Canal Square. This successful project led to many others that adaptively reused ordinary commercial and industrial buildings as well as significant historic structures. The free adaptation of old buildings for completely new and different uses takes liberties with both design and traditional form. This early activity coincided with the birth in the 1960s of a popular dynamic constituency for that approach to preservation, an approach which developed an audience and became the first and only architectural movement to achieve manifest political recognition and power.

Complementing the adaptive reuse portion of my work are stories about the seductive glories and privileges inherent in the act of restoration. Restoration has been the beneficiary of the political power of the preservation movement. Tax relief for such projects was and remains regulated by strict enforcers who favor a pure restoration approach which brings a building back to its original just-finished state. Balancing the obvious public benefits of this work are some of the underlying attitudes implicit in restoration, including a growing tendency toward a kind of preservation fundamentalism that is atavistic and regressive and disdains the vast majority of our built environment.

We all have become inured to what is arguably the ugliest human-made environment in history. The majority of the world's less-than-landmark buildings are neglected and therefore routinely altered by absurd remodelings, commercial overlays, and other examples of egregious insensitivity, creating stupendous visual chaos and suggesting underlying societal issues, some dark, but most merely poignant. In the chapter *Preparing for Downtowns,* I offer from my studies of downtowns some visual evidence of the vast ocean of buildings that are grievously neglected and abused. Mocking the sorry fate of these authentically old buildings is the growing acceptance and the embarrassing phenomenal commercial success of false, historically themed, replicated, or simulated environments which challenge the very core of preservation. What is the value of real preserved buildings versus new fake old buildings? What is the value of truth in architecture?

I also want to show how legible a regular block of individual buildings in a typical downtown is as a narrative of the cares and issues of our civilization over the last century. Most older buildings were done in styles which expressed precise philosophies and can be interpreted as hortatory visions of the future. What happened to them over the years can be read both as an accurate record of society's agendas and as a predictor of the future.

The perspective gained from these observations and the success of early projects led to the enlargement of my scope from individual buildings to whole downtowns by means of a strategy that combined the public popularity of preservation and the concept of the linkage of reused buildings, permissive and artistic uses, and water-based amenities. This very practical approach to downtown revitalization necessarily focused on forging incremental, doable, comprehensible, and financeable projects into a development chain, expanding, the architect-preservationist-planner's role into one of communicating and translating the design strategy into practical and political actions and articulating the long-range implementation steps and processes that can be carried out by local community groups.

These good and not so good experiences taught me to appreciate the various forces that pull at the city and to assay what future city centers probably will look like without intervention. From this work and the work of others I have been able to synthesize some interventionist propositions that seem to have worked in certain city areas.

Some of these out-of-the-ordinary and rarely discussed tactics arise from personal reflections and observations over time and present challenges that I believe can be uniquely met by the wide variety of preservation solutions. The notion of a range of less restricted, more permissive functions extending to even sexually oriented uses can be part of an economically viable strategy for important but unique and threatened old downtown districts and part of a new authentic way of thinking about cities.

Every urban environment has all too many missing elements, dysfunctional or hostile features, and missed or abandoned resources for which preservationists, civic activists and architects are uniquely suited to work out answers. This is a stretching of the notion of preservation into a kind of civically inspired city-wide action. In the chapter *City Preservation,* I try to illustrate via my pro bono publico planning and urban design projects in Washington how there are voids in the general public's and even the professional's approaches to problems in any city which can be filled by these civic activists, particularly if they conceive of such improvements as preservation in the largest scope–a metropolitan area–and are ready to see their pursuit and achievement as political acts.

Anyone wanting to make beneficial changes to a city cannot afford to take or adopt anywhere near an elitist position. Much as I might enjoy sharing the subtleties of coquillage and the latest in distorted geometries or clucking over America's tackiness with my colleagues, to effect change one absolutely must join the assembly and work in the marketplace. If the goal is to save a neighborhood or revive a downtown, there is no option but to work with and within our profoundly money-directed system. One of the many lessons of living in Washington is that one must always be able to explain to any interviewer (usually coming off a congressional story) why the proposed physical change is clearly of measurable economic and/or social benefit to a significant number of people.

There is only an occasional word in this book on the technologies, techniques, nuts and bolts, and tricks of preserving or restoring an old building and only a few words on artistic intention, because I want to focus exclusively on the political, social, and economic contexts of change in our cities, on some solutions to their plight, and on expanding the purview of preservation.

I have relied on my extensive photography collection and what the memory sieve of time has left in the pan, and so it is not only possible but highly probable that I have left out places, people, and events or have recalled them differently than others involved.

My arguments are deliberately not crafted to cover every epistemological crack and joint where the precise critic's chisel can enter but are deliberately generalized instead for the widest applicability; for example, fakery and its challenge to preservation constitutes a major trend affecting millions of people. Jacques Derrida and some philosophically immersed architects say that everything is a sham and that we are surrounded by fictions, but most of that discourse is presented through stand-alone assertions whose solid manifestations to date have been some woolly and disliked architectural experiments that have had virtually no effect on any major environmental issue. Of course these architects would say that they go beyond such surface trivia, but I disagree.

I feel strongly that we do not need more conjectural haute-couture philosophic architecture but require more ready-to-wear thoughtful constructs leading to actions which can reverse the widespread destruction and aesthetic pollution of our physical environment. It all may be a sham, there may be even smaller particles than the theoretical quark, and there may be many universes beyond the visible universe; these things matter and don't matter. The philosopher Thomas Nagel credits us with being able to hold and respond to two apparently diametrically opposed concepts at the same time, such as our utter insignificance when confronted with the cosmos and our scheming to get a daughter into a good school. It is with this latter side of our nature, which deals with mundane, quotidian human-scaled problems, that the most immediate meaningful urban improvements can be made. I therefore focus only on the most practical, most widely applicable, and most doable menu of preservation actions. I appreciate that in reaching for accessibility and applicability I run various risks of contrast to current academic writing about architecture, buildings, and cities, but I want to assert strongly the value of on-the-ground and in-the-street experiential knowledge as at least one perspective that seems to be in short supply. In fact, it is only now, after all these projects and countless others that would not fit in this book, that I feel qualified to comment. I hope also to communicate that I care deeply about abused architecture, am committed to battle for preservation, and simply like old buildings and see them as old friends.

In the last chapters, I distill some observations from my work experiences in adaptive reuse, restoration, downtowns, and pro bono preservation. From this review I suggest a synthesis of the various methods, approaches to, and advantages of freer and more permissive and expanded notions of preservation by attempting to show how new approaches could form the foundation for new creative directions in design and make the public more aware of and involved in the opportunities in our ordinary and fairly recent building stock. Finally, I would like to renew, elasticize, modernize, and refresh the value of a preservation strategy for the reclamation of our endangered cities.

In 1943 Sigfried Giedion wrote, "Cities cannot be simply discarded, like worn-out machinery; they have too large a place in our destiny. But . . . this fundamentally provisional and feverish institution must soon be brought within narrower limits. Whether the work will be done by intelligence or by brute disaster cannot be foreseen." Fifty-five years later the decision is in: Brute disaster is winning by more than a nose. It is precisely this feverish quality that I enjoy every day by living in the middle of one of the greatest of all traffic jams. At night the thousands of cars around my home look like a cross fire of tracer bullets; above, the frequent beat of helicopters is topped off by the whine of jet aircraft on their final approach to Reagan National Airport. Something of this buzz invests all urban communities, and it is precisely this frisson which quickens the pulse, lifts the spirits, gets more blood flowing to the brain, and makes city life exciting.

Since this book is partially a professional memoir, it calls for at least one memoir-like sentiment. As I look back, I certainly want to feel that it was all worthwhile, that some part of my work, some contribution, has been in some way beneficial. With this in mind, I have tried to think about and respect the original architects of structures that I restored, renewed, and adapted, just as I hope future preservationists will respect my new and renewed projects and in so doing will make my work worthwhile.

Arthur Cotton Moore

Since I started my firm in 1965, hundreds of architects have worked with me, among whom are the following, who made a special contribution to the firm and its projects, for which I thank them: Kent Abraham, Robert Adams, Harold Adler, Rick Archer, Shalom Baranes, Earl Bell, James Berkon, Andrew Borja, Thomas Bourke, Ellie Wynn Briscoe, Patrick Burkhart, Dale Ciapetti, Eric Colbert, Andre Copeland, David Cox, Archie Cromer, Michael Deckert, Robert Dudka, James Dudney, David Esau, Ory Eshel, Joan Fabry, David Fede, Glenn Chen Fong, Jan Frankina, Paul Froncek, William Geier, George Gordon, Barry Habib, Cynthia Hamilton, Peter Hapstak, David Harris, Hattie Hartman, Christopher Heaven, Kevin Hildebrand, Ik Pyo Hong, Brian Hunt, David Jones, Michael Kallay, Elissa Levin Kellett, Yongwon Kim, Fred Klein, Tara Lamont, John Livingood, Steven Luria, Mark Malloy, Gary Martinez, Ronnie McGhee, Robert Miller, John Murray, David Olesen, Gregory Olving, Theodore Osborne, Richard Oziemblowski, Boro Popovitch, Larry Ranly, Belinda Reeder, Jeff Rindin, Darryl Rippeteau, Dexter Seiss, Cal Schorer, Milton Shinberg, Kenneth Simmons, Austin Smith, Margaret Axtell Stevenson, Thomas Sze, Mallory Reynolds Warner, Margaret Weidlein, Anthony Whale, John Yanik, Farouk Yorgangiolu, and, in memoriam, Pierre Paul Childs and William H. Young.

In addition, I thank the following engineers who worked on these projects: Thomas Carcaterra, James Madison Cutts, Zivan Cohen, and Rick Edelson for structural engineering, and Harold Glassman for mechanical engineering.

Also, I would like to acknowledge the professional participation of the following firms in projects described in this book: ELS of Berkely on the Foundry; Pound & Flowers on the Columbus Trade and Convention Center, Barge Waggoner Sumner & Cannon on Nashville, Richard Frank/PUDI on the Library of Congress and the Old Post Office, and McGaughy, Marshall and McMillan on the Old Post Office.

Since the art of architecture begins with a client, I would like to thank especially the following clients: George White FAIA, the Architect of the Capitol and the Librarians of Congress Daniel Boorstin and James Billington for the Library of Congress; Laughlin Phillips for the Phillips Collection; Robert Larson for the Cairo Hotel and the Foundry; Franklin Thomas and John Doar for the Bedford-Stuyvesant Restoration Plaza; Richard Bernstein, and the Diocese of Charleston for the Cathedral of St. John the Baptist.

I would also like to acknowledge the help of the following people on these projects: Peggy Cooper for Ellington; May Dean Eberling of Nashville; Nancy Hawk, Tunky Summeral, and Nancy Stevenson of Charleston; Genevieve Ray of York; Rosier Dedwyler of Columbus; the Arts Center of Winston-Salem; John Cullinane of Louisville; Thomas Beuchner of Corning; and Kenneth Sparks of Washington.

In particular, I thank in memoriam Wolf Von Eckardt, former architecture critic of the *Washington Post*, for his help and guidance and his friendship to my practice.

[ADAPTATION]

CANAL SQUARE

Washington, D.C.

Early on a September morning in 1970 my wife Patricia and I were kneeling on cold hard bricks because it took four hands and many fanny-wrenching jerks to yank up the 5-foot-wide, 70-foot-long cheap phosphorescent red indoor-outdoor carpeting J. Willard Marriott—founder, CEO, and legendary chairman of the giant Marriott Corporation—had personally selected to be taped down from the street to the entrance of his new restaurant in Canal Square.

We had had skirmishes before, when his too-long-over-the-fryer mind had collided head on with our shaggy old warehouse mind-set, but this was serious. It all began when he devised the name Port O' Georgetown for his restaurant and we, trying to uncute the name, would return his drawings with a fresh "f" after the "O." In my opinion, Mr. Marriott had a somewhat peculiar approach to our old warehouse, now standing with renewed dignity worthy of its century-plus age. All his graphics and promotional materials featured a logo of a jolly jumping sailor dancing at the Port O'. To reinforce the concept, he had an actor dressed in a striped shirt and bell-bottoms do Jolly Jumping and Yo-Ho-Hoing at the restaurant entrance, which he had improved by means of the aforementioned indoor-outdoor carpeting. I, by contrast, was enormously proud of the new square and its specially cut brick laid out in a painstakingly constructed pattern slightly reminiscent of the great Campo in Siena and felt that the carpeting was not an improvement.

Inside the warehouse was my major invention: a concealed fire-rated comprehensive structural-mechanical system that legally allowed the massive heavy timber beams, the 3-inch thick planking, and the powerful brick columns and stone walls to be uncompromised and clearly revealed. All of which Mr. Marriott covered with wall-to-wall nautical artifacts and enough fishnets, oars, brass fittings, cork floats, lanterns, wheels, harpoons, dinghies, and mounted dead fish to refit Cape Cod.

"Okay, inside is his turf," I said, full of youthful self-importance, "but in my square, never."

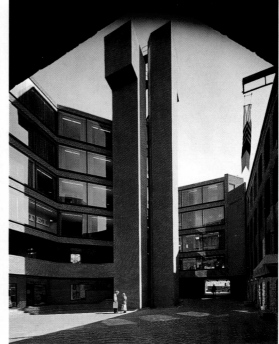

1-1. *Canal Square.*   1-2. *Elevators.*

In 1965 I had left steady employment soon after passing the weeklong architectural license exam and opened my own office on a wing, a prayer, and a small residential commission which died the day I finished the preliminary drawings and my client looked in her bank account and saw that it was bare. My prospects were a tad cloudy.

During those worrisome nebulous days well before Canal Square I had one bright spot, a client who was a movie star. Not too big a star and by now a Trivial Pursuit celluloid footnote, Nina Foch always seemed to play the other mature woman, dispatched in grisly fashion halfway through the picture. But that didn't slow her down at all. When she came to see me, it was with an opulent feather boa swishing about her neck and a rejuvenatingly young about-to-be husband in tow. Improbably, he had just become the youngest director ever at Ford's Theater, and even more improbably, she was going to buy and renovate a house in Georgetown to be near him.

The house was one I had already begun to remodel. In fact, when the workers pried off the first-floor fireplace mantel, releasing a batch of dusty old yellowing calling cards, the one that came to rest faceup was, astonishingly, my mother's before she married, Miss Beatrice McLean. When I told her about it, despite a famously faulty memory that at times included the proper names of her children, she said that of course she recalled the house and remembered paying a call some fifty years earlier on the Looker sisters, for whom it and an identical adjacent eclectic Second Empire Victorian had been constructed by their builder father. I am not much into tea leaves, but this might have been an omen.

The star had bright new ideas that required a sharp left turn in my plans. Her aged and infirm parents would be moving into the rear semidetached carriage house, which I was firmly instructed to detach completely, severing all connections, including inactive telephone lines; I also was told to wall up any orifice with indestructible metal soundproofing in areas where solid masonry was not possible. Next, and something which I thought was remarkably forward-thinking considering her maturity, was the provision for children. The attic was to be totally gutted and lined with seamless Orlon sloped to floor drains so that, as she puckishly put it, the whole place could be hosed down with acid. Finally, warming to the whole project and moving with the steady majesty of an ocean liner approaching its throng-filled home pier, she described with splendidly sweeping gestures and Shakespearean diction the entire ground floor as one vast unencumbered open space: I want to be whipping up an omelet in the kitchen area while entertaining Mr. Cecil Beaton in the living area with the latest news, was her curtain closer.

The structural magic needed to hold up in the air a large Victorian house with hefty internal load-bearing walls to create such an uninterrupted esplanade was not her problem and would have been too tedious for me to mention. A month or so later I was saved from the impending need to deal with this virtually impossible requirement because the generationally challenged union of star and boy director did not get stellar reviews on its out-of-town tryout, and the star went back to Los Angeles.

Eventually I finished the house but retained those bothersome bearing walls. The rear carriage house rejoined the main house as the dining room, and by moving the entrance to the side, the typical cramped narrowness of this sort of Victorian was converted into an appropriately grand residence.

After this tantalizingly brief affair with a real client, things got bad. Desperately, I rattled around chasing additions, jacking up porches, puffing up kitchens, expanding closets, doing custom mailboxes—anything—but still my practice, if it could be dignified by being called one, dwindled down to a single cardboard sign job for bus directions at a druggists' convention. I will never forget staring at the press type spelling out "RIDE WITH NARDA" and thinking that this was how my architectural career would end, with this damn sign.

Canal Square was my first major project, ending my brief career in signage. Perhaps the first time always induces over-the-top intensity, but I had to struggle with my client, the managing partner of Canal Square Associates, of which I was a limited partner. Before Mr. Marriott and his carpet in the square, the client, pinched for cash, declared that he was going to asphalt the square. How do developers always intuitively know exactly where the nerve endings of the design are, those supersensitive areas which, if merely mentioned, make an architect start to howl like a moonstruck dog? The experience of having an aesthetically blind, numerically minded client select for elimination precisely those items the architect is ready to die for is one of the few common bonds in the practice of architecture. Virtually every design feature, innovation, and subtlety arrived at wearily from head-pounding design work came under the managing partner's bombsight. Perhaps that's why I was not sorry that he eventually went to jail. (Years after we had parted ways, he ran into problems with fraud, larceny, theft, embezzlement, and other difficulties.) As the press started to notice the project, he was the most surprised of all to hear that it was anything but some numbers on a ledger sheet.

The old warehouse had become a forgotten footnote in history. It was the birthplace of the predecessor of IBM—the Tabulating Machine Company of Dayton, Ohio, and Endicott, New York. The 1890 Census was compiled there by Herman Hollerith and his amazing new card-collating machine. His partner, the legendary Thomas Watson, somehow wound up with control of the invention, went off to New York, and renamed the company IBM, which eventually contributed a small plaque commemorating the site of its beginning.

Canal Square has been kindly credited as a forerunner of the popular preservation movement for a number of reasons, mainly for its expansion of the notion of historic preservation to include a range of ordinary working industrial and commercial buildings, making them reusable by means of beneficial but then-unrecognized development economics. At that time the accepted wisdom was that any preservation effort required an onerous, academic, and very expensive restoration program. In contrast, through a process that came to be known as *adaptive reuse,* Canal Square showed how preservation could yield both aesthetic and financial rewards exceeding those of replacement. Reuse was more appealing and therefore more rentable and had lower construction costs (due to a credit for the shell) than did new construction; it achieved this through a systematic insertion of required modern services and equipment without aesthetic compromise to the original structure. This argument, widely published at the time, was bolstered by verifiable construction numbers. As I traveled around the country talking up preservation, I was always shown many fine and worthy buildings and told about others that owed their continued existence in part to the example of Canal Square.

1-3. *Warehouse in 1900.*

4

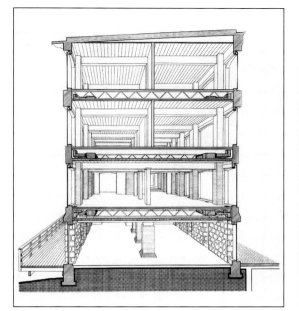

1-4. *Perspective section of warehouse.*

1-5. *Office interior.*

The awakening to the country's great resource of industrial equity occurred at the same time that many such buildings were becoming surplus as the economy began shifting to service and information and modern assembly-line techniques. Canal Square not only showed the adaptability of old blue-collar structures to modern and pleasurable uses, it also was a prototype in the continuing and often troublesome issue of new additions to old buildings. Its public space was formed by joining new and old construction into a compatible whole, without stylistic imitation, and by clearly emphasizing the textures and "oldness of the old" played off against the "newness of the new." Its vibrancy was created by contrast, and its compatibility was achieved by an original type of steel plate detailing and common colors and materials.

Even today it is still an example of the good manners of urban design. In massing, its smaller parts relate to the smaller scale of the neighboring street and push its major mass to the rear, where it is largely obscured by the smaller old and new parts. In areas where the new parts are exposed to the street, the architecture adopts a more courteous treatment to further blend in. Its bulk is masked by a linkage of old and new sections which created the first privately owned, purely pedestrian public gathering space in the community. This represents for classic urban design a reversal of the figure and the field relationship in which the building is seen as poché, fully occupying irregular city lots, and the formal design lies in the carving out of the shape of the void—the open plaza.

One of its principal entrances, from M Street, was simply punched through an existing building. When all the applied panels and signs were unbolted, the underlying brick was a muddled mosaic of bad colors and ugly stains, and so I made a solution of brick sealer and walnut stain which the painter applied with a small brush per my instructions yelled over the traf-

1-6. *Balcony shops.*

1-7. *Detail of the joining of old and new.*   **1-8.** *Looking toward 31st street entrance.*

fic from across the street. The brownish result obscured time's insults to the front but gave rise to wisecracks that we had rubbed it down with horse manure or worse.

1-9. *M Street entrance.*

The most important lesson of Canal Square in regard to today's urban crisis is the capacity of such a new-old project to stimulate areawide urban investment. Architects and preservationists may not like to talk about it, but profit-seeking investment is the engine of our capitalist society, and the level of such investment is widely accepted as the true measure of its success. In the old slummy broken-down Georgetown waterfront district, an area the size of an average downtown, Canal Square triggered more than twenty-five other major development projects that represented private investment of between one-half billion and a billion dollars—concrete testimony confirmed in concrete. In our society money doesn't just talk; it sings and dances.

In its almost seamless integration with the townscape, Canal Square is an early and continuing example of the benefits of contextual design, particularly in a historic district. At the time it was the largest new construction the area had seen for decades, yet even the passionately antidevelopment citizens association gave it a special commendation. In 1968 the only other new project in the entire area was an all-new large Neocolonial clunky office building across the C&O Canal. It was half empty at low rates. Assisted by a lot of good publicity, Canal Square was 75 percent leased nine months before completion, at almost downtown rents. From the local citizens' somewhat hypersuspicious antichange point of view, this unexpected achievement was going to set off a wildfire of development in the old moribund waterfront. For those of us drumming our fingers on the table, however, it gave the term *killing time* new meaning before the building's success became contagious, nudging along further development. When the moment arrived, it was certified by an announcement in the *Washington Post.*

But first there was the million-dollar misunderstanding. One of the tenants in Canal Square, whose business was a bit obscure, was having a drink with the managing general partner when a Wisconsin developer of the tenant's acquaintance entered the bar. The tenant introduced the two, and after some extensive lubrication the managing general partner began to rhapsodize on the future, but nevertheless certain, cornucopia of riches that would soon be gushing forth from Canal Square. The developer had just concluded a subsidiary arrangement with a very large midwestern company, Inland Steel, and was hunting for prospects. It was greed at first sight, and a deal was done in a few days. Perhaps the tenant felt left out, perhaps he felt his fellowship was priceless, perhaps it was all a misunderstanding, or perhaps he was just trying to cover the rent; in any case, he sued for a finder's fee. I was shown a copy of the suit, which was, given most legal discourse, an uncharacteristically brief brief that concluded with the simple sentence "The normal fee for this service is one million dollars." Well, as they say, it was worth a try, particularly if the attorney was on a strict contingency basis. I was beginning to get an insight into architecture's constant companion, the legal profession.

THE FOUNDRY
Washington, D.C.

In the early 1970s, a corporate itch to get into the real estate game afflicted companies that should have known better. Chicago's Inland Steel was persuaded by the previously mentioned Wisconsin entrepreneur and the example of Canal Square that just making steel out in the midwest was not as sexy as saving and developing the most visibly trashy area in the most famous section of the nation's capital. So it came to Washington and bought 11 acres of industrial slum land stretching from the canal to the Potomac.

Expecting that a grateful populace would fall over in a swoon of gratitude, Inland proudly announced its purchase in a massive press release distribution. Only a few days later the local Maloney Concrete Company, scratching the same itch, announced that it would build a very large, sloping, angular faced office building on its property. In reaction, the citizens geared for battle with the rallying cry "No matter how you slice it, that sure is a lot of Maloney."

Armageddon in old Georgetown, the smell of money on the waterfront, screamed the community newspaper. The switchboard at city hall lit up like a scoreboard after a hometown victory. The zoning commission declared an emergency and set the first of what came to be a long and hot series of late August hearings on the future of the Georgetown waterfront.

Stepping out of its new suit of shining armor, Inland realized that its next move was to hire a bunch of lawyers. I attended a meeting at the firm of Wilmer Cutler Pickering, even then prefixed by the label "influential," at which Lloyd Cutler listened to the bruised feelings of the Inland executives and, looking with fond approval at his perfectly manicured nails, said, "Frankly, gentlemen, this is a sticky wicket," got up, announced that he was off to Wimbledon, and left. Inland was getting a crash course in Washington ways, and I was getting an all-expenses-paid postgraduate course in the politics of real estate development.

One of my first discoveries in this brand of politics was that under the cover of an allegedly noble cause such as Fighting Evil Development, otherwise fine upstanding honorable citizens are quite prepared to lie. In the face of clear incontrovertible fact, they will baldly misrepresent the height, size, use, and design of a proposed building without a flicker of shame. There was a local architect who would photograph our renderings in the public record, overdraw a silhouette of a much larger structure, and get it published in the community paper with a caption saying that the new outline was what we were really planning to do. Other local architects, who could read plans quite well, would tell the citizenry that our proposed development in the low-rise district was two and three stories higher than our drawings actually showed. Antidevelopment sentiment can easily rise to a form of almost religious fanaticism that justifies anything and everything. Public hearings revealed that all the hoopla was over only two new buildings, Maloney's and Inland's, proposed for the 100-acre waterfront area, certainly no emergency. However, future public hearings, too fun to miss, were scheduled anyway.

Inland's site along the canal was occupied by the Busy Bee Auto Repair Shop, an old foundry, and a distressed abandoned Lincoln Continental that served as the primary residence of one of the waterfront's less flush floating populations. We decided to save only the two-story brick Duvall Foundry, but first we had to move it in order to blast out the granite directly under it for a parking garage. The mover brought his large family from southern Virginia, along with garden chaises, picnic baskets full of crunchy deep-fried chicken, and thermos jugs, so that everyone could watch Daddy move the building. He did it Egyptian style, placing rolling pins under the longitudinal beams as the huge masonry structure traveled down the street. Carefully slowing the enormous moving tonnage, he parked it on a pile of wood cribbing and six months later rolled it back without cracking a pane of glass.

The foundry's main contribution came after a lengthy and tail-chasing design process conducted both in-house and with the Berkeley firm ELS. The final complicated massing solution begins with a dominant diagonal form that terraces out sequentially to adjust the larger mass to the scale and size of the historic foundry. This step-down three-dimensional shaping both accommodates and joins the foundry to form—new with old—an informal casual public gathering place. We had worked all this out for a building of only seven stories, but our client refused to give up any of that precious permitted height and ordered me over my screams of protest to submit a full 90-foot-high building to the Fine Arts Commission. On the commission was Gordon Bunshaft, the gruff commanding presence of Skidmore, Owings and Merrill,

1-10. *Temporarily relocated old Duval Foundry.*   **1-11.** *Concerts on the Canal.*

who said, "Give 'em a permit, it's a good building." But to his lasting credit, Carter Brown, the chairman, said that we had to lop two floors off first. We were very lucky to recover most of the square footage in the deleted floors without losing too much of the hard-won nonstandard quality of the urban space along Lock 3 of the canal.

Two years later, just as the bandleader was hoarsely saying "And now for something completely different," the gates of Lock 3 opened and the canal barge, full of startled tourists, was rope pulled slowly by National Park Service employees dressed in old-timey canal workers' costumes out of the lock and into the brown water basin, which was completely surrounded by a huge thick mass of cheering clapping humanity dressed almost entirely in blue denim. The front of the Foundry is not only the launching area for the Park Service's mule-drawn canal barge tours but also the site of Mobil Oil's summer Concerts on the Canal, which I've always wished could be continued in winter with ice-skating in the lock basin.

As a backhanded testimony to the Foundry's immediate success, the National Capital Planning Commission proposed an area-specific regulation in an attempt to appease the agitated citizens, stating that no building would be allowed that had other than right angles; fortunately, it was not adopted. Eventually, the citizens were partially right: a sort of miniavalanche was coming. Of the twenty-five new waterfront area projects since Canal Square, we did eight, including three others on the canal, two on the next block (CFC Square and Georgetown Mews), and the all-new construction Washington Harbour.

1-12. *Foundry with canalside seating.*

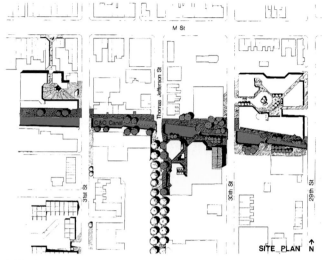

1-13. *Area plan.*

THE CAIRO HOTEL
Washington, D.C.

My second project for Inland Steel also involved preservation, but of a far larger building. The Cairo Hotel was once "the Plaza of Washington," whose guest list included glitterati such as Thomas Edison and F. Scott Fitzgerald; however, by 1974, when we arrived, it had reached its nadir and was a one-building crime wave. A Washington writer whose first job in this country was as the hotel's telephone operator observed that the bellboys by then had developed a heavy dating service on the side. As the Cairo declined, its plummeting room rates made it a favorite of school groups coming to town for their civics lessons. Bursting into the dark decadence would come fifty pennant-waving, screaming, shouting, pushing, shoving, twirly-beanie-wearing kids who were totally oblivious to the den of iniquity. Upon their departure, the oozy swamp of turpitude would silently close without a trace until the next busload arrived. On my first site visit the day after being hired to remodel the building into apartments, a body, killed by a drug overdose, was being carried unceremoniously down the building's grand front steps.

As we struggled to make the renovation work on paper, the building's slide became precipitous. What was left of the decorative marble, fountains, and interior detail sequentially disappeared. To counter the rampant vandalism, the owner installed guard dogs to roam the building, and whenever we would innocently open a door in the dark interior, a huge malevolent growling wolflike thing would spring out of the gloom. These attacks and the overpowering fragrance of dog poop considerably reduced the popularity among the staff of being

11

assigned to the project. Eventually, occupancy dwindled to one demented old woman who kept herself slightly thawed in the icy building by holding her feet over a portable electric cooktop; her only other activity was trying to have our already apprehensive young architects arrested when they went to make basic measurements.

Everything had to be measured because the only information in existence on Washington's first and last example of a steel-framed tall building, the city's only embryonic skyscraper, was one torn shop drawing from Carnegie Steel Works dated 1893. The architect, Thomas Franklin Schneider, was also the Cairo's developer, as he was of many other Washington buildings. For both the energy with which he pursued his projects and the regard with which he was held by the local citizenry, it would not be unfair to liken him to a nineteenth-century Donald Trump. In fact, the Cairo had so infuriated the establishment that Congress passed the Act of 1910, forever limiting the height of buildings in the nation's capital. It almost seems now that this majestic commandment was handed down as in a Cecil B. DeMille movie on a tablet of stone while choirs of seraphim sang "Ave Maria," but the source really was just Mr. Schneider's old Cairo. Eighty-seven years later there are still factions in the city that after ritualistic bonding genuflections to the act raise their fists and blood pressure in its defense at the mere whisper of the sacred words *height limitation.*

When I went to city hall to get the building permit for the renovation, the District's not quick building department discovered to its horror that the Cairo violated the hallowed Act of 1910. Holy L'Enfant, I had the most illegal building of all! Fortunately, the terrorized neighborhood and the overworked police department saw the remodeling in a far different light, and the developer was allowed to proceed after much theatrics in front of the D.C. Board of Zoning Adjustment.

The fact that the Cairo received a review in *Architectural Record* magazine in 1895 under the banner "Architectural Aberrations," I consider in its favor. Although it is much beloved now, its creative melange of gargoyles, arabesques, reptilian forms, and various esoteric exotica seemed at the time to show an imperfect grasp of high-rise Egyptian architecture; perhaps the lack of precedent was at fault. In any case, the style did not catch on, and as far as I know, the Cairo is

1-14. *Aerial view of the Cairo.*

1-15. *Last tenant in lobby.*　　　　　　　1-16. *Typical hotel room.*

both the first and the last example. One of the formidable elements of this style is a Brobdingnagian cornice which on close inspection resembles the Maginot Line constructed out of sheet metal. This very hard to repair cornice bordered the roof, once the home of a panoramic but nonrevolving restaurant which closed when several high-spirited patrons pelted pedestrians fourteen stories below with roof gravel. To avoid similar problems, the general contractor put a lock on the door to the roof which had to be replaced almost daily.

The Cairo was the largest market-rate 221D4 that the Department of Housing and Urban Development (HUD) had done at the time, and Inland had selected the general contractor from HUD's approved list. For safekeeping, we presented him with a box of the building's unique spherical hefty marble doorknobs that we had rescued from the pillaged interior, only to hear later that there were a few left at an antique shop on Capitol Hill.

1-17. *Cairo gargoyle.*

Without our knowledge, the construction superintendent used a smallish bulldozer to clean out the building which in charging around loosened, cracked, and ruined all the plaster, dictating exposure of the original backup brick exterior walls in the finished building. The floors were supported by a flat tile arch held in compression between purlins. This late-nineteenth-century structural system is very brittle, and the image of a heavy earthmoving behemoth roaring down on and capsizing whole sections of masonry walls which could collapse like a thunderclap on the old floors haunts me to this day. The superintendent was, shall we say, inattentive. He had all thirteen stories of new drywall installed on the interior partitions before tearing off the roof, which he timed perfectly to coincide with a major storm. Drywall is just that—dry; it disintegrates when wet, which is what it did. It also turned out that the

1-18. *Renovated Cairo entrance.*

1-19. *Renovated tower.*

superintendent was not so super, working two jobs as he was, the other being in the more remunerative street pharmaceutical business. In the denouement of the construction he would return in shackles under escort from an Atlanta prison to testify about his novel construction techniques.

The Cairo's greatest obstacle, however, came right at the beginning: just getting it to pencil out as a barely break-even investment. As with most economically driven old building projects, finding fallow space within the building envelope was the key to its salvation. At the ground floor there had been a restaurant, regularly closed by the health department, which had spread its aluminum-trimmed aquamarine Formica decor like a fungus over most of the grand old salons; the basement was completely empty with a dirt floor, except for the restaurant's garbage, which it had piled inconsiderately around the bases of the main steel supporting columns, where the acid in the decomposing wet garbage could eat away at the steel. I remember standing in the basement after the well-aged garbage had been hauled away, absolutely frozen and stupefied by the scene. In effect, this huge tall building was being supported by what looked like small patches of rust. The notion of rust as the ultimate supporting high-rise structural component, along with my next discovery of some smoldering ancient Egyptian wiring, gave me some bad nights.

In any case, we found that by cutting out the restaurant and parts of the basement, we could extrude the form of the building down, creating two-story town-house units with private gardens; the revenue from these additional generous apartments swung the project into the plus column. In the end we were not just rehabilitating a building, albeit a famously infamous one, we were doing a neighborhood. The area around the Cairo had

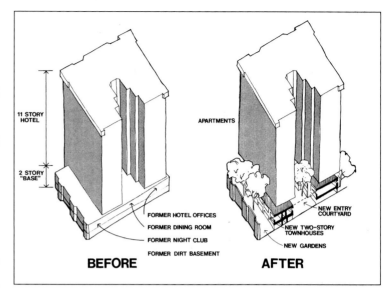

1-20. *Diagram of two-story garden units.*

been one of the city's worst; when the project was finished, it started a resurgence, and today it is easily one of the most vibrant areas in town.

BEDFORD STUYVESANT RESTORATION PLAZA
Brooklyn, New York

Around 1970 John Doar, a well-known civil rights lawyer who was later to be Hillary Rodham Clinton's boss as counsel of the House Judiciary Committee hearings in connection with the impeachment investigation of President Nixon, read an article in the *Washington Post* on Canal Square entitled, and I am not making this up, "Miracle on 31st Street," written by its architecture critic, Wolf von Eckhardt. At that time John Doar and Franklin Thomas, later to head the Ford Foundation, led the Bedford Stuyvesant Restoration Corporation, newly formed by Robert Kennedy (just before his assassination) and New York's Senator Jacob Javits. The corporation had just bought a full city block of old industrial buildings on Fulton Street which shared some similarities with Canal Square.

I had decided to move our offices from the old Canal Square warehouse right after the general contractor had removed the roof membrane two stories above without bothering to inform me, just in time for a summer storm. It had been a fun afternoon, running around like a bunch of little boys trying to stick fingers in a collapsing dike to protect our paper possessions from the deluge; it cemented the realization that it was time to leave.

The office was moved into a former auto maintenance garage which had been previously used with almost no change as a drapery manufacturing sweatshop and remained an unfinished cavernous cryptlike space. To provide some interior definition, we bought a lot of cheap Sears metal shelving. Architects use very heavy books such as Sweets catalogues, dense building codes from many jurisdictions, and fat systems manuals. Just as the dapper Stephen Smith, Senator Kennedy's brother-in-law, was being escorted to the conference area to interview me for the BedStuy project, someone must have hiccuped, because we experienced catastrophic structural failure. Like a long snaking line of dominoes, one after another, the shelves buckled into each other in a lengthy ascending roar. Feigning nonchalance, I walked proudly first up and then down the heap of tangled metal and debris to greet my visitor, who graciously acted as if nothing had happened. Confidence in the stability and security of one's architect being of paramount importance, to my amazement we got the job.

To take preliminary photographs, our first team sent to the site was led by a young architect so groomed and squeaky clean that he brought his own carpet to the office to keep his feet from making rude contact with our naked concrete industrial floor. He returned with fuzzy, totally blurred pictures snapped from remarkably oblique angles; this, he explained, was a result of running from panhandlers the whole time. It turned out that in a Faustian effort to appease the first contact group he had shelled out real cash, news of which spread, and more than a few fellows had come like wasps to honey. After his debriefing (he was a former naval officer), he rolled up his rug and quit.

BedStuy was a certifiably tough place in those days. The only sign of healthy economic activity was across the street from our block in what we always assumed was the corporate headquarters of Carlo Gambino, whose presence was signaled by two Dobermans chained on either side of the front door. At the beginning of construction each floor of our newly installed plate glass warehouse windows was christened by a neat high-powered bullet hole. When these stopped, we feared for the worst, but it turned out to be a kind of local welcome wagon formality, after which we were either silently accepted or just ignored. A quite civilized etiquette soon developed for all visitors to the site connected in any way with

1-21. *Old auto maintenance garage.*

the new project: As long as one stayed on the sidewalk around the entire perimeter of the block, no one would be bothered; however, step into or cross the street and one became accessible.

There were some rough patches inside the block as well. I particularly remember the day I was to present the full conceptual plan for approval by the entire collection of officials and boards of the Bedford Stuyvesant Corporation, which included luminaries from Wall Street, members of Congress, Ethel

1-22. *Remodeled ACM/A offices.*

Kennedy, and other members of the clan. I arrived at the main conference room clutching my tray of slides and projector, and my anxiety turned to panic when I saw that it was blessed with an enormous glass skylight ceiling through which the summer sun was fiercely blazing. In an effort to stall in the pathetic hope of an unseasonally early sunset, I suggested that we begin by making an educational visit to the site. After marching the increasingly agitated self-important group through what was plainly a time-killing repetitive, almost figure-eight pattern, I could tell by the volcanic red face of Senator Javits that it was time for the show to go on. As I flipped through my carefully prepared slide presentation, I could just make out a barely perceptible shimmer on the screen in the 1,000 candlepower of the room. The audience must have thought it all rather odd as it watched me vigorously jumping about to point emphatically to parts of a dead white screen; it was the flip side of a silent movie—all talk and no pictures. At least there were very few tough questions.

The most unusual aspect of the design was the retention of the facades of the front walls of a series of burned-out tenement houses for functional reasons of security and circulation, as an urban design device to preserve the integrity of the street wall, and for symbolic reasons. The emphasis of Restoration was the care and upgrading of building fronts in the neighborhood as an economic way of creating pride and self-identity and showing visible improvement. I wanted to reference that goal but also celebrate the rich symbolic connotations of this ordinary piece of historic vernacular housing and memorialize and elegize the thousands of lives once spent in those old tenement houses.

Now, twenty-eight years later, we have installed the finishing touches on the old wall: homey domestic accents such as window flower boxes and curtains made from a composite of

1-23. *Old tenement wall.*

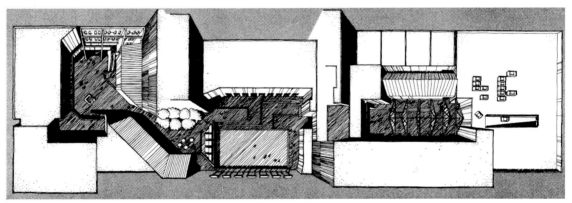

1-24. *Plan of squares in the block.*

1-25. *Curtain sculpture, old tenement wall.*

1-26. *Stark warehouse.*

1-27. *First square.*

1-28. *Third square.*

1-29. *Opening day.*

rigid ceramic material and fiberglass, bracketed out so that they will seem to be blowing forever in an imaginary breeze.

My overall plan was to subdivide the long, narrow city block into three large, comfortably scaled outdoor rooms formed by old existing and new infill buildings, a new-old partnership. The first room/plaza was framed by retail stores and offices, the second by recreation, and the third by entertainment and a supermarket. Since John Doar is from Minnesota, the recreation was a skating rink, now being replaced by a bandstand and dance area. The project continues to be a place of safety and sanctuary where one can buy groceries and other necessities or just hang out and relax with little apprehension. I feel extremely lucky to work on it again, adding a few of the important finishing details that often get lost in the final shuffle and financial squeeze of completion.

Nowhere near as depressed as BedStuy, our next work area was the quite remarkably dejected Main Street of the nation.

THE OLD POST OFFICE
Washington, D.C.

For the preservation movement, the 1971 battle to save the 1899 Old Post Office Building (OPO) was Gettysburg, Waterloo, and Hastings combined. On the country's main ceremonial boulevard, Pennsylvania Avenue, the new grassroots movement confronted the mighty federal government and its armies of regulatory agencies, which all had agreed to the demolition of the second tallest (330 feet) landmark in the capital. Actually, in the best Washington tradition, what they had all agreed to was a ridiculous compromise.

From its birth the OPO had been the subject of scorn and ridicule. At the time of its completion the *New York Times* called it "a cross between a cathedral and a cotton mill." Offending throughout its history in small and large measure, it was nicknamed the "Old Tooth" and showed up on everyone's demolition list. Its main offense was that it interrupted the Grand Circle planned for the Federal Triangle by the classically mesmerized McMillan Commission in 1901 under the assumption that this Victorian Romanesque monstrosity, just two years old, would be gone. Changing tastes in architecture have always proved stronger than granite and steel.

The new Pennsylvania Avenue Development Commission, inspired into being by comments from John F. Kennedy during his inaugural parade, was hypnotized by the same hoary tradition as the McMillan Plan. In 1970 the commission decided to get on with the job of completing the Grand Circle in the classical Beaux Arts tradition of noble geometric shapes which are appreciated principally by migrating birds.

The boneheaded idea that was uniformly seized upon was to demolish everything but the tower, which was to be glued onto a new building for the Internal Revenue Service, completing the Grand Circle. Several obstacles stood in the way of this triumphant progress: a ragtag group of preservationists who had organized under the self-explanatory banner "Don't Tear It Down," the complication of the proposed construction, and the patent absurdity of the result.

In 1971 Senator Mike Gravel of Alaska, chairman of the Subcommittee on Public Buildings and Grounds, was looking for an issue. Through the civic-minded generosity of Wolf von Eckardt of the *Washington Post*, my plans and idea to turn the building into a hotel were published, followed by a public demonstration in front of the building mounted by Don't Tear It Down. I then lobbied Senator Gravel and each member of his subcommittee for hearings on the proposed demolition.

A very glum General Services Administration (GSA) administrator and his staff glowered from the back of the hearing room while several architects presented what must have seemed to them improbably featherweight sketches of happy people cavorting through the Bastille-like building. In a more pragmatic vein I presented drawings showing that if the building was really surplus under the law, it could be transferred to the D.C. government, which could lease it to a developer for public use as a retail center whose upper floors could house a tourist hotel to serve the throngs of visitors to the Mall; in addition, I submitted letters of interest from a developer and the president of a major hotel chain eager to redevelop the building.

The subcommittee split, and I was stuck. Help came from my wife's former roommate, soon to visit from San Francisco, who was an old friend of Senator John Tunney, son of the famous boxer and the swing vote on the subcommittee. A party was planned so that I could meet the senator with drink in hand and lobby for the Old Tooth on the avenue.

By a vote of three to two the subcommittee denied funding to demolish the building two weeks before its planned demolition. Long after the battle people at GSA remained nostal-

1-30. *Old Post Office two weeks before projected demolition.*

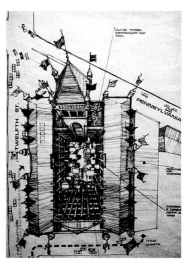

1-32. *Sketch to save the building.*

gic about the best bid they had ever received: $400,000 to knock down the OPO. The wrecker had figured on chopping it up into little souvenir pieces and selling them to preservationists.

Victory was not sealed, however, until Nancy Hanks, the first head of the National Endowment for the Arts, told GSA that her agency would happily be a tenant in the building. The last tenant had been the local office of the FBI, which had loathed the building like the long line of previous tenants, with real passion and justification. A black cloud seemed permanently fixed over this edifice since the day of its dedication, when the postmaster general had fallen down his private elevator shaft and died.

The U.S. contingent of Victorian-age architects was an enormously inventive lot, but unfortunately, many of its inventions simply did not work. Willoughby J. Edbrooke, the original architect, who as a government official initiated the design of over forty public buildings, some quite similar but smaller, designed an enormous atrium, called the cortile, covered with a huge glass roof to bring natural light to both the executive and the clerical staff and, through a second glass roof, to the blue-collar mail-sorting operation on the first floor.

From the beginning the glass roof fried workers in summer, froze them in winter, and leaked year-round. The lower glass roof served mostly as the final resting place for the deceased ancestors of the ever-enlarging colony of pigeons cooing and mating in the upper trusses. In frustration, the government covered the glass roof with a metal skin, plunging the vast space into a Stygian gloom. Tenants dragged filing cabinets into the open corridors as protection against the evil spirits that surely resided in that ominous black hole. The metal roof was also not watertight, and the steel cabinets rusted onto the marble floors. Piles of bird parts also hinted at other possible ejectamenta that could not be seen as one slunk and sniffed about the infernal dungeon.

1-31. *Exterior of Old Post Office after cleaning.*

Saving the most prominent structure halfway between the Capitol and the White House had greatly empowered the preservation movement, whose popularity and influence soared, but GSA was left with a hot potato. Mostly through the good offices of New York's Senator Daniel Moynihan, special legislation designed for general implementation but really aimed at this building—the Cooperative Space Use Act—was enacted to permit large-scale commercial use within a federal office building for the first time. The infusion of retail and restaurant activity, which I had shown in my original scheme, was an essential first step toward getting the public into this fabulous relic.

Perhaps as a sign of recognition of the specialness of the building, GSA cast aside its standard procurement process for the selection of the architect and dreamed up an exhaustive procedure called a Level Three Competition, a huge ordeal with stepped eliminations. As the design architect I put together a joint venture, spent over $125,000 on the process, and eventually won the design competition over 105 firms that had entered from around the country.

I had always envisioned the OPO as an opportunity to bring together the two faces of Washington—the national capital and the local city—separated by the 70-acre wall of busy bureaucrats known as the Federal Triangle. To welcome the annual 20 million hungry and tired

1-33. *Interior of Old Post Office, before.*

tourists from the Mall, I created a new rear south plaza and entrance by cutting through the old loading dock to open up the mostly empty basement level. At the northeast corner the design made a city entrance from an enlarged shallow window well to invite people in from Pennsylvania Avenue and downtown. Through these two new entrances the old unused basement became the meeting ground of the two Washingtons and the primary new floor for commercial use.

In the atrium interior we reglazed the old cortile roof with sun-reflecting glass to reveal the sky and the tower and removed the dead-bird-bearing lower glass roof covering the former mail-sorting room, leaving in place its richly riveted muscular trusses as a historical reminder suggesting the new duality of public retail and federal offices. In its new life the truss array has become like a large site-specific sculpture that makes one more conscious of the exhilarating volume while adjusting and mediating the space to human scale. The floor of the old mail-sorting room was cut to open up the basement level and reveal the absolutely stunning stepped pyramid mass of the rough old granite foundation of the tower and was shaped for a theatrical space with boxlike balconies, focusing on the tower with a new stage at its base. New railings abstracted from the original ironwork define the cutout shape and are bordered with special oak linear heating grills, with decorative lights and brass strips producing a warm theatrical sparkle.

The cortile wall below the tower was repainted in the original colors to make it more obvious as a continuation of the shaft, which is now seen soaring through the new

1-34. *View from the fifth floor.*

glass roof. Old wood screens were refinished and missing ones were replicated to provide porthole views into the atrium for visitors coming in from the side entrances. The entire concept was radically different from the original building, where no one could actually physically be in the vast center space of the cortile (a person would have fallen through the lower glass roof) or even experience it except from the upper, nonpublic floors. Elsewhere we invented new designs in conjunction with the restoration work, principally in all the lobbies, the corridors, and the highly decorated strict restoration area of the executive fifth floor, which contrasts with the free adaptation of the new retail space in the basement and the whole new floor for the President's Advisory Council on Historic Preservation in the never-used ninth-level roof truss space.

The third component after the federal office and the retail uses was the development of the decoratively empty (except for pigeon guano) tower, which Edbrooke's successor, William Martin Aiken, had changed so much that historians feel he should properly be credited with its design.

In 1975 Sir David Wills, heir to a British tobacco fortune, had graciously provided the bicentennial gift from the United Kingdom to the United States: a replica of Westminister Abbey's peal of massive bells which rang to sustain hope for democracy during the Blitz of Britain. He had the idea that they could be hung in the dome of the Capitol, but that dome is made of cast iron, and one swing of the thoroughly impressive ten bells would have put the Capitol's hat down on the Mall. Capitol Hill already had a not-much-liked carillon (the Taft), and Congress wasn't inclined to encourage this

1-35. *Commercial area under trusses.*

sort of gift, knowing that an avalanche of further gift giving that would include something like a Samoan war canoe would not be far behind.

As the person with the only available tower around, I was summoned to the British embassy for a meeting. It turned out that Sir David had gone ahead and cast the bells, storage costs for which in the Whitechapel Foundry were steadily mounting. Tardy acceptance of the gift by Congress was becoming diplomatically embarrassing, and so Nancy Hanks, in her famous honey tones usually reserved for cantankerous Texas congressmen, asked, "Arthur, couldn't you do something about this?" Feeling the eyes of various representatives, the ambassador, and assorted federal officials focused on me, I said sure, and everybody smiled.

James Madison Cutts, our structural engineer for the tower, was not so sure. After touring bell towers in Britain, he found that many of them, even in heavy masonry, swayed so much on ringing that even a 300-pound man could not hold the rope. We conducted a sway test, which our tower flunked all the way down to the tenth-floor level. The method of getting the sound out of this solidly enclosed level was pure Rube Goldberg. In simplified form, we devised an acoustical inverted pyramid to deflect the upward sound of the bells that ring out through the old clock faces, whose illuminated translucent glass panes were replaced by white speaker cloth. This freed up the twelfth-floor open arcade for an observation deck, which I terraced in anticipation of a historical photography exhibition to be mounted on the piers which visitors could compare to the large arched window-matching views (more on the observation tower appears in Chapter 5). The funding that a relieved Congress provided for the tower allowed the

1-36. *Cutout shape of the first floor.*

1-37. *New glass roof.*

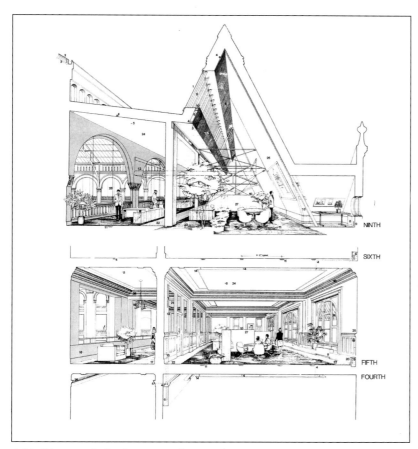

1-38. *Diagram of adaptive reuse and restoration areas.*

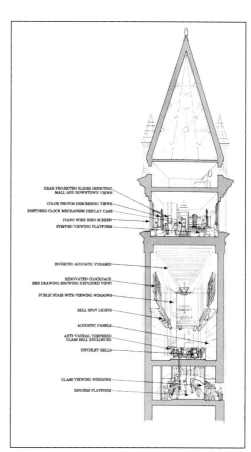

1-39. *Section through tower.*

completion of the basic transformation of the Old Tooth, whose retail areas were then leased out by GSA.

DUKE ELLINGTON SCHOOL OF THE ARTS
Washington, D.C.

It was a swelteringly hot night in the fully packed theater because the high-tech new energy management program in the computer had emphatically, with superb timing, shut down the air-conditioning system. But this paled as a problem given that our special hydraulic adjustable-height orchestra platform was frozen at the bottom of the pit, stubbornly ignoring all commands. This also seemed minor compared to the fact that the fire curtain in the proscenium arch was refusing to rise, which meant that the entire Ellington Orchestra (which happened to be led by Duke Ellington's son) and its soloist were jammed onto the little sliver of stage forward of the balky fire curtain.

A whole parade of celebrities had come to celebrate the city's first school devoted to training talented teenagers in the performing and visual arts in a renovated school building appropriately renamed for the great Washington-born musician. As the architect, I was seated in the front row, from where I could appreciate in a direct sensory way the chorus of performers teetering, sweating, tooth gritting, and cursing on the 3-foot-deep stage. The dance numbers were a trapeze act of brinkmanship.

Normally, the architect is relegated to recognition just below the third assistant accountant's intern. Only a few months later, for example, I was at a luncheon celebrating the opening of our Old Post Office renovation where everybody was saluted and toasted for his or her inestimable contribution down to the washer of the coffee pot, but not the architect; coincidentally, that very same evening at a gala celebrating the opening of our Washington Harbour, hour after hour of gaudy gaseous tributes were given to scores of people without one passing gaudy gaseous reference to me. In 1997 the same thing happened at the opening of the Library of Congress, but during this gremlin-filled evening I was not so lucky. After enduring a prolonged performance of the Laocoön-like group struggles on the precipitous stage, the announcer was inspired to pause in the festivities for a special presentation and recognition of the architect, not a moment to remember.

The underlying cause of the snafus was that construction had been delayed and then rushed at the end because of the Great Steel Problem. I was converting a famous old school

1-40. *Aerial view of the Ellington School.*

1-41. *New front entrance.*

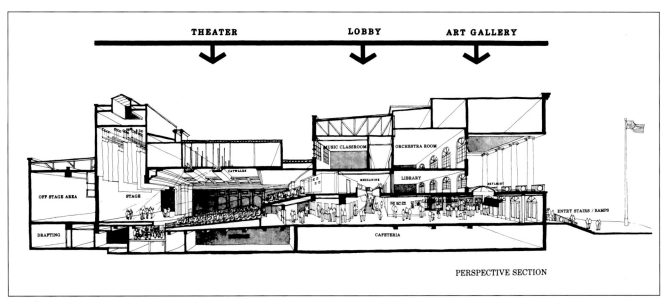

THEATER   LOBBY   ART GALLERY

OFF STAGE AREA   STAGE   CATWALKS   MUSIC CLASSROOM   ORCHESTRA ROOM   MEZZANINE   LIBRARY   SKYLIGHT   ENTRY STAIRS / RAMPS

DRAFTING   CAFETERIA

PERSPECTIVE SECTION

1-42. *Perspective section.*

1-43. *Gutted interior.*

1-44. *New auditorium.*

originally designed by Harry B. Davis in 1896 that, largely because of its stately Greek temple portico front, looked a lot like a compromise between the White House and a warehouse. Into this imposing and complicated old pile had to be inserted a completely professional theater for the new arts school, requiring that a fairly elaborate steel structure be threaded into the heart of this old temple of learning. Just as the large-scale spiderweb of big steel beams was delivered to the site, the D.C. project manager noted that markings on the steel identified its source as South Korea. For unknown but suspicious-looking financial reasons, the D.C. government, bound to made-in-the-USA procurement, was in possession of foreign goods. Everything came to a sudden stop. Time was set aside for adequate finger-pointing between the general contractor and D.C. officials. Voices were raised. Officials went to their offices for days, weeks, angrily scratching at the stack of papers in their inboxes. The construction schedule went out the window. It was very confusing to all concerned because Korean steel basically looks remarkably similar to the domestic stuff.

The final built design shows a simple and direct processional scheme. The dominant temple front, despite its clear appearance, had not been the real entrance for years. Instead, students and teachers slithered in through one of several minor side doors. Making it the real entrance required major gutting and rearrangement. First we aggrandized the temple front with new doors, steps, and flanking handicapped ramps culminating in large urns which concealed floodlights to illuminate the imposing portico. From this grand new approach visitors are led through open partially skylit gallery spaces designed to show the paintings and sculpture produced by the students to all coming and going traffic and to serve as the intermission space for the theater. The galleries connect to the main cross-hall, which leads to the dance rehearsal spaces, studios, and classrooms. Proceeding ahead, one arrives at the ticketing foyer which admits the visitor to the main theater. Now direct and clear, the flow of the arts at the school has become a recognized force in the cultural life of Washington.

THE CAR BARN

Washington, D.C.

While being kept waiting in O. Roy Chalk's outer offices, like all humble folk, I could not fail to admire the marvelous antique Flemish tapestry that spanned the length of one wall. One day during an especially tedious wait I tiptoed over to marvel at the stately talisman. It appeared on close inspection to have been emphatically and thoroughly and industrially stapled directly to the wall just under the lay-in T-bar Armstrong cork simulated acoustical tile ceiling and the surface-mounted fluorescent lights. But what made my jaw drop was the fact that the tapestry was a wee bit too tall for the room, so the bottom few inches were dragging on the waxed vinyl asbestos tile floor and countless passes of the floor tile buffer machine had worn down its lower portion pretty much to burlap bag status. Call me picky, but I just couldn't believe anyone anywhere would do that to a heroically proportioned centuries-old priceless object.

When I would be escorted into the Great Man's windowless inner sanctum, I was always struck by how, once my eyes penetrated beyond the cloud of mementos, awards, trophies, and toys inscribed to him "with great appreciation," I could see that the walls, under the same cheap lay-in acoustical tile ceiling were lined with beautiful old oak panels richly carved in delicate rocaille patterns. Mr. Chalk proudly told me that they once had been part of a lovely old French chapel.

If our meeting was proceeding according to Mr. Chalk liking, he would frequently take me into his boardroom, which contained an enormous massive oval table crowned at its center with an absolutely stupendous model of a Spanish galleon at full battle stations. I always felt at a disadvantage here because surrounding the table were suits of armor clutching menacing halberds, maces, and other fiendish medieval bashing devices; when I once peeked inside a helmet's visor, a wax face with bulging eyes stared back. I always sensed those warlike waxy eyes boring right into my back whenever I was about to deliver some unfortunate—that is, realistic—news; the ebullient Napoleonic Mr. Chalk liked only good news.

After years of inventing prospective uses and doing conceptual designs for the transit company real estate he had cleverly sequestered while selling a fleet of worn-out broken-down old buses to the fledgling Washington Metropolitan Area Transportation Authority and seeing others carry out my ideas, I was finally commissioned to do over the Car Barn, the central transit headquarters station itself. Once grandly designated Union Station, the 1895 building was a flamboyantly detailed landmark by a local Washington hero, Waddy Wood, who clearly had been untroubled by Georgetown's small-scale Federal Colonial-style past. He was also the architect for what became the Woodrow Wilson House, built next door to my great-grandfather's house at 2300 S Street.

Originally, each floor of Union Station was filled with waiting rooms and trolley maintenance to serve three different streetcar lines. The one to Virginia was never built, and the interior had long before been changed by repeated layers of gypsum board into barely third-class office space, mostly for Mr. Chalk's transitless D.C. Transit Company. In 1911 the romantic picturesque roofscape dancing about its monumental tower had been squared off to create more

1-45. *Car Barn, originally built as Union Station.*

1-46. *Car Barn decades after the change of 1911.*

office space, resulting in a monumental block surmounted by a giant spike. I reinstated the picturesque roof profile with a new pavilion recalling the old brick turret and dormer roof forms. The fact that we were allowed to enlarge an old nonconforming office building, already the biggest thing in commercial development–hating Georgetown, was said to testify to my wiles gained from years of construction combat but actually was due more to an intimate knowledge of the eccentric D.C. zoning code. The droll secret was that part of this immense structure was legally nonexistent, that is, technically below grade, because it was in effect the retaining wall keeping the adjacent streets and buildings from falling into the river. Therefore, fat as it was, it could get fatter.

One of the original building's main functions was to receive the trolleys traveling along M Street at the ground-floor level and raise them via a giant elevator some 50 feet to the roof level at the cliff top, Prospect Street, so that they could go along the palisades out to Glen Echo, Maryland. One of the nicest features of our scheme was the conversion of the upper street-level industrial roof (which by 1985 had become a 1-acre acrid gravel desert strewn with the bones of dead air-conditioning equipment) into a budgetary approximation of formal gardens extending the plane and prospect of Prospect Street.

At the base of the building's massive north retaining wall was a shooting gallery where legend has it many late but not lamented South American police chiefs were trained in efficient crowd control through firepower and persuasive electrical testicular interrogation techniques in courses offered by Robert Kennedy's Justice Department. Later, the story continues, this facility was used on occasion by President Lyndon Johnson, who would recharge his batteries or let off a little steam by blasting away at pictures of Republicans. In keeping with this dark history, alongside the Car Barn, ascending the cliff, are the seventy-five steep knee-killing steps featured in the final climactic scene with the Devil in the movie *The Exorcist.*

1-47. *New pavilion on roof.*

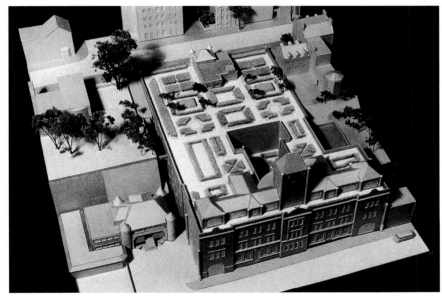

1-48. *Model of roof garden.*

1-49. *Roofscape, before.*

1-50. *Roofscape garden.*

Mr. Chalk's method of financing was almost as bizarre as his taste in interior decor. On a visit to his house he said I should look at the profile of Thomas Jefferson on a nickel in my pocket and then look at a white plaster bust that appeared very nickellike, saying it was the original by Houdon. A few months later he announced that he had sold the Houdon at a New York auction for $3.5 million to finance the remodeling. (A questionable tale since the original marble Houdon is thought to have been in the Museum of Fine Arts in Boston since 1934.) Perhaps the Devil had not been completely exorcised, because the mood-swinging Mr. Chalk, tardy in his mortgage payments, reportedly refused an offer of $28 million for the remodeled building and then lost the whole thing to his lender.

Actually, his taste in decor was still the strangest thing of all. I could never show the building's interior without fear of giggles and guffaws because of the generous Chalkian eclecticism, where trailer park lamps, vinyl grass cloth wall covering, moose heads, Grandma Moses murals, and patches of marble mixed with colored plastic were quite originally cojoined.

THE FORD PLANT PROJECT
Alexandria, Virginia

What do the settlement of non-Russian land claims in Alaska, innovative industrial design for automobile manufacturing, and the deeply colonial and very proper Old Town Civic Association of Alexandria have in common? Absolutely nothing, it turns out. They are like dogs and cats and Republicans. The primary cast of this improbable farce was an association of Indian tribes from Anchorage, preservationists who dependably fainted in ecstasy at the sight of either Art Deco or pioneering industrial buildings, and a community totally obsessed with the Right Kind of Real Estate, which detested Art Deco and industrial structures. In actuality, there was a supporting cast of thousands with many juicy conflicting interests.

One of the minor players was the U.S. government, which in settling the Alaskan Indians' claim that the only thing the United States had purchased from the Russians in 1867 was the turf actually occupied by the Russians, leaving an unpaid bill to the native inhabitants, offered, instead of cash, chits that the recipients could exchange for surplus federal property. Perhaps thinking that disposable federal property meant old brown dented filing cabinets, eye-ease green partitions, and cigarette-burned furniture that once had suited GSA's fine taste, most tribes took the money. Our client took the chits instead and began showing up at auctions of surplus federal land; one was the improbably located Ford plant, which had been taken over by the government during World War II for military purposes. The war being comfortably over by 1982, GSA had put it up for sale, and the client, using chits, outbid others using real money.

1-51. *Aerial view of the Ford plant and site.*

In 1932, for reasons known mostly to himself, Henry Ford had felt that in the old failed port he at least had access to rail lines and deep water, and so he commissioned his River Rouge plant designer, the famous industrial architect Albert Kahn, to design an assembly and parts distribution plant at the foot of Franklin Street. Neither Henry nor Albert knew that they were doing this on future Indian territory or that their assembly building would be surrounded in the 1990s by hostile, Brie-nibbling, chardonnay-sniffing, self-righteously energetic super neocolonialists who remained totally unawed by advances in industrial design.

Preservation for the folks in Old Town simply meant straight-up Colonial architecture with the grudging admittance of some Victorians. There seemed to be genuine surprise that the words *preservation* and *twentieth century* could be used in the same sentence, but horror knew no end when the labels *industrial* and *Art Deco* were joined. In fairness, courtesy of the U.S. Navy, the plant had been disfigured by the addition of an enormously ugly, pugnaciously cantilevered blockhouse which occupied almost the total view that the Old Towners could see and was one of the first elements we pared away. Like meat to a tiger, that demolition seemed to temporarily satisfy them, but soon they were hungry for more.

Meanwhile, the client had been on the roller coaster of development in the 1980s. Its first attempt was a joint venture with a land developer in Connecticut; just as I was getting the entire $100 million 10-acre development approved by everybody, the Connecticut developer saw its shadow in the market and decided to get out of real estate. The client next teamed up with the eighth largest home builder in the country, who filed for bankruptcy shortly after joining the project. The market had crashed for our client and ultimately for my plan.

Those are the bare bones, but not the full body, of this play. Getting such an enormous development accepted by the battalions of government regulators and the various constituencies (quite unsympathetic to each other's agendas) turned out to be similar to running for political office. I gave so many presentations that they became stump speeches which I pitched slightly to each group's main interest. In the end such a program had to get through not one but many public review sessions—the city council, followed by the planning commission, followed by ten meetings with the board of architectural review, preceded and followed by every possible subinterest group—before the whole parade would have to be marched through again. Along the way were the staffs of the various agencies, members of which are statistically likely to dislike something or somebody or to be forever reminding you that you took the head of the citizens association to lunch but did not take them.

It is an axiom that hostility to development increases exponentially with the size of the project. Alexandria had just fought off a billionaire and his stadium and a railroad and its new in-town town, and the citizens had just sued, stopped, and brought to its knees a nearby waterfront project. In others words, they had tasted blood, savored victories, and shared their feelings about development with very receptive politicians and bureaucrats. The Ford plant was more visible and seemed bigger to Old Town than the previous vanquished projects. It took two years to persuade thirty-seven government agencies and every man, woman, and child standing within earshot, but by 1988 we were fully approved.

The secret was that the plan was simply appealing. I had picked up the fundamental idiosyncratic quality of Alexandria's old industrial waterfront, specifically the repetitive interpenetration of water, piers, and land. Historically, the old piers were like the spokes on a long comb stroking through a mixture of boats and water. We toothed together land and canals and inset harbors, interweaving a rich range of architecture and building types, all interspersed with public walks and bridges. Everyone agreed that it would have been a wonderful community, but we had bad luck and bad timing.

The battle of the bulge came at the old Ford plant, in part because some preservationists had metamorphosed back to their old cocoons. In the beginning caterpillar stage of preservation, the restoration of historic landmarks was the entire goal. Then came that butterfly of adaptive reuse—as in Canal Square—which opened up a whole new range of vernacular architecture, but as preservation became more popular, most of the available stock was done over, adaptive reuse seemed too compromising, and a return to the cocoon of restoration without intrusive or compromising modern elements had occurred.

It was as if adaptive reuse were only grudgingly allowed as a holding action, to stop the infidels as it were, and now we could return to our true love: the pure unadulterated past. To the lovers of the Albert Kahn Ford plant only something incredibly similar to real automobile manufacture was satisfactory, obviously not a program the client was keen to take on; they also wanted the long-gone old giant Ford sign replaced and were even critical of the removal of the battered and dented old water tower. The neocolonial citizens, who were overtly pushing for total demolition, were adamant that at the minimum the only use of the property could be residential.

1-52. *Model of proposed development.*

1-53. *Rendering of proposed development.*

Although Albert Kahn is known as a great industrial design architect, this was just one of about a thousand buildings he did for Henry Ford and other automakers, basically a stock design which was built with little alteration in many diverse locations, including Sweden. During the war he could knock out one of these plants in two weeks. Still, the program of housing in a 1932 automotive plant structure held such pathfinding possibilities for freestyle adaptation that I was excited by the challenge.

I do like big living rooms, but the 200- by 440-foot size of the plant is a bit agoraphobic even for me; sliced up, the short dimension would yield kitchens the size and shape of bowling alleys. Clearly, only alteration and removal of some of the plant's interior bulk could have made the mandated residential use work. Since the navy had no compunction about bashing into the building, we felt that those parts (mostly the north wall), significantly altered, could be changed to admit residential use and permit the dropping in of a low-rise apartment structure around a small inset harbor, which for complex structural reasons made the whole thing constructable. Having the original drawings and specifications supplied by Kahn's still-operating office, we also proposed to reconstruct exactly the highly visible western wall that had been destroyed by the navy. The newly unified main plant could then be internally subdivided into town house loftlike units incorporating and displaying the existing unique light monitor truss system not only through the units but over the parking and the harbor without altering the industrial facades. The state historic preservation officer agreed with us after site visits. Intolerant of such a design compromise, some nonaccommodating preservation protesters came from outside the city to form a pincer action with the prodemolition citizens at the crucial public hearing, which we survived by only two votes.

A bum actor of our saga was the client's employee who did amusing things such as hiring other architects without our knowledge to debase and cheapen the design, one of whom

1-54. *Entrance to units in the Ford plant.*

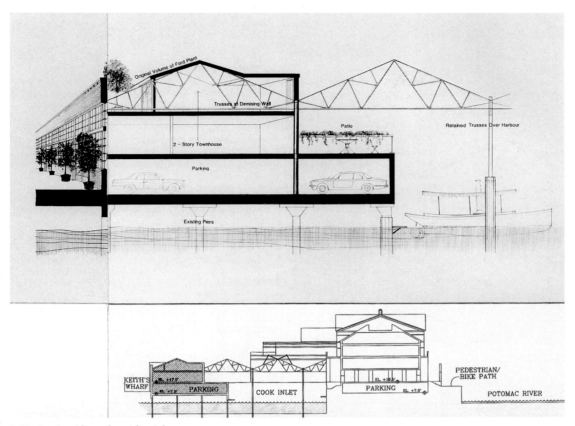

1-55. *Sections through residential use.*

1-56. *Sketch of boat basin.*

saved himself some money by blatantly duplicating my copyrighted drawings, eliminating some of the quality elements, and whittling down the rest. The real culprit of this project, however, was bad luck (developer partners pulled out) and bad timing (the market for expensive homes, the bricks of our plan, completely collapsed). Only fifteen houses were built and sold. The Indians sold the land to another developer, totally uninterested in preservation, who hired his own architect. Albert Kahn's plant was torn down in 1996, partly

1-57. *Ford plant, now demolished.*

a victim of purist preservationists and partly a casualty of the 1990s real estate collapse.

STAR CARPET WORKS
Washington, D.C.

If I had to select just one from all of my encounters with ordinary working buildings to illustrate how a preserved historical presence from the uncelebrated recent past can be brought together with contemporary needs and forms to make a new composite that reflects both eras, it would be this project.

Georgetown in 1930 was the oldest and most deeply unchic area in Washington at a time when being old was widely considered to be tired, worn-out, and cosmically undesirable. It was a period when steel and paper mills and putrid rendering plants were the norm in lower Georgetown and the residential northern area was a rummy slum infiltrated with commercial and low-grade uses. Some of this remains today as a healthy zoning-incorrect interspersal of grocery and convenience stores which gives the area its small town ambiance, convenience, and urbanity. But some of these insertions were just plain low-grade marginal industrial uses that were there because of cheap land prices. The Star Carpet Works was certainly one of these, there being no other explanation for why such a crummy industrial service plant would be located in the very middle of a purely residential block. In later years it had even descended to temporary trash storage.

Forty-seven years after its completion Star Carpet Works could not have stood out more from its surrounding area, which had become one of the country's first and most successful gentrified and restored historic districts and one of the most desirable communities on the east coast; it was now the skunk at the garden party. The obvious solution for most new owners looking for a more conforming single-family house would be demolition and the construction of a new but probably Federal-looking row house with lots of shutters, but we had a different idea and a different client.

The anomaly of the Star building had become like the nail that the tree grew slowly around. As the adjacent houses were renovated, it partially supported some of their back additions and porches; trees, bushes, and vines had become entwined with the 1930 structure. Ripping it out would have been like extracting a piece of shrapnel from a long-healed war wound. Even then, we were sensitive to the too popular eradication of the recent past, and the Star was a genuine artifact from the too close and unpleasant preceding bad times. It wasn't a nineteenth-century handsome old heavy timber warehouse, but it was guaranteed unpretentiously authentic.

While fully occupying a site that provided 11,000 square feet of floor space on two levels, the boxy old plant still managed to be a polite neighbor by presenting a low profile to the street and revealing its full bulk and 30-foot height at its back end only to a few private rear yards. Its high ivy-covered side and rear walls accorded neighboring yards a privacy cherished in any dense urban setting.

The design premise was to form a new-old hybrid out of an interplay of opposites. The bounding factory walls were retained in their entirety and conserved in a way that exposed the 1930s typical backup material, structural clay tile, and the ad hoc patches of brick where changes had been made over the years, such as windows that had been filled in. In the remaining windows, the mostly broken glass was cleaned out but the industrial sash was retained. The construction began as a process of subtraction. In areas where the structure and floors were removed for the courtyard, entry court, and backyard, the unbraced walls were supported by a line of plainly exposed contemporary wide-flange steel soldier columns. The rough shaggy tactile nature of those braced surrounding walls was then contrasted to the new skin of soft smooth precision white stucco, extruded curvilinear Plexiglas, and aluminum glazing hardware.

To preserve the integrity of the exterior, the industrial sash of the old show window was converted into a fence and gate protecting the new entrance court. By keeping the complete but paneless metal windows throughout, the intertwining of climbing vines with the delicate grids of the industrial sash evoked a surprising sense of romanticism.

1-58. *Old carpet works, before.*

1-59. *Old carpet works, after.*

1-60. *Star Carpet Works sign.*

Passage through the entrance court leads to the first of two building pavilions within the walled compound, where the original structure (concrete frame and wood roof) was kept intact to contain the main living spaces. The new house shapes within the factory walls were expressed as buildings within a building, articulated from the old walls to heighten the sense of contrast. Retention of the bounding walls not only minimized the impact of the renovation on the surrounding neighborhood but recalled a sense of defensive design, like a castle wall, protecting the vulnerable interior organic, bubbly humanistic shapes, which despite their apparent freedom are precisely keyed to the old structural bays, an aspect clearly seen in the exposed honeycombed concrete columns and beams that contrast with the smoothness of the interior partitions. The formal inverses and juxtapositions of the design complete the metamorphosis of a superordinary twentieth-century modest commercial structure refreshed by contemporary forms and materials into a new-old hybrid.

1-61. *Interior used for storage.*

Why does the Star Carpet project have importance? I think it is noteworthy because the basic stuff left in our withering cities consists of ordinary twentieth-century modest buildings like this old carpet factory, and if this is what we have in abundance, we should turn it to an advantage and approach it as a resource, a stepping-stone to the future. The project offers an example where materials of the time—a concrete frame and structural clay tile walls—became the foil and catalyst to a new composition, just as old brick and heavy timber framing were used at Canal Square and numerous other nineteenth-century mill reuse projects around the country.

This type of freely adapted preservation involves new architectural interventions which are designed to have not only autonomy from but appreciable visual and functional rapport with the existing structure and in the process yield a heightened understanding of the historic material with which they are joined. Compatibility and subsequent interpretative meaning can

1-62. *Courtyard looking at main house.*

1-63. *Courtyard.*

1-64. *Children's pavilion from rear yard.*

1-65. *Kitchen.*

1-66. *Dining room.*

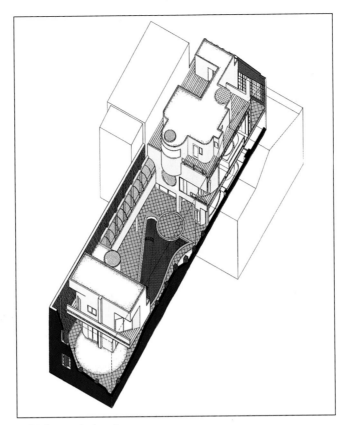

1-67. *Isometric drawing.*

1-68. *Aerial view.*

be achieved through contrast and distinction as they are here or through a system of references and interrelationships, mimetic elements, and even very abstract spatial and structural patterns.

Robert Venturi's 1977 criticism of false simplicity and proffering of a more inclusive architecture of real complexities changed thinking throughout the architectural community. In *Complexity and Contradiction in Architecture* he argues that complexity leads to positive artistic tension and multiple interpretations. While the theory is by now a milestone in architectural history, I have found its practice in contemporary architecture to have mixed results at best. The play of both-and and the promise of the complexities have not been widely engaging or meaningful in Venturi's or his followers' work to the layperson or the professional; these complex messages have been somewhat elusive, abstruse, and too recondite for general communication. It is almost like a palette of black and white producing only subtle imperceptible shades of gray. But freely adapted reuse, by combining genuinely old fragments with modern fragments, generates enough readable contrast to communicate to a major part of the public yet offers all the rich possibilities and more for which Venturi was looking. A freer style of preservation works with a full color palette that can combine the materials, colors, and forms of the past and the present in infinite ways. These new time-based combinations would not constitute a false picturesqueness or contain contrived juxtapositions and complexities that would require a guide from the inner circle to explain. There would be a purpose to the complexity, producing a clarity to the observer that invites further exploration and appreciation of the full aesthetic effect. Moreover, this form of freestyle preservation has the capacity to use our predominantly twentieth-century remaining urban equity and turn these neglected resources into components of a force for the revitalization of our cities. The more recent the building adapted, the more evident the partnership of old and new; in reusing nineteenth-century buildings, the old was most of the seeable result, and in restoration it was more like 99 percent. More recent building combinations would be closer to 50-50 and provide a good prospect for the exploration of intriguing complexities.

THE UNSTABLE, THE IMPROBABLE, AND THE UNDESIRABLE

Swept along by the ecstasy of early successes, everything became grist for the preservation movement's mill. Indicative of the euphoria, I was pressed into service on some of the most shaky and unlikely projects, of which the following are just a sampling.

The Cannery gets the prize as the most unstable because it was closest to spontaneous catastrophic collapse. The owner of this homely object, understandably unaware of its historic value, had tried to knock it down to put it out of its misery but had been stopped at the last moment by alert preservationists. We had to find a brave contractor to place enough shoring and scaffolding in the building to even inspect it. Not only was it not going to make it through the winter, it looked as if a heavy dew would bring the whole thing crashing down. This mundane shedlike remarkable defiance of gravity was the remnant of a 1917 corn and pea canning plant and the very modest beginning of the exploding commuter suburb going on Edge City known as Gaithersburg, Maryland. For the inhabitants of the former corn and pea fields, which were full of plastic shuttered split levels, ranchburgers, and estatettes, the Cannery was deep history, and in 1988 we were grossly overpraised for stabilizing the barely vertical pile, which awaits a recovered real estate market. Indisputably, the Cannery represents identifiable living proof that everything and any building can physically be saved.

I have also had some acquaintance with the improbable and the undesirable. On arrival in Louisville, I was taken directly to the central jail because many years before, in a quick visit to the city, Eero Saarinen had proclaimed that the old fortresslike prison was the most beautiful building in town. Taking this as a compliment, some of the city's activists were determined to turn it into condominiums. They were aided by a judge who had decided that incarceration in such a place was cruel and inhuman punishment and had ordered it vacated. A handsome massive rampart, it gave the impression that long after Louisville had capitulated, it would have held out. Inside, burned cabbage and other perfumes that one did not want to identify wafted through the echoing floorless space. Essentially, the building consisted of a perimeter wall and a catwalk around a self-supporting series of stacked metal cages. I, of course, expressed my enthusiasm for its ready adaptability and for how it just said "condos" to me. The scheme we did in 1977, inevitably called the "Louisville Slammer," did not proceed because I suspect that most of the enthusiasm was related to the reverse chic of having Kentucky Derby week festivities in such an amusing venue.

1-69. *Unstable structure of the Cannery.*

Although the jail's smell was probably a deterrent to its conversion, absolute first place for odoriferous challenges must go to the old main sewage pumping station on Columbia Point in Boston. The University of Massachusetts had built on once-desolate Columbia Point (it now has the Kennedy Library) a contextually barren and sterile

1-70. *Proposed renovation of the Cannery complex.*

megastructure surely designed to terrorize and subdue the wildest and most undisciplined students. So successful were the architects in creating an unforgiving angular futuristic world that in 1974 the student-inmates seized on the only old friendly building in this Orwellian land for their student center, the by then obsolete main old sewage pumping station. It was a ruggedly attractive old stone castle from a distance with the wind at one's back, and we approached it with our customary optimism. Inside, we were told and could immediately sense that it was sitting on approximately 75 feet of effluent residue of Boston's finest, accrued over a hundred years. The thought of the already put upon students munching cheeseburgers on top of a humongous stone septic tank was too much even for me; I communicated a lack of enthusiasm, and we were not hired. As of 1997, the project has not started. I wonder why. The lesson here is that almost everything can be a candidate for adaptive reuse.

Occasionally even one's best efforts are doomed to failure. In 1987 we were commissioned by one of the world's richest men to remodel and make suitable for royal visits one of the largest homes on Foxhall Road in Washington. Worthy of the title *mansion,* the house was named Dunmarlin and was deemed grossly inadequate to the new owner's needs.

To properly prep us for the task, we were flown to Paris to be shown a couple of the client's recent acquisitions. After a trip to Rambouillet, where we toured a very charming *Architectural Digest* spread of old redone water mill buildings that could bed down twenty to thirty guests, we were taken to the most fabulous *maison particulière* I have ever seen. Access to this palace was through massive doors in a large apartment building forming one side of the Place Jena, Sixteenth Arrondisement, a good address but petit bourgeois compared to what was inside. Driving through the building, through a formal garden and then through an enormous espaliered triumphant arch, we arrived at a veritable jewel. Overlooking the Seine, with an excellent view of the Eiffel Tower, was Mr. Eiffel's own house. Eiffel may have been a structural engineer, but he clearly had a sweet tooth for architecture. The detailed ornamentation, the elaborate entrance canopy, and the colorful rich materials made this quite large building seem like a scrumptious piece of candy. The confection was on the market ten years ago for a mere $25 million. Encouraged by all this, my design for the client's Washington property added three wings, one partially subterranean, in a fashion which hugely enlarged the existing mansion without taking away its character and complemented the enormous dwelling with grand formal gardens descending to a new lake.

On a sweltering night on the fantail of the client's yacht anchored off the Hotel du Cap, my presentation of the design was interrupted when the armed men who were all around the ship ran to the railing with weapons out and frighteningly ready because a speedboat was racing in our direction; it suddenly, fortunately, changed course. At dinner afterward, as his large retinue of suave cultivated debonair lieutenants fell strangely silent, our extremely warm and gracious client talked politics to make us Washingtonians feel at home.

To make sure we understood his program, the next day he helicoptered us to another of his homes, this one above Saint-Tropez. We were met at the landing site by armed guards who surrounded the heavily armored Mercedes Benzes waiting to take us to the house, past sentries with automatic weapons posted on every hilltop. The whole scene made James Bond seem possible.

After two more enlargements of what to most Americans and the neighborhood was a grand manor house, word came back that the problem was the old house itself. While not Blenheim Palace, it was one of the most impressive estate buildings on Foxhall Road and certainly surpassed most of the other big piles along this main line of Washington's palatial dwellings, including the nearby Rockefeller and Brady estates; nevertheless, it was not up to the client's standards. Through his lieutenants I implored via various schemes to at least use the old house, even as a garage and maintenance facility, to support a totally new house elsewhere on the estate. One day I got a call that the client had decided that the house had to go, and the next day it was gone.

Later he showed me a model of his proposed new house that had been prepared by his corporate conglomerate. Pointing to a 75,000-square-foot version of Versailles sitting on top of more than the average-sized acropolis, he said that the king could stay here. It has not yet been built, the land is still empty, and the city is poorer for the loss of Dunmarlin.

HE WHO PROPOSES NEVER DISPOSES

I was often hired to do studies on delightful old buildings that later were flipped to be developed by other people who had chosen other architects. Despite my disappointments, I began to

1-71. *Existing mansion expanded.*

realize that this was a necessary phase in the beginning years of what could be called the democratization of preservation. As an early activist in the new freestyle reuse movement, I was asked to deal with problem buildings that years later, largely as a result of those studies, became important local projects. Also, I just could never stop (still can't) pointing out reuse opportunities which too often proved fruitful for others, giving Wolf Von Eckhardt reason to admonish me that "he who proposes never disposes."

As one example, at the end of 1975 the good news that even somewhat brutal industrial buildings could be candidates for reuse had reached the planning department of Alexandria, Virginia. At the foot of the city's main street was the most brutal of all, a complex of ten buildings collectively known as the Torpedo Plant that had been bought by the city in 1969 from the federal government with the intent of demolition. These were fierce government-issue concrete structures allegedly designed to withstand the accidental explosion of a torpedo. After being asked by the planning department to do a reuse study on what could be done with these menacing blocks, I met with a group of artists who had been sniffing around the area and decided that having artists making and selling their work in the rugged tough bones of those buildings was a natural fit and a sure traffic generator equivalent to, but more appropriate than, a department store. We made an informal alliance.

In studying the government drawings, I realized that munition manufacturing had dictated such massive loads that the resultant pile cap fields (the foundations) were so dense that after demolition one would be forced to virtually recapitulate the structural frame. On even further investigation, I decided that demolition was both expensive and foolish. With minor modification of these bastions I could make a waterfront plaza with the artists as the main attraction and with complementary retail, parking, and some residential structures, and I drew plans and renderings illustrating that concept. I was instructed to show my study to the planning commission.

In a council chamber empty except for the five members of the commission, I presented my scheme. After answering a few desultory questions, I started to gather up my boards, when the doors at the end of the room suddenly burst open. In swarmed a horde of people who ultimately filled every pew in the hall. The chairman wryly asked if there were any comments on my presentation from the just arrived audience members who had missed it. One by one they trooped to the microphone, angrily bashing my idea of retaining any part of the loathsome complex. After quite a number of speakers had exhausted the prime subject, new testimony shifted first to my other projects, all of which were reputedly in ruins, and then to me personally, ending close to 1 A.M. with repeated vein-popping shouted declarations that I should stay on my side of the Potomac and never darken the sacred ground of Virginia again. It was the best ass stomping I ever got. After a while I got into the spirit of the evening with a little countertestimony; the chairman opined charitably at the close that I gave as good as I got. The good news about preservation with industrial structures had a bumpy start in Virginia.

1-72. *Torpedo Plant.*

Beginning in 1983, over eight years later, the ten buildings were renovated by others with different forms but with a use profile similar to my initial idea. The artists in the Torpedo Plant are now known as a metropolitan attraction, and the retained plant buildings form the much-liked center of the waterfront in Alexandria.

There are many similar stories. In 1971 I did a concept for a retail center in the old maintenance warehouses of D.C. Transit; in 1981 it became the Georgetown Park shopping center. In 1972 I conceived of and presented to the Arlington County Board a new density infill around the existing retail buildings of Shirlington, a development hub in northern Virginia, which was partially realized in 1989. In 1979 I convinced the D.C. Board of Education that the Sumner School could be a combined restoration and development site; in 1986 it was done. In 1975 I envisioned a residential adaptation for an undercapitalized group of the old Lansburgh Department Store; it was done, reusing only the shell, in 1992.

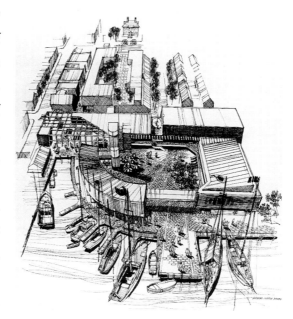

1-73. *Sketch of the Torpedo Plant.*

I share these stories to illustrate that in preservation, locating and envisioning reuse possibilities constitute an important part of the collective contributory effort. It is a sort of beneficial preservation pathfinding and project spotting which I can only take as consolation for the "he who proposes" axiom. The searching for and the visualizing of opportunities constitute a forward observer role which anticipates the expanded concept of proactive urban preservation that is discussed in Chapter 5.

REFLECTIONS

There has been recent popular criticism of having commercial uses in fine old buildings such as Faneuil Hall in Boston and Union Station in Washington which states that the cheap touristy goods being sold debase the grandness of such structures. The assumption must be that the activities the buildings housed in the past were unremittingly noble and never involved filthy lucre, which of course is absurd. Faneuil Hall always incorporated a market, and I grew up schlepping through the original Union Station near Capitol Hill, whose interior contained a motley collection of seedy gift shops, bookshops, barbershops, newsstands, shoeshine stands, and eateries ranging from bad to toxic. The fact that there are somewhat more of these shops now is more than offset by their vast increase in quality. Introducing commerce into a good building may make its stature grow by contrast, and the advantage of more people experiencing an old building's quality should be more than a little persuasive. Obviously, it is how it is done and not the fact that someone may enjoy some delicious profit that is important. The other part of the criticism is that the cheap and shabby goods being sold gain stature from the old building. This benefit is minor but good, because it might make merchandisers more disposed to move into revived old city quarters rather than into suburban megamalls and therefore become a force for the preservation of other worthy structures. It is telling that the criticism consistently refers to the shops as selling cheap and shoddy goods for tourists. Would the attitude be different if all the shops were run by Cartier? Does the sponsorship of the Metropolitan Opera by Texaco hurt the Met? When I created a stage for the Old Post Office Building, I had reveries of hearing a string quartet playing lilting chamber music while a hushed audience enjoyed its meal in silence but found that the operator favored heavily amplified pop acts over the luncheon din. This is the real world, and the anticommercial critical bias seems a bit touched with economic snobbery, ennui, and priggery. We live in a commercial world and must operate within a market-driven economy.

Despite some forgivable errors, preservation remains the late twentieth century's only widely appreciated and genuinely popular architectural movement, the only one to gain a significant constituency, and therefore the only one to have any real political power. As a consequence, government processes and institutions have been created, laws have been enacted, and tax subsidies have been given to help preservation efforts. But far more important, people truly interested in preservation remain a democratic force in a democratic society that has and knows how to use the power, and at the same time it is procity and proarchitecture. Preservation has its problems, but its popularity and successes have put to shame all other architectural movements. In the face of these realities, the American Institute of Architects (AIA) has never given its prestigious twenty-five-year award to any preservation project, only to all-new buildings. The architectural press too often thinks of preservation as merely a matter of repairs and remodeling, work architects get in hard times when nothing new is happening. Is it any wonder that compared to any other political advocacy group the AIA is dependably impotent on specific problems and pressing issues in the city, in the profession, and in the country in general? Survey commentators must think that preservation is simply retro, since several recent anthologies on architecture in the twentieth century do not even mention it.

Preservation, particularly the creative power of adaptive reuse, not only is a modern movement in architecture but has survived the dustheap of worn-out fashions and remains one of the most important movements for the future. Indeed, there is one form of preservation that is universally loved inside the profession and is also wildly popular among the general public: the pure restoration of great landmark buildings.

[RESTORATION]

Restoration, as is often stated but little practiced, calls for a true sublimation of ego. The modern architect's role becomes that of a mole, burrowing around in the innards of a building to make his work invisible; while there is considerable invention in this effort, in the end success depends on the perception that he has not even been there. Part of the popularity of restoration derives from the same reason we celebrate dead painters, writers, and other artists: These formerly driven, competitive, challenging people are no longer threatening, being safely dead while we are in the superior state of being alive and can comfortably, even a bit condescendingly, shower praise on a reliably nonreactive target. The original architect can therefore be treated as the star of the show, an unthreatening name, and the invisible modern architect can be patted on the head for his or her unegotistical ways.

There are two schools of thought in restoration: the Whites and the Grays. For the Whites, the only direction is toward a thorough and strict return to how the old structure was exactly when it was freshly built, literally brand new; cleaning goes far beyond the removal of dirt and grime to the re-creation or replication of surfaces. The grays, in contrast, believe in trying to make the original building whole again but are much more tolerant of the visible effects of the aging process; surfaces should be cleaned, of course, but not to such an extent that hard-earned time-created nicks, sheens, and patinas, its *craqueluer*, will be eradicated. In effect, the Grays hold that an old building should still look old and somewhat worn, its verdigris intact. Telltale imperfections from long use and decades of weathering should be accepted if they present no serious problem, because they substantiate the building's venerability. Aging and death are part of life in humans and in buildings.

The Whites have produced stunning work, particularly in their spectacularly ornamented structures, but have also produced objects which seem unreal, plastic, and almost Disneyesque. Subliminally we miss the clues to age, and instantly wonder how much of what we see is new, that is, how much of an allegedly old building is old and how much is nouveau fake.

Dirty buildings are important for this discussion because the perceptible identifiable difference between the real old and the fake old may come down to the dirt stains naturally created by wind, sun, rain, and pollution over a long period. Our eyes quickly pick up this evidence, and we say that a building really looks old; indeed, these patinas of age are reassuring, confirming the fact that we are looking at a truly historic piece. At the same time, I believe buildings should be cleaned primarily with sweat, soap, and water, although there are other methods, but shouldn't be scraped and skinned of time and weather's basic recoloration embedded in the epidermis of the materials.

The differences can be rendered in more pragmatic terms. The White attitude has consistently been shown to cost much more than a whole new building and so can never be a viable approach in the general marketplace, remaining an option for something so special that there is no bottom to the pockets. The Gray position, which focuses on a selective repair program which has at its basis a falling in love with as many existing conditions as possible, is more often less expensive than the cost of a new building and therefore can be a salable approach with wide applicability in the general economy. Except in the very special case of richly ornamented structures, I am in the Gray camp. The following are some of my more White projects.

THE CATHEDRAL OF ST. JOHN THE BAPTIST
Charleston, South Carolina

The bishop of Charleston needed more room for a variety of services, including the consecration of priests, because that ceremony requires that ordinands prostrate themselves before the altar; since many men are more than 6 feet tall, they presented a quite unecclesiastical image to the congregation. The bishop simply wanted to move the altar and most of that end of the church to the rear. Casually ordered, it was like someone saying that Boston should be moved over 6 feet. Having this as his unshakable goal, the bishop knew he could bargain the parishioners' support if he included repair of the extensive termite damage, fire protection, and, most seductive of all, air-conditioning—in effect directing a total renovation.

Fire protection was an issue because the original cathedral had been consecrated in 1854 and only seven years later the entire structure with its soaring 200-foot-high spire had burned completely to the ground. The replacement building had been done by Patrick Charles Keely from Ireland and Brooklyn, a specialist in Roman Catholic church architecture who carefully followed the original plans but unfortunately did not live to see its completion in 1907. Perhaps because the architect was not around to defend the design or for the usual money shortage reasons, the spire became expendable.

The cathedral was an all-around handsome Gothic edifice except for that missing spire. It hurt so much to see its stump that I made a rendering of a steeple on the cathedral and

2-1. *Restored interior of the cathedral.*

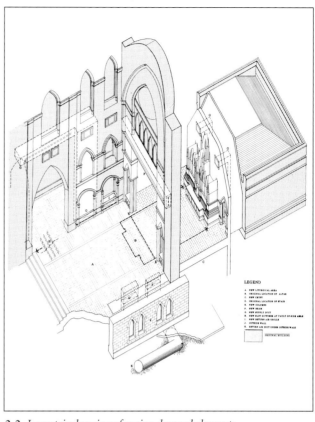

2-2. *Isometric drawing of major changed elements.*

2-3. *Installations inside the cathedral.*

2-4. *Restored interior.*

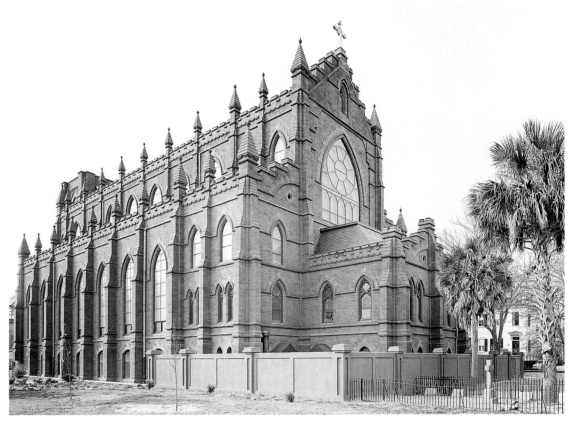

2-5. *Exterior of restructured back end of the cathedral.*

showed it to the bishop. He reacted like I was waving around a cosmic top-secret document and grabbed it so that the other priest in the conference room could not see it. He muttered that he would think about it, but I am sure that with his other financial priorities, my sketch wound up in a dumpster somewhere between Virginia and South Carolina.

While Mr. Keely was clearly wired into the Catholic hierarchy, I, who am not Catholic, got the job through our Jewish structural engineer and in the spirit of ecumenicalism assigned it to one of my project managers who is Korean-American and Buddhist.

Among all the crucial new systems—audio, fire, television—the supremely bulky enormous return air ducts provoked the most head scratching because there was simply no place for them in the delicate beloved Gothic interior passionately remembered by the parishioners. Like a good mole, I took them outside, buried them in the ground, and ran them beneath the sidewalk to our new gothically walled equipment farm set beyond the rear of the church. After ripping great long gouges inside for the lesser ductwork wiring and pipework and mindful that any restructuring of the interior had to look absolutely original, I designed new compositions of arches and columns formed and accented by details molded directly off the existing decorative features of the foliated imposts, the sconcheon arches, the reredos, and the rossetted ribs on the quadripartite vaults. This molded decorative kit of parts was used to camouflage the steel pipe columns supporting the hefty steel beams that carry the bottomless stained glass rose window and create the niche for the relocated massive marble altar. With the exception of downright irresistible additional gothicized flourishes concealing registers and ductwork and a nave painted in ascending lighter shades of blue, it is hard even for me to see what was changed in the enlarged cathedral. Even as a restoration, it was humbling to work on such a project, because for an architect a cathedral remains the highest level of architecture, a symbolic Supreme Court.

When the rebuilding was practically finished, Father Roland, the project priest, gathered up his courage and took the formidable bishop on a tour. We were told to address him as Monsignor Roland afterward, and so we figured the bishop was pleased.

2-6. *Detail of the moved altar.*

THE LIBRARY OF CONGRESS
Washington, D.C.

I was wary about working for the Congress, but my experience certainly was better than that of the library's original architects. Almost right off the boat, Smithmeyer and Pelz had gotten the American spirit quickly, trumpeting their intention to do grand buildings like those in Europe, but better. In 1873 they won first prize in the national competition for the library; the next year the competition was reopened, and they won again over submissions from H. H. Richardson, William A. Potter, Thomas U. Walter, and Edward Clark, the Architect of the Capitol. Congress ultimately fired the two sequentially but first made them grovel and submit revised designs over twelve years (Gothic, French, Italian, German, and Modern Renaissance); then, incredibly, it refused to pay them, even fighting all the way to the Supreme Court, sending Smithmeyer into such a decline that he attempted suicide. Eventually, Smithmeyer died destitute and Pelz had to borrow the money to bury him. Yet what they gave to this country in 1897 was a building second to none, with its originally gilded dome once rivaling even the adjacent Capitol.

2-7. *Central Reading Room.*

2-8. *Central Reading Room during reconstruction.*

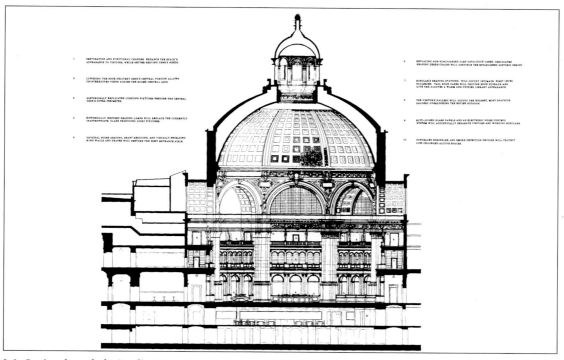

2-9. *Section through the Reading Room.*

2-10. *Restored Great Hall.*

2-11. *Former office partitions in the Great Hall.*

When I started design work in 1980, the interiors, largely the work of Pelz's successors, General Casey and his twenty-eight-year-old son, were no longer glorious. The entire building had become a giant honeycomb of tiny beaverboard and drywall cubicles for several thousand people. Acoustical tile ceilings, at the basic minimum height of eight feet, had been hung from wires casually screwed into the intricate plasterwork of the towering, majestically arched halls far above. When I poked my head up above the cheap T-bar lay-in tile grid, I blinked at a panorama of flamboyant and ornately decorated barrel- and groin-vaulted Olympian chambers with allegorically painted tympanum tableaux that had not been seen in fifty years. In part patterned after Garnier's Paris Opera and incorporating elements from many of the sensationally baroque revival structures of the Belle Epoque, the Jefferson Building of the Library of Congress is arguably the most elaborately volumed and decorated structure in the new world, and it had been completely trashed. The problem lay in the library's basic mission: As the world's greatest repository of information, it was attempting to contain in a finite building the most dynamically growing thing of all—knowledge.

The library's third building, the Madison, an unloved and almost windowless vast marble leviathan, contained enough space to relocate most of the offices in the Jefferson Building, allowing us to rethink and restore this national treasure. Demolition of the miles of beaverboard was greeted by genuine expressions of astonishment as we became like a gang of archaeologists uncovering a long-buried nineteenth-century version of the Baths of Caracalla tarted up like Versailles. We made multiple discoveries as the layers of accretions were stripped away, but none was more sobering than finding that this magnificence and its miles of shelving containing everything from Stradivarii to Laurel and Hardy movies to a Gutenberg Bible was protected by a few handheld fire extinguishers. The

2-12. *Hidden vaults and tympanum paintings above the hung ceiling.*

2-13. *Office partitions below ceilings.*

2-14. *Restored northwest curtain.*

2-15. *View of the Capitol from a corner pavilion.*

apparent lack of palpable concern was all the more remarkable because the library had a history of two major conflagrations which had caused considerable damage to the collections. The fire in 1851 had consumed Jefferson's original contribution, which had formed the seed of the library.

Among all the library's treasures, and they are manifold, the greatest is the Thomas Jefferson Building itself. My first important design decision was a no-build determination for the entire array of grand spaces on the western entrance side, whose halls, I maintained, had to be restored, protected, enhanced, and, most important, taken out of active library use, reserving those palatial rooms for public functions and exhibitions. Restoration of those halls of a grandeur rare in America involved incorporating the full range of needs—basic wiring and sprinklers, security systems, lighting, and air-conditioning—but all in an unseen way. The mosaic and marble tile floors were trenched for wiring and then carefully replaced because the mountain the marble had come from no longer existed. Sprinkler heads, emergency lighting spots, and miniature air diffusers were camouflaged in the rosettes centered in the panels of the vaulted coffering. Baseboards were replaced by double-celled snap-out wiring chambers and then faux painted to look exactly like the original wood. Tour guides play a game of "try to find the sprinklers" in the lavish impasto layers of florid decoration, which contain such rarities as gilded imbricated tori, guilloche bands, vermiculations, encarpi, and outside ethnocentric keystones.

Each grand space presented an escalating challenge to our inventiveness at conceal-ment until we were completely defeated by the extraordinary strata of gilded decoration fused directly onto the building's monolithic structure in the Members Room. Here we had to run the sprinkler pipes right on the surface, but when I point them out today, they seem so much a part of the intended moldings that they are almost impossible to discern. The removal of parti-tions and the restoration of the Members Room revealed a long narrow room anchored at each end by columned marble fireplace surrounds that support elaborate didactic mosaic murals. One shows law and the evils of nonlaw; the other depicts history and celebrates the great histo-rians. The ceiling delights through a long series of diaphanously painted maidens representing the muses of enlightenment and inspiration. The members for whom the room was created were the members of Congress, who were to take refuge there, buttressed by wise law, empow-ered by the sweep of history, and inspired by the ceiling muses to create noble legislation. (How far this is from today's adage that the making of legislation and the making of sausage are two things one does not want to see up close.)

Past attempts at cleaning and patching the building had been disastrous, and so an elaborate couplet of drawings was done for each space throughout the Jefferson and its annex, the John Adams Building, depicting in rectified photography and diagrams the damage and the existing condition on one sheet and a detailed delineation of the restoration work with elabo-rate cleaning codes on the other.

Risk management consultants and fire control studies done before our arrival had called for the spectacular, stupendous, and truly magnificent Central Reading Room—the heart of the library—to be compartmentalized into small fire control areas. Absolutely appalled by the nightmare image of new fireproof partitions of gargantuan scale slicing up this match-

2-16. *Members Room.*

less heroic space, we sought out more sensitive experts and together came up with the idea of Roman arched sprinkler lines concealed inside the arches in the surrounding loggias, from which a vast fire-suppressing deluge could be delivered. To create a hushed atmosphere, I designed a specially imprinted carpet to muffle footsteps and contained the tourist visitors in a soundproof glass box on the third level. Aside from all the accumulated former junky accretions that we removed from the Reading Room, I would estimate that about half of what one now sees is new. Formerly occupying a full third of it, the card catalogue system was retired and computer index terminals were housed in the card catalogues' carved wood frames in the nearby search area. Extensive restoration and replication of existing desks and lamps to complete the circle, decorative painting, and other features make this incomparable empyrean space well worth a visit.

But my main task was preparing this old treasure house for the twenty-first century and ensuring that the destructive past was not repeated. With the most precious volumetric spaces restored, protected, and conserved for public exhibitions, we had to create a way in the working parts of the building not only to accommodate some of the library's dynamic growth but also to contain the knowledge explosion from trashing anew the newly restored interior. My solution was a set of subordinate reading rooms occupying the north and south grand halls

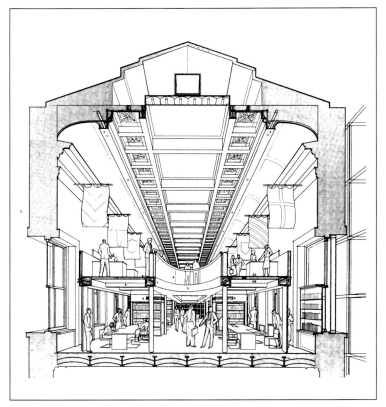

2-17. *Hollow structural elements in office colonnade.*

(known as curtains) devoted to a specific cultural region, a subdivision that would improve approachability and comprehension of the staggering 112 million items. These balconied reading rooms, subdivided by sloping bookcases (which are also staircases) into study areas, help soften the impact of the two-level building inside the back half of each curtain. This new inner architecture provides for future expansion on the upper level and contains the offices (and their attendant noise and clutter) of the specialists, curators, academics, and librarians in each discipline. Conceived of and designed as large pieces of furniture in dark mahogany, these minibuildings, while providing needed services (power, light, communications, and air-conditioning), were made of hollow members, permitting an almost infinite variety of wiring and access for unknown twenty-first-century information delivery systems. Like furniture, they can be replaced without compromising the restored interior.

During the build-out I was invited by George White, the Architect of the Capitol, to carve my designs for the decorative tops of the first-floor reading room bookcases and the railing supports for the second-floor reading room so that they could be cast directly by the foundry. Amused by this foray into hands-on architecture, my office bought a lot of hobby shop self-hardening clay so that I could begin my career in decorative sculpture. The small intermediate rail support went so well that I was flicking my potter's rib around as if I were conducting the Boston Pops. On the morning after I had shaped the major railing support, however, I discovered to my horror that in self-hardening, the clay had cracked and moved around as if in death throes. It took me all day to patch everything back up, but when I came in the next morning, the clay had again cracked and was rambling in unpredictable directions, and the same thing had begun to happen with the giant medallions. It was the clay from hell, and I began to think that my craftsmanship career should have begun with something less august than the Library of Congress. Day after day I would repair cracks and put things back in place, and so ultimately these pieces became composed more of glue and wood putty than of clay. I began to have dreams about clay hands grabbing me by the throat, but after two weeks I

2-18. *View of satellite reading room and colonnade.*

2-19. *First-floor bookcase stair.*

2-20. *Architect's clay maquette of medallion.*

2-21. *Architect's clay maquette of intermediate support.*

2-22. *Balcony-level view showing railing supports.*

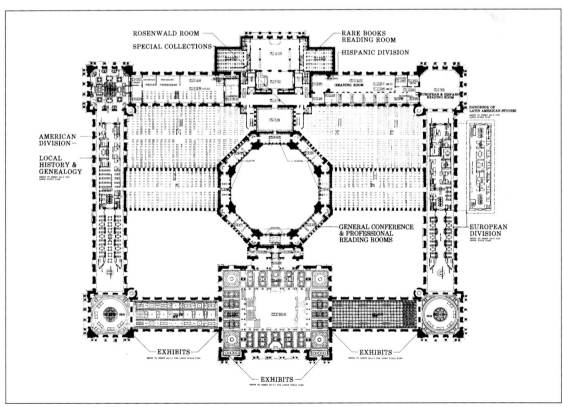

2-23. *Second-floor plan.*

started to get the upper hand, although the main support made one last massive crawl before it hit the foundry. Even though these pieces were abstracted from existing motifs, it was extremely gratifying to me to add some small-scale contemporary decorative detail in the most decorated of all American landmark buildings.

The aspect that most struck me about the Jefferson Building, which was heavily criticized after its 1897 opening but became inordinately loved, was its inventiveness and innocence. Not only are the tunnel system interconnecting the buildings (where I someday want to display the dust jackets from the yearly sum of books submitted for copyright) and the balky vast book conveyor (now also presented as an exhibit) intriguing, but also the Victorian way of using warm colors on the north side of the building and cool colors on the south side, in a sort of environmental mitigation by hue.

Through allegory, taxonomic iconography, and a rich panopticon of symbols, the building represents the Neoplatonic idea of embodying all knowledge in a single structure. Naturally it also particularly incorporates and celebrates American achievement up to 1897 in its exposition of world culture. The relentless translation of every subject into a geometric shape with symmetrical parts where each subclassification is represented by an architectural

symbolic element is downright dizzying and requires a knowledgeable guide to be even partially understood. Inscribed, carved, and painted everywhere are allegorical symbols and references, sage sayings, wise epigrams, learned mottos, and hortatory maxims urging reading and learning which seem almost unbearably quaint in our cynical times, for example, "They are never alone that are accompanied with noble thoughts."

The librarian's office, a dome-vaulted gem, has two entrances so that a visitor can come in on one side, ask the librarian. "What's new in ornithology?" and then go out the other side to collect the book in the Reading Room. This is a nice arrangement for a small branch library but is not as useful with so large a collection.

I worked on the library for seventeen years, and it seemed at times to be almost a Czechoslovakian

2-24. *Restored first-floor hall.*

2-25. *Librarian's office.*

restoration. In the cold war era the countries of Eastern Europe developed an excellent but languid reputation for historic restoration. The Czechs or the Poles would begin a restoration by moving onto, say, the king of Prussia's front lawn to construct substantial brick homes for their families where children would be born, grow up, and eventually join Daddy and Grandaddy in the restoration work on the king's palace. The construction trailers at the library had acquired that solid dug-in look reflective of their incredibly long presence, during which children have been born to people who worked inside, recalling that gone but not forgotten Czechoslovakian tradition.

We also worked on the 1939 Art Deco annex behind the original building, the John Adams Building by Pierson and Wilson. The inventiveness of these depression-era architects also offered us challenges. Across the rear wall of its reading rooms was a blocklike mysterious synthetic material that defied analysis, attracted and absorbed dirt like a sponge, and mysteriously could not be washed. It turned out to be an acoustic precast stone, popular in the 1930s, that could be cleaned only by careful vacuuming with soft bristles. The architects had won an award in a national plastics competition for the use of the new material Formica in the Adams Building; while we were not awestruck at this achievement, at least the material, edged in aluminum, proved easy to find, fix, and replace. Probably not very obvious to most visitors are our

2-26. *Stair in the Great Hall.*

2-27. *Restored Great Hall, Main West Pavilion.*

minor interventions, which largely play off or are hidden by the Art Deco chevron motifs characteristic of the building. It is a fine building, but perhaps, like its namesake John Adams, it suffers in comparison to the glow of the original building and its namesake, Thomas Jefferson.

THE U.S. TREASURY BUILDING
Washington, D.C.

The Treasury Building could be said to have set the mold for that legendary penurious camel of a government building designed by a committee, only here the committee of architects worked on it sequentially over thirty-five fractious years. In 1836 Robert Mills, who had just won the competition for the Washington Monument, was hired by President Andrew Jackson to do the new Treasury Building, but he completed only the east side and his position was terminated. Then Thomas Ustick Walter, who was one of the winners in a competition to extend the Capitol, did the design for the north wing and eight other government buildings, for which he was never paid, dying almost broke. Ammi Burnham Young completed the south wing in 1860 and then was fired and replaced by Isaiah Rogers, who designed the 1865 west wing and then quarreled with his assistant, Alfred Bult Mullett, who replaced him. Mullet also designed forty other government buildings, including what is now the Executive Office Building, for which he was not paid, and completed the Treasury's north wing in 1869. Like Smithmeyer later, Mullett unsuccessfully sued the government to collect his fees, but unlike Smithmeyer, he was successful at committing suicide. Clearly, there was a lot of architectural woe and cantankerous stepping on of toes, and the government proved to be a remarkably bum client. Also, it is just possible that they all had a whack at each other's work, making this a true camel.

Although the building is miraculously unified on the exterior, as can be seen on the back of any ten-dollar bill, the inside reflected committee work compounded by the tender mercies of GSA and the fact that what had been a small impecunious agricultural country in 1836 now spends and hocks the future in trillions of dollars. As many people were happy to point out, the dark, narrow, confused, congested, archaic, inefficient, and cluttered interior perfectly reflected the federal government hard at work. Even though the gold bullion bars and cold cash have long gone to Fort Knox or off-shore, security for this paper-pushing Kafkaesque morass seemed tighter than that for the White House.

Our task was to sort through all this and come up with a master plan for restoration of the multiple architects' work, new uses for fallow spaces, and, incredibly, the possibility of more additions. We were excused from engineering, presumably to avoid increasing the national debt, and so our plan was entitled "An Aesthetic Master Plan for the U.S. Treasury Building."

Symptomatic of the problems of the building was the issue of how one got into it. Treasury boasts two grandiloquent, chest-thumping grandstanding temple front entrances that fairly shout "Come in here," but the real entrance was through a nasty little rathole on 15th Street. After a welcome just short of a strip search, one noted that the inside had narrow and dark corridors leading to a maze of mean little labyrinthine spaces. Did I not say this was the model for future government structures?

As one would expect from a stretched-out committee of architects, the building runs the aesthetic gamut from Robert Mills's spare and noble Erechtheum Ionic colonnades to record-setting ornate pendant light fixtures embellished by a snarl of agitated cougars, biting rattlesnakes, and Indians in pursuit of buffalo. I confess to for once being happy that budgetary constraints prevented us from having to re-create those beauties.

I discovered that part of the umber dinginess of the corridors was due to surplus army camouflage colors and an energy-saving lighting program probably designed to impress President Carter. The distribution of miners' helmets was suggested, but we held out for a color

2-28. *Existing 15th Street entrance.*

scheme closer to one of the originals, renovated and electrified several almost boring
original late nineteenth-century brass fixtures,
and proposed a simple cleaning of the worn
but marvelous checkerboard marble floors. As
a result of a mysterious event in Treasury's
copy room, a budgetary shortfall in the U.S.
Treasury, and a political minuet, the corridors
are all that have been realized from our work.
I was told that the day after its submission my
large, well-documented master plan simply

2-29. *Proposed enhancement of 15th Street entrance.*

disappeared from Treasury's copy room (perhaps with a routing slip to Jimmy Hoffa), never to
be seen again. An attempt to secure funding for new copying ran afoul of the discovery that the
government was short by $212.2 billion in 1985, and the copy department would have to do its
part to see the country through the embarrassment. Finally, as happens in administrations, we
experienced a cabinet musical chair dance with Secretary Regan, whose inspiration was behind
the plan, switching seats with Chief of Staff Baker, whose idea it was not.

On any project I do, even a pure interior restoration effort, I can never just stay on the
inside but always look for possible connections to the rest of the city. At the south end of

2-30. *Proposed renovation of corridor in Ustick Walter's wing.*

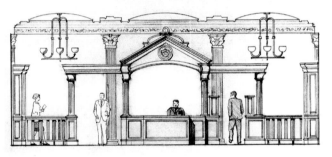

2-31. *Proposed security station with integrated metal detectors.*

Treasury was an accretion of precast concrete lumps, generally known as Jersey bunkers, strewn about in an impotent attempt to inhibit terrorist car bomb attacks. Demonstrating the ineffectiveness of the strategy were hundreds of cars of executive branch commuters parked in among the bunkers. At the same backside of Treasury the visual axis of Pennsylvania Avenue ends in a most unsatisfying manner. (In their book *Buildings of the District of Columbia*, Pamela Scott and Antoinette J. Lee incorrectly ascribe to me the idea of closing East Executive Avenue, the street on the west side of the Treasury and the east side of the White House; my recommendation was for major changes to the south grounds of the Treasury and nothing on the west side.)

In 1836 President Andrew Jackson had ordered that Treasury be sited in a location which interrupted L'Enfant's line from the White House to the Capitol. In recent years the majestic axis of the nation's Main Street has been terminated by a sometimes English-speaking vendor and his cart overflowing with made-in-Taiwan plastic Washington Monuments, buttons, keychains, and pennants, all carrying primitive representations of the first family and a fine collection of streetwise epigrammatic T-shirts. It is fair to say that the unresolved nature of this heavy and stentorian problem, given another round, would be like a shot of speed to the local architectural and planning communities. Clearly the largest amphetamine response to date was the initial Pennsylvania Avenue Temporary Commission's proposed heroic National Square, a Tiananmen Square–like colossal space requiring a multiblock demolition program and at least 10,000 constantly jumping synchronized gymnasts to feel in service. At the time, to earn a little moonlighting money as a young draftsman, I did the rendering of this vast hypersquare and nearly went cross-eyed drawing all those tiny happy-looking people to make the space seem even somewhat used.

During the Treasury project my solution was a relatively modest replacement of an existing never-used south terrace with a curved recessed plaza that would comfortably accept

2-32. *Vendor and concrete bunker ending Pennsylvania Avenue.*

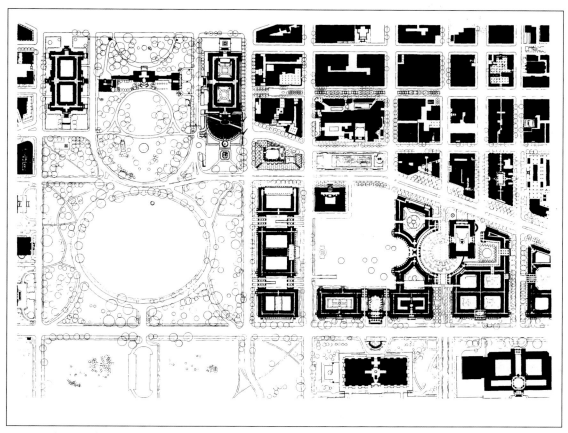

2-33. *Plan of proposed plaza ending Pennsylvania Avenue.*

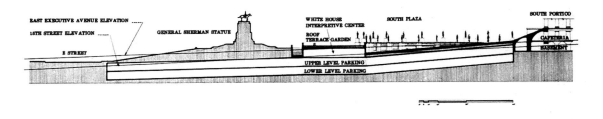

2-34. *Section of proposed White House visitors' center and parking/plaza.*

2-35. *Rendering of proposed gates to new plaza.*

the angular thrust of Pennsylvania Avenue, rotating the geometry like a sundial to the White House. Under the plaza was to be an extensive and secure executive branch parking garage placed so that the southeastern section of the presidential enclave stopped looking like a suburban mall parking lot at Christmas time. A semiunderground visitors' interpretative center where tourists could wait, for once out of the rain, before being x-rayed for the White House tours defined the plaza's shape. Embellishing all this and replacing the Jersey bunkers as terrorist vehicular impediments were to be statues of the presidents, two of which, Lincoln and Washington, at a larger scale, would bracket the gates and define the axis.

The thought of a hopped-up Iranian terrorist crashing a bomb-laden rented Chevette into a perpetually stonewalling granite Nixon has always tickled me. I also always hoped that the plaza could function as a Washington version of London's Hyde Park Corner, an agora of protest where people could stand on the axis and shake their fists at either or both ends of Pennsylvania Avenue, and am hoping now that when the budget is balanced, a small part of the surplus can be made available for copying this still-not-out-of-date plan.

2-36. *Aerial view of proposed plaza.*

THE PHILLIPS COLLECTION
Washington, D.C.

Even charming institutions have their bad days. This was particularly true during 1983 when the staff had to go out and explain to a busload of tired and rumpled Canadians who had been driving nonstop for three days from Saskatchewan to see the famous Renoirs, Bonnards, Degases, and Klees that the museum was closed and the paintings were in Japan. Apparently even our calm friends to the north can get quite apoplectic and dangerous. The paintings were visiting Japan as a way of raising the funds to pay for the first phase of renovation of the old house-museum.

As the National Gallery is majestic and huge, the Phillips is small and winsome. The first museum devoted to modern art in the country, it was created in Duncan Phillips's own house and thereafter retained the captivating quality of art displayed in a domestically scaled family-friendly environment.

The original house was designed by Hornblower and Marshall, who were exceptionally good club members (Cosmos, Metropolitan, Chevy Chase, Army Navy, and three in New York), with a practice that consisted mainly of houses and additions for wealthy Washingtonians. Until 1883 Marshall worked as a draftsman for A. B. Mullett, one of the architects of the Treasury Building (north wing). The house was finished in 1896, after which came two addi-

2-37. *Restored museum-house and new addition.*

tions, in 1907 and 1912, by the clubmen. In 1920 some New Yorkers named McKim, Mead and White added another addition and converted the house to an art gallery. In 1960 a less well-known New York firm, Wyeth and King, once practitioners of Addison Mizner's flexible version of Spanish Colonial, added the somewhat modernistic blockhouselike addition across the alley.

2-38. *Former art storage.*

For a number of reasons there was a need to turn the Phillips into a professional museum. Space was so tight, for example, that storage shelves in the office-level bathrooms were jammed with pieces from the collection, all wedged together and certainly insufficiently humidified by the nearby occasionally open toilet. On the john, one could contemplate the edges of paintings which would have thrown Sotheby's into a greedy orgasm; also, paintings were known to walk out of the unprotected old house, with one finally being returned in 1997.

In the first few years I worked with Laughlin Phillips, the founder's son, who had also started the *Washingtonian* magazine, where I wrote occasionally as the contributing editor on urban affairs. He and his directors and staff provided a very civilized and congenial working atmosphere where decisions were made almost by consensus; we all did our best work in those days. The Phillips was run like a genteel family business with cooperation and toleration in great and easy abundance, but it was not to last. The need to raise funds for the addition and institutionalize the gallery forced an influx of trustees and a proliferation of committees with gangs of spring-loaded legal advisers that shattered the productive working calm and serenity.

The Phillips had quickly become a security teddy bear for too many of these new controllers with selective memories who saw every microscopic change after the multiadditioned building had been totally gutted, all the requisite modern security and environmental systems had been installed, and the former interior had been carefully replaced. The old brown music room ceiling sparkled with added details and four different colors chosen to enhance the three-dimensional effect and conceal the sprinklers and emergency lighting. Yet I was chastised because the D.C. fire marshal, with statutory authority, required one fire door to be actually visible. Before I was allowed to proceed on the new fifth addition across the alley (the Goh Annex), an artistically blind enforcer and a famously heavy but not friendly law firm were assigned for a while to give us guidance. When it became obvious that neither knew a finial from a festoon, they just sat there furiously twisting their lower vest buttons. Finally, the board

2-39. *Entrance to renovated music room.*

empowered a special committee unshackled by any experience in design or construction to watch our every move.

For the new Goh Annex I designed the contemporary interiors to have the same volumetric dimensions that felt so comfortable in the old house, with large galleries similar to the old music room, medium-sized galleries like the old dining room, and small galleries like the old Klee Room. The small galleries became specific shrines for the Rothko paintings and the Phillips's signature piece, the *Boating Party* by Renoir. (During a subsequent trip to Paris I made a pilgrimage to the restaurant in the painting, but construction crews were pouring new concrete blockhouses nearby, and the ambience just did not have that rosy Renoir glow.) To encourage movement through the buildings but avoid dominating the special character of the galleries, I placed a skylight-lit open elliptical windowless staircase off center so that one would come to it after a natural progression through the galleries. Generous landings and the unusual rectangular steps inside the oval form make it an easy climb for tired art lovers.

Most of my mildly adventuresome ideas for the exterior were quickly rejected by the building committee, people who in discussing Michelangelo's St. Peter's would focus on how many times it leaked. Even the choice of brick for the new addition required multiple testy meetings mostly devoted to the discussion of whether it was too late to scrap the entire design

2-40. *Gallery for Renoir's Boating Party.*

2-41. *Elliptical stair in new annex.*

2-42. *New annex across the alley.*

2-43. *Music room performance area.*

even while the construction was proceeding. I had dared to insist that the brick for the new addition match the brick of the old building so that the entire complex would look like it belonged to one entity. Violently opposed by some members of the committee, that brick, complemented by sandstone, copper, and slate details, visually forms the binding glue that holds the complex together. In all the tours I gave after the opening, everyone thanked me for holding out.

REFLECTIONS

Why is preservation so appealing? People often answer with an enumeration of what they dislike—usually modern design, particularly glass reflective boxes, giant looming blank walls, Bauhaus-stingy detailing, and the whole International Style—but it could be any contemporary abstract project. One indicator of why there is so much antipathy to the modern comes from the movement itself. Since World War II modernism has attempted to reinvent itself more often than Billy Clinton. With great fanfare, the New Sensualism, New Brutalism, poststructuralism, New Metabolism, New Minimalism, and neorationalism are announced, with each shedding of skin leading to a shedding of audience down to the recent celebration of destruction which looks to much of the public like self-destruction, but calls itself deconstruction.

Modern architecture has just not gotten it. In a democratic society there is a fundamental relationship between popularity and potency, and while I would never suggest that modernism sell its soul to be popular, it has so consistently gone out of its way to achieve unpopularity that it has become a singularly impotent force today. In his book *The Shock of the New*, Robert Hughes wrote, "Memory is reality. It is better to recycle what exists, to avoid mortgaging a workable past to a non-existent future, and to think small. In the life of cities, only conservatism is sanity. It has taken almost a century of modernist claims and counterclaims to arrive at such a point. But perhaps it was worth the trouble."

Incorporated into the negative image of modernism but really apart from it is the plain dislike of the here and now. The ugly, in-your-face reality of what we see all around us is dismaying; subconsciously people resent it and, I think, turn to preservation for relief. People like preservation because it seems a time-out from right now, a way to reject today's society, whose endless parade of ills consumes the morning newspaper and dominates the evening television news. Some of the interest in preservation begins with a flight from today's realities.

To accent the positive, people genuinely like the old. In contrast to the absence of craftsmanship so evident in most quick-buck modern speculative projects is the enjoyment of the handmade quality of many old buildings and all that such personal care represents. Ostensibly the product of honest human labor, craftsmanship subtlety suggests moral values and theories of redemptive work that go back to William Morris and John Ruskin. Yet some people are content simply to appreciate aesthetically the colors, irregularities, textures, and patinas that come with age. Jonathan Hale maintains in *The Old Way of Seeing* that older architecture is appealing because on some level we perceive the pleasing geometry inherent in the composition of the facades, which, according to the author, can be found only in buildings erected before 1830, when facades were important enough to be composed. The vast majority of available preservation material currently consists of more recent utilitarian structures whose exterior wall compositions are more often the product of aleatoric functional requirements. If they offer a satisfying opportunity for diagrammatic analysis, that is a rare accident and represents only a contributory argument for reuse.

By now the argument that preservation is an antidote to sprawl, ecologically beneficial, energy-saving, and a contributor to the idea of smart growth is well known and need only be reiterated as the assumed strong fundamental argument for it. Moreover, preservation not infrequently involves a building that is itself the result of a previous evolutionary process of untutored indigenous building, tearing down, and rebuilding, which is the consummate adaptation to a place or region. The use of local materials and artisans and the responsiveness to light and climate throughout this maturation process make many preservation subjects the best examples of regionalism.

A rarely mentioned support for preservation lies in its widely perceived higher social status. Despite endless efforts by the National Trust for Historic Preservation, it is seen as, if not a rich person's game, a field for the affluent and prestigious. Prince Charles is a preservationist. The past's golden glow is almost always pictured in books and movies through the eyes and trappings of the aristocracy. In a way, by engaging in preservation one becomes an associate of that privileged class. Therefore, membership in preservation groups generally is seen as a social plus.

A strong resource for preservation (proved by its frequent denial and constant denigration) is nostalgia. The nostalgic return to a reliably better time far from today is essentially a romantic movement. The longing for things and qualities not present is partly satisfied by sentimental scenes of old architecture which let memory launder the bad and make the past seem a far rosier time. It also harbors the sweet notion that it could happen again.

Old buildings are powerful mnemonic devices. The sight of a house that once was a home and even of secondary places such as schools and offices is enough to trigger a tidal wave of memories, making us dewy-eyed. Old architecture prompts recollection of the personal histories which define us; the song "Going Back to Nassau Hall" has made millions for Princeton University. The clientele for nostalgic preservation quite naturally consists mostly of middle-aged people to whom the future doesn't look so good and who can reasonably expect their coming years to feature increasing physical deterioration, pain, sickness, and death. In a dream-like nostalgic setting we stay the hands of time, stave off the inevitable, and escape to rummage around in an everlasting timeless past; we can set aside the present, place death at bay, and play in a womb of comforting certitude. Is it any wonder that Jane Austen is so popular today? Preservation can be likened to trying to maintain a sand castle on a beach. Aren't dissolution and death an integral part of the natural process? Is the very fact of transitory existence, like the short bloom of a cherry blossom, part of its beauty?

If we look to the Japanese notion of permanence, we see wooden temple buildings that are expected to decay and rot and be periodically rebuilt when the natural deterioration becomes severe. Clearly, what is being retained is not the physical building but the architectural concept and purpose; the basic idea and form are preserved as a culturally agreed on perceived value through rebuilding. Things get worn down, but their beauty is encapsulated in their idea-form and will die only if it no longer holds that collectively perceived value. In this sense, beauty is at least semieternal and is not supposed to die. In preservation we continually repair, rebuild, and adapt a building before it disintegrates, because we perceive that it has such core value.

It has become fashionable to say that the very popularity and interest in preserving old things have tended to suffocate new ideas and current perspectives. However, a mature notion of most preservation efforts, particularly adaptive reuse, is a pouring of the wine of contemporary ideas into old vessels. This is not a burdensome past but a truthful present. A building that might, in the economic system of its day, have been built by slaves is not preserved in whole or in part to celebrate the work of slavery but as a piece of the truth of all history, good and bad. To remove it for such a reason is a form of lying, like regimes which obliterate the works of their predecessors in order to avoid recognizing any debt or sharing the spotlight with past leadership. Making use of some of the equity of the past keeps us aware of the fact that we are a product of the continuum of history, that we were not born yesterday. At the same time, however, we must reinvigorate the past with the imperatives of the present and, in our best works, even a hint of the future.

Restoration and adaptive reuse, preservation's two modalities, developed such an audience that in 1981, responding to this new groundswell of pressure, the federal government enacted laws giving it tax breaks so generous that by 1985 they were under attack by the Treasury. At that time I was developing a small apartment building which incorporated into its design the fronts of two canal workers' houses, which were all that effectively remained after fires had gutted the property. Thousands of people commuted daily past the construction, including then-Treasury Secretary James Baker's tax staff and members of Chairman Dan Rostenkowski's Ways and Means Committee. Their discussions of the tax breaks became so heated that Baker's staff bet the Ways and Means staff that I was retaining those two sad old fronts for blatant tax reasons.

One day Rostenkowski's staff called, and there was a resounding whoop of relief when they were told I did not apply for a preservation tax credit for these small historical artifacts that would enrich the quality of the new apartment house. Ultimately tax benefits were reduced for historic preservation but not eliminated, as were many other real estate deductions, as part of the 1986 tax reforms. In the final accounting we cannot expect preservation to be subsidized by the taxpayer; it can and should succeed on its own considerable merit. Nevertheless, tax benefits tend to move preservation projects into a restoration mode. The Internal Revenue Service looks to the Park Service for strict adherence to the regulations, and since something is being given away, the natural tendency is to be uncompromising.

The common thread running through fundamentalism around the world is the need for simple answers. To manifold problems and complexities it offers a reductionist answer: "Inshallah" ("if Allah wills it") to the Muslim and "God's will" to the Christian. It is that simple. Preservation has a touch of religious fervor about it; in an attempt to gain converts there is always the temptation of the simple message, and there is nothing simpler than the idea of pure restoration. But restoration is not literally historic preservation. Restoration as practiced by the new fundamentalists is full of value judgments about what should be preserved, often erasing more history than it restores. What is erased is perceived as bad history, usually the years of abuse and disuse, but it can also be beneficial changes to the structure that occurred before it became a candidate for restoration. Only good history is wanted, and that history is frequently only a scrap of time when the building was first born, a kind of reductionist fundamentalism.

What is needed is some courage about design judgments. Some changes over the life of a building, even minor ones such as aging patinas, can be supportive to the final result, while other changes can actually fly in the teeth of the original design intent. Historians do not like reliance on something as subjective as design evaluation and prefer the security of more clinically applied rigid tests. Some years ago in Savannah, a scoring system was proposed for design elements such as the positioning and proportions of windows and the height-to-width ratios of facades so that an accountant with a measuring ruler but no architectural training could approve or reject a design. Of course, it is the very profusion of idiosyncratic variations that attracts us to preservation, making certain that no such rigid system can ever be anything but an exercise in stultifying conformity. Certainly preservation implies that an implicit design judgment has already been made; what is needed is to encourage receptivity to the aesthetic premises inherent in an existing building and to be open to design changes. For the main work-load in the future—ordinary twentieth-century buildings—a purely historical approach is unrealistic, and review professionals and review boards need to become more receptive to experimentation. If that can be achieved, many more good and deserving but unrecognized contributing structures will be put back into service, and this should be a goal of all preservationists.

What the fundamentalist approach crowds out, among other things, is the cross-fertilization of adaptive reuse. When finely decorated grand structures are the subject, certainly a restoration approach is required; for the Library of Congress and the Charleston Cathedral, I was enthusiastically for restoration. But the vast majority of existing buildings that can be economically reused in whole or in part will benefit from the cross-breeding results of an adaptive reuse approach, taking advantage of the freshly transformed architecture that comes out of the dynamic synthesizing of apparently irreconcileable dichotomies.

If we can accept the notion that there are few instances where a totally new environment is fully created and that there are few absolutely totally restored old buildings with no new elements, we can acknowledge that we are always, to some extent, in the hybrid new-old design conflux of adaptive reuse. These heterogamous designs can be seen as mature transitions to a future that confidently includes the stabilizing legacy of the past; in the largest spherical lens, we are always only making additions to the existing patrimony and the community of built things.

The manifold charms of grand restoration are so hypnotizing that preservationists have tended to overlook the widespread and epidemic abuse of more ordinary buildings and the challenges presented by the new proficiency and popularity of fake historical building environments.

CHAPTER
THREE

[PREPARING FOR]
DOWNTOWNS

ATHENS, THE EYE OF GREECE, MOTHER OF ARTS

AND ELOQUENCE.

{ John Milton, *Paradise Regained* }

Well, Athens must have needed new glasses the day I managed to survive the careening traffic of Syntagma Square only to come upon the offspring of a union of real estate and historic preservation that not even a mother could love. Cringing under the crushing weight of a multistory jumbo apartment building, cruelly imprisoned by its barlike piloti, was a tiny, clearly historic relic of an old church. If Athens was being eloquent that day, it was shouting, "Who left this creepy old little nothing on the road to greater cash flow?" As can be seen in this case, noncontextualism is a common route to the world of the absurd.

3-1. *Noncontexualism in Athens.*

THE ARCHITECTURE OF THE ABSURD

I have often been puzzled about why there seems to be simultaneously a wholesale uncritical popular love of some old buildings and an equally wholesale uncritical popular indifference to others. First let's look hard at the world around us. If we travel down any but the most exclusively residential street, we see what has been not too rashly judged to be the ugliest man-made environment in history. While this may seem an overly harsh condemnation, a growing number of people have realized that bombardment by the increasingly strident parade of attention-seeking building antics has doped them into insensitivity to the widespread conversion of our surroundings into a kind of Architecture of the Absurd.

87

3-2. *Building by H. H. Richardson in Chicago.*

"MEET ME AT THE HAM N' EGGER THE BITE THAT'S RITE MORNIN'–NOON & NITE" splattered in 4-foot-high letters across the decorative spandrels separating the Roman arches of a real Chicago H. H. Richardson Romanesque building should have given us pause, but it seems that a sight like this no longer has the power to shock. The Shazam arrow yelling "FLASH PIZZA" that impales the keystone in a Beaux Arts classical facade may hurt, but apparently not enough. Maybe the giant "BINGO TONIGHT" sign doesn't totally deconsecrate the old starched New England Congregational church, but the nervous jumping signs on high doses of amphetamine proclaiming "FLAME STEAKS" and "XXXX PRIVATE PREVIEW BOOTHS" often decorate everyday manifestations such as the following: Greek Revival fronts pancaked with bleached extrashaggy cedar shake shingles, Moorish Revival facades undermined by glued-on permastone bases, front elevations that have been 80 percent blinded by screwed-on painted steel corrugated panels, and Edward Durell Stone knockoff architectural aluminum grillwork. The list is endless. Years ago Philip Roth pointed out that a novelist with the most vivid imagination could no longer surpass or even match the crazy things ordinary people do; likewise, this reality is far more bizarre than anything an architect could invent.

The worst and most common abuse is a shallow show window front addition slapped onto an old facade like a thick-crusted pie in the face. Enough of the original building rises behind these flimsy one-story additions that the whole ludicrous composition is fully exposed, like a man with his pants down. But you just can't beat for real tackiness Barrel House Liquor's 12-foot-high simulated wood barrel crushed deeply into the sternum of an old Victorian shopfront, or the two-story-high crab screaming "EAT ME" that really torques a building's symmetry, or the beer mug that mildly affects the solemnity and dignity of a once carefully composed classic Edwardian facade.

The Victorian whose upper windows are obliterated so that the latest celluloid gooey monster with a giant orange tile mansard mustache can be portrayed over its formerly elegant marquee has become commonplace among old residential or commercial structures that have

3-3. *Storefront additions.*

3-4. *Major change to a one-story Victorian building.*

3-5. *Classic facade in Baltimore.*

been repeatedly physically attacked by waves of savage remodelings and let-her-rip signage in an ever-increasing competitive effort to grab attention in a pitiful attempt to capture sales.

It may be an accident of history that America's fruition as a great mercantile power coincided with a sudden explosion of cheap choices in oppressive megawatt lighting and unnatural materials foreign to its original buildings. The long view of this new world phenomenon is that no large European city was founded after the sixteenth century and no American city was founded before that; this may explain the old world's semiresistance to the seductions of neon, ultraviolet, high-pressure sodium, mercury vapor, tungsten halogen, metal halide, and other high energy lighting, *and* to Dryvit, Kreonite, Galva-foam, Fypon, Synboard, Trex, Eternit, Kwik-wall, and Presto panels, *and* to Kemlite, Vistawall, and gold reflective glasses with Rite-hite, Roto-swing, and Permaloc aluminum trim. However, even that resistance is eroding. It has become common for people to say, "We were in favor of progress until we saw what it looked like."

Adaptive abuse is characterized by the wretched excess of salvaged porticoes stuck on gas stations (the country's best example is in Charleston), the unfortunate conversion of movie theaters to parking garages, and technically preserved churches whose symbolic interiors are infilled with floors for the storage of dead records or are converted to discotheques. In a hopeful mode these could be considered holding actions, but more often what is happening is simply the turning of fine old buildings into what looks like left-behind junk, which leads to their being literally junked. It is a blind spot not to realize that this is a form of demolition just short of the wrecker's ball. As is often exemplified in minor abuses such as the backdating restoration game (Victorians morphed into colonials to lubricate sales with fashion), partial demolition occurs when buildings are transmogrified, that is, made into an absurdity. This can be a contagious disease throughout an area that suggests the neologism *transmography*. The Architecture of the Absurd is the by-product of a complete fascination with the present and a total lack of interest in the past.

The casual violence of remodelings, usually on the ground floor but progressively creeping up the entire facade, can be seen everywhere in old downtowns. Shiny plastic, Fosroc, Marblelite, and Specstone tile facials are stamped on turn-of-the century French copybook facades, which thus are rudely jerked into a 70-year update. In some cases it appears to be a fate worse than death. The resultant visual war becomes invisible only as the area itself becomes increasingly invisible. Adaptive abuse is regrettably very real, and its widespread presence is a challenge to the efficacy and soul of the preservation movement.

One particularly poignant little example is a small building in Washington's Chinatown where the crime of the nineteenth century was planned. Now afflicted by indiffer-

3-6. *Portico attached to gas station in Charleston.*

ently applied but dominant Chinese graphics presenting Go-Lo's Restaurant, the building was called "the nest where the egg of treason was hatched." Here the plotting of the assassination of President Lincoln and his cabinet took place. Mary Surratt, the woman who ran the boarding-house at the time, was hanged as a coconspirator. The current owner should be forewarned of the fate of his predecessor and the penalties for transmography and historicide.

One obvious aspect of transmography is the blatant conflict between the canon of architecture associated with traditional western civic, religious, and cultural values and the spread of an apolitical consumerist supranational commercialization originally associated with America but by now an almost worldwide phenomenon typified by grafted-on, incessantly upbeat, and relentlessly happy

3-7. *Coined pizza shop in Washington.*

3-8. *Overlays take over a facade in Dublin.*

3-9. *Only the very top remained in Providence.*

images—the battle between the Caryatid and the Cartoon. These composite images reveal an underlying surrealistic engagement with massive shifts in scale and a kind of subconscious delight in bad taste and the ridiculous. Despite being significant financial investments, these altered buildings reflect a street-smart awareness of the need for eye-catching playfulness, although some of the best humor is unintentional.

Transmography speaks loudly of the absence of feelings about the plight of central cities and the basic economic health of old commercial row structures, because such abuse usually means that a building has one foot in the grave. Indeed, the clash between an old building and its new overlay would be comic if it were not so dominant and ubiquitous. Although this style of spontaneous absurdity may have been invented in America, like the transnational corporate consumerism it more and more represents, it now can be seen almost everywhere in the world. Certainly in terms of mindless colossal semiotic excess, America was long ago surpassed by Asia, particularly Japan. We now have global formulas which with the automobile-dependent generic glass office building box have been whipped up into a universal homogenized mush to such a depressing extent that the loss of much of the rich minestrone of cultural identities is a foregone conclusion.

Clearly, I am focusing on the most common and widespread condition, where the conflict between the original building and its recently applied elements is the most painful. There are unique places where the architecture has simply disappeared and therefore the conflict has

3-10. *Painting by the author of supersigns.*

been conveniently concealed under a blanket coating of electronic signage in what could be called urban photospheres. The world has been able to afford very few of these places—Times Square, Piccadilly Circus, and the Ginza, with some minor variations in Las Vegas and Shinjuku. Like a blinding chain reaction, they present an overriding pulsing display of energy in superconcentrations, obliterating any inconsistencies. But these areas are rare, requiring crushing population densities to achieve ignition. Most places lack anything like this density and its resultant figurative consistency, and this is why the resurgence of Times Square and other hyperdense commercializations are not really instructive for most cities. New York commentators in particular too often assume that the tourism and entertainment pull of midtown Manhattan represents a model for other communities when this is of course the great exception.

Returning to the transmography of noncontextualism, anything done with blinders on results in some stumbling, and it is also natural that deep reverence and concentration result in a certain length of tunnel vision. The strong historicist bias of many restoration efforts tends to exacerbate this narrow exclusionary focus with a revealing museumlike orientation. In a museum exhibit it is customary to set the revered object on a pedestal surrounded by a frame, floated on a panel, and stripped of any context, to be appreciated purely for itself alone; too many preserved historic treasures have been treated in this way.

Except for a few special monuments and manor houses, real usable architecture in an urban context usually was predicated on reacting to or linking with the surrounding real estate. A row house stands naked and alienated without the rest of the row. Many preserved buildings in isolation have an almost startled look, as if they were guilty survivors of a catastrophe. This beached whale syndrome can produce a rather strange malaise, like unpleasant reminders of a Guernica-type bombing raid, and the resultant preservation effort seems oddly perverted.

As early as the 1960s books such as *Townscape* by Gordon Cullen pointed out that most historical buildings could be seen from only a few select views and always as part of an assembly of other structures with which they had a symbiotic relationship. Stripped of their urban context and seen in the round, some preservation efforts tend to recall not old times but a fast-

3-11. *Historic firehouse preserved in isolation.*

food franchise building on the strip equally isolated by its field of parking. Buildings saved without regard to their settings invite unintended juxtapositions, creating a sense of overwhelming that can make the preserved look absurd. Beyond these peccadilloes is the unsurprising message that a significant number of people fundamentally don't like the old—old people or old buildings, despite the popularity of the preservation movement. As we approach the twenty-first century, the preservationist position is certainly being challenged by the feigned, the inauthentic, and the frankly fraudulent.

Consider an honest example of modern architecture, the Department of Health and Human Services' Hubert H. Humphrey Building, much ballyhooed in 1976 as a masterpiece by one of the great leaders of modernism, Marcel Breuer. Despite having the world's worst urban plaza—hard concrete benches arranged in a circle reverentially focused on a standard-issue Park Service trash container—it was a celebrated, multiawarded effort to bring modernism to Washington. Today, more than twenty years later, it is not appreciated partly because of its tired brutalism but mostly because its precast and poured-in-place concrete collects and shows dirt and stains more than any other material would. Yet other much older places are loved not only for their oldness but for different values, including paradoxically the cleanliness that usually coincides with newness. This is why the fake old is so popular today; it offers the appeal of the old and the cleanness of the new.

3-12. *Urban design at HHS.*

3-13. *Dirt stains on the HHS building.*

THE CHALLENGE OF FAKERY

At the Copyright Office of the Library of Congress I asked who the little girl in the picture was, and the woman said that it was her daughter, Authentico.

Why are Santa Barbara and Santa Fe so appealing, and what do they have in common beyond Spanish names? They are both architecturally themed creations, pleasantly mature fakes to be sure, but counterfeits nonetheless. Back when these two towns decided they didn't want to be like the rest of the country, they outlawed typical ordinary American-looking buildings and mandated that all future structures have a specific architectural style. Santa Fe chose the Adobe style, Santa Barbara chose Spanish Mission, and they have been wildly successful ever since.

Orlando, the capital of sham environments, has added alongside Disneyworld, Universal City, and Spongerama, Chinese, Egyptian, African, Mayan, and Parisian replicated "lands" as well as a simulated and sanitized Key West, even though the real thing is hardly remote, being about a day's drive to the south. But even the real Key West is now holding on to its raffish dipsomaniacal Hemingway reputation with new artificially dirty, feigned funky, and synthetically distressed saloons with very clean modern bathrooms and kitchens. The future promises to be not only relentlessly themed but inclined to blur the line between reality and the fake. In *Travels in Hyperreality* Umberto Eco describes this American phenomena as follows: "The 'completely real' becomes identified with the 'completely fake.' Absolute unreality is offered as real presence."

The most visible new trend in architectural commissions is theming, a grown-up mutation of amusement parks, wax museums, and roadside curiosities. All over the country, and surely soon throughout the world, themed environments—sanitized, Disneyfied, simulated places—that attempt to capitalize on the success of the great American theme park and other fantasy places are being created. A few years ago Disney planned to simulate American history outside Washington, including features such as a slave auction, where wretched parts of our past would take place twice daily in entirely hygienic conditions. The new $1.3 billion Centro megamall in Germany will be anchored by Planet Hollywood and an artificial lake containing an artificial adventure island. Among the pyramids, volcanoes, and castles out in the Nevada desert is a one-third-size simulation of Manhattan with an extensive cast of its iconic buildings, Central Park, Soho, and forty-eight-story skyscrapers that is advertised as New York without the problems: no crime, no congestion, no unpleasantness, no dirt.

These ersatz places are focused, coherent, planned, and safe. They provide the best setting in which to mass-market products, and they are clean because they are new. These are the qualities that most people extol, but they are only part of the story. Themed environments, particularly when they are done well, send vacation messages even if only for the duration of a minute's stroll down the MCA CityWalk's re-creation of Los Angeles right in downtown LA. The trend is exemplified by colossi like the amusement park cum shopping center Mall of America, which definitively fuses retailing with entertainment; these generally are architecturally themed, fun places where people voluntarily choose to spend their leisure time. Shopping trips become minivacations.

On the surface we don't appear to want oldness; we seem to want themeness, cuteness, funness, above all a differentness that allows us to click into a vacation mode where society's rules are relaxed; for a time we can eat that extra dessert, drink that extra drink, and think and even act out those forbidden thoughts. Themed environments are congruent with vacation, play, and, most important, nonwork, triggering a form of reverie associated with unconventional uninhibited activity. Theming is a means to an escape from an oppressive reality.

Our culture is saturated with the faux, from marbleized vinyl floor tile to infomercials and contrived news exposés. But this is a slippery subject. What, after all, do we mean by fakery? Are revivals fake? Are buildings that have been repieced together out of a few surviving shards fake? Are restorations from drawings fake? Is a building modified and added to over time to meet the changing needs of its occupants fake? Maybe none of these are fake, because they do not have the basic intention to deceive, whether for profit or for mischief. Considerable confusion can be avoided by simply separating eclecticism (the choice of period styles) from pure fakery, which involves imitation, parody, or the replication of something real, formerly existing, or existing elsewhere.

Would-be latter-day Tocquevilles such as Umberto Eco and Jean Baudrillard describe themselves as royally amused by the seaminess and fakery of the U.S. landscape, but what they unintentionally do is convey is a kind of superior Gauguin-like report on the droll cultural savages in America to a Europe threatened by the dominance of the American century. By saying that America is happy with the fake, they are saying that Americans are charming (wink) but stupid. But is fakery, implying the intention to deceive, really the right word? When visitors to Universal Studios are attacked and about to be eaten by a five-story-high *Tyrannosaurus rex,* they are perfectly clear that dinosaurs haven't been around for a while and are not under any delusion that the make-believe beast will swallow them. Pretending is entertaining and, depending on what is being pretended, even downright enchanting.

In the past most people spent their entire lives in work and basic survival-related activities. But we have seen in the twentieth century the steady development and expansion of leisure time and the invention of predominantly entertainment uses to fill that time; in fact, we have long been told that it is healthy to make a separation between the stressful dailiness of our lives, which requires working, going to the doctor, getting educated, paying taxes, serving on juries, and catching a bus, train, or plane, and our vacation and leisure time, which might involve going to a resort, casino, shopping mall, sports event, or restaurant. The buildings which serve these two parts of our lives reflect these differences directly. It is inherent in buildings whose main purpose is to amuse that they have a make-believe, illusionistic, out-of-the-ordinary quality. Perhaps it is the explosion in the size and number of these fabrications that has caught the attention of so many critics. But theming, outrageousness, pull-out-the-stops fakeries are the forms that logically serve an entertainment function, and I venture that few people are being seriously deceived or morally warped by all this in America. At the same time, in our regular lives we don't want to worship in a church that looks like Donald Duck, have a coronary bypass operation in a pirates' lair, or attend a public hearing in a giant orange. The fact that America leads the world in the manufacture of entertainment and therefore the production of entertainment buildings certainly does not mean that this constitutes the majority of our architecture. We easily separate work time from playtime and are not in love with the perfect fake; actually, I believe, the case is quite the opposite. But first I want to deal with the issue of reusing old styles.

If architecture is, as some critics have maintained, analogous to clothing, why is the man emerging from his subdivision pseudo-Colonial house wearing a modern Brooks Brothers suit? Why isn't he bedecked in a powdered wig, frock coat, leg stockings, and three-corner hat? It is clearly duplicitous but acceptable to live in a historically costumed house, but it is also clear that the man does not want to go around wearing a historical costume. One is acceptable by society; the other is not.

On the east coast, the Neocolonial tract house is so pervasively the norm that it is almost deviant to be housed otherwise. Virtually every developer's offering is a variant of the Neocolonial style, and each builder's brand X Colonial, generally executed in cutout plywood arches, nail-on shutters, and neverbend columns, is depressingly similar inside and out. (Presumably as a response to market research, one often sees hanging over the master bed in the decorated model a Lady of Spain painting of a mantilla-wearing, dusky smoldering señorita with a fuzzily rendered sombreroed Lothario skulking in the background.) It would take not only deep architectural conviction to build but even deeper pockets to sell a modern-style tract house, and a purchaser would have to be brave to buy one. Part of the explanation may be that the important symbolic role of tract house architecture originated to represent not the individual but the family as a whole and to suggest on behalf of the family, particularly the children, that in our constantly moving society the family has roots; thus the Neocolonial style has come to convey a protective association with traditional values. My continual surprise is that the minimal artificial trappings used to theme the typical subdivision house, such as snap-in plastic muntins, are perceived to be sufficient. At its most basic, this is just a continuation of the tradition of nineteenth-century stylistic eclecticism, choosing the best (as perceived by the chooser) from the available roster of styles for its associative values; collectively, the builders and buyers in the last part of the twentieth century along the east coast have almost unanimously chosen some version of Early American Colonial.

The real hard-nosed enforcers of tract house stylistic conformity are the homeowners' associations, often armed with architectural covenants. People are all too aware that purchasers do not buy a house but instead buy into a neighborhood, and the surest way for a neighborhood to retain its appeal is for all houses to have the same Colonial style, all equally maintained and landscaped. Owners today consider their suburban houses as temporary investments to be cashed out of someday, creating intense pressure for all to be the same brand X. The Neocolonial house has become an ordinary and thorough cliché, certainly not admirable but so totally integrated, like canned laughter on sitcoms and King James English in religious cere-monies, and so ubiquitous that we can only notice its absence.

Although I subscribe to the tenets of modernism, I also accept the idea that we must communicate with the public, and the public thinks of modernism as a style. I remind my fel-low architects that after decades of earnest preaching and screeching harangues, the message that modernism is the only mode has not been even slightly convincing, and certainly in the residential arena it has been conspicuously rejected. The reason why postmodernism has had such a good run (too good for some) is that when practiced as an isotope of modernism, it can soften the edges of the International Style and achieve some of that dreaded and loved popular-ity. In addition to the suburban home with its putative family reputation, a connotation com-municated by traditionally styled architecture, there are other building categories, such as churches, banks, and some government buildings, where the purpose in selecting a style is not to make a fake but just the opposite. The choosers of period styles for these building types hope to tap into an enduring traditional lineage and confer a pedigree on a building that is as con-vincingly true as possible.

An important distinction between choosing a style and making a fake is that the selec-tion of a style represents the choice of a whole vocabulary of distinctive features, forms, spaces, attitudes, and expressions which are put together in enterprising and original ways to produce a totally new creation, as has been done many times. By contrast, fakery generally involves the relatively unimaginative manufacture of individual simulations or replicas of an existing or formerly existing original.

The fact that styles are so often used predictably is unfortunate, but because these buildings contain the possibility of creative originality, they are in a different category from obvious replica fakes. Since they have this mitigating quality and since it is essential to commu-nicate with a public that thinks and believes in styles, we should set eclecticism aside.

Maintaining the moralistic fervor formerly required to sustain the modern revolution against stylistic work sidelines architects from the primary struggle between fakery and preser-vation and prevents them from seeing eclecticism as including a choice of modernism with all its strains and variations.

Make-believe settings originated in the entertainment world and follow it wherever it goes. The reason why we have such a burgeoning of simulated thematic environments is that more and more activities are touched in some form by or are directly in convergence with entertainment; we no longer use the term *theme park,* but instead use the new industry-approved term *location-based entertainment.* Resorts, casinos, and amusement parks are becoming like the Stratosphere in Las Vegas with its wraparound 900-foot-High Roller coaster on top of the usual array of gambling rooms. Recreation has become less participatory and more of a spectator sport that consists of watching entertainment. Politics used to have unintentional amusement value, but now with television star journalist round tables and gonzo radio talk shows, political discussion, as it is still called, has become almost purely intentional entertainment. Religion has always made use of entertainment in the form of ceremony and pageantry, and music and learning and teaching are increasingly presented in some form of entertainment package. Schools are more and more apt to employ television programming, and much has been made of the alliance between entertainment and the computer. But entertainment as a lure to a serious purpose is not to be confused with its core function, which is to free us from our real lives into the escape called vacation time.

Entertainment is play. The majority of people hate the requirement of work and prefer the freedom of play; people who like to work are the exception, and they usually have work that for them is play. The banality and resolute earnestness of most real places are inhospitable to play because they are too familiar, too serious, and too diffuse to create an upbeat mood. The new play settings are places where the theme is consistently unreal, an almost relentless and convincing fantasy world.

If the Architecture of the Absurd expresses a decline in values, it is only another confirmation of what the media present every day in a never-ending procession of cheating celebrities, amoral crimes, lying politicians, murdering mothers, outrageous business practices, and a scattered sexuality that makes adultery seem quaint. Heavily promoted sermons calling for a restitution of values can be interpreted as an even more secure confirmation of our moral slippage. Many people believe that all this stems from Nietzsche's nineteenth-century proclamation of the death of God, meaning of course a recognition of the widespread death of the belief in God, resulting in trickle-down skepticism and cynicism which, together with our corresponding trickle-down and unprecedented affluence, have conveyed a double permission slip to lose that formerly all-controlling Judeo-Christian guilt. Forget the Protestant ethic. Don't work; go into debt and play. A woman who had severely defrauded her friends in a Ponzi scheme used as her defense the argument that a bad gene made her do it. The 1990s phenomenon of letting everyone off the guilt hook is well documented but acquires its ultimate steam from biology's apparent discovery that the genetic code at least somewhat predetermines our behavior: There is a gay gene, substance abuse and obesity genes, and a criminal behavior gene; nothing is your fault, so go out and play. That message, however derived or contrived, seems to be one more reason why the entertainment industry is going through the roof.

But at the same time that this acknowledged tidal wave of entertainment/vacation time/fakery threatens to swamp western values, I believe there is a burgeoning hunger for real-ness, a search for authenticity. Many observers have been puzzled by the built-in blurring of reality and unreality in America's themed environments. These smudges are not confusions but products of economics; even if the developers would prefer transplanting real old stuff, they can't because it would be prohibitively expensive in practically all money-making ventures. The inclusion of some real elements to show the roots of authentic and grounding pasts has moder-ated the taint of fakery which, I maintain, is on several levels perceived as a threat to our self-image and integrity. Although it is all right for parties and vacations, we are simply uncomfortable wearing a totally fake historical costume every day. Blurring reveals that there is a search and a degree of hunger for authenticity in this sea of virtual reality.

To mark its 150th anniversary, the Smithsonian Institution created a traveling exhibi-tion that consisted of a selection of highly prized items from each of its sixteen museums, including Lincoln's top hat. This worn-out old hat would be totally unengaging if it were not the absolutely genuine hat that once sat on top of the martyred president's head. People stop and almost reverentially genuflect before this mundane piece of stiff cloth because they believe it to be a silent witness to real history. Essentially the show is full of other humdrum things which also derive their claim to our interest from an assertion of their authenticity. In the auc-tion of Jackie Kennedy Onassis's possessions even the most ridiculously prosaic object took on incredible value because it was guaranteed to be the actual thing once owned by Mrs. Onassis. Perhaps preservationists should redouble their efforts toward publicizing the provenance of buildings and issue certificates of historical authenticity for structures, which might help, although the main remaining candidates for preservation—twentieth-century structures—would offer less than thrilling historical backgrounds.

Further testimony to the latent hunger for the really real is provided by a new phenom-enon in retailing, the (Nike, Sony, Disney) superstore. Only a few years ago commentators believed that stores were on their way to becoming obsolete, to be shoved out by mail order cat-alogues, television purchasing such as QVC and the Home Shopping Network, and retailing via the Internet, making buying from the home easy chair an easy convenience. But the new super-stores, besides being another example of the convergence of entertainment and a formerly con-ventional activity, provide enough attractions in their astounding interiors to get people to travel through traffic, parking, crowds, urban dangers, and hassles. The two-dimensional simu-lated reality on the television or computer screen, no matter how digitally perfect, is bloodlessly unreal. We don't feel it around us. We can't exclaim to ourselves, "I am really here." Perhaps constant overexposure to endless nontactile pixel microsmudges on phosphorescent planes becomes too insistently a dry mechanical artifice. As electronic wizardry increasingly bombards us with sounds and images from every vector, we will come to value the authentic being-there experience even more.

As an architect, I know how critical actually being there is, particularly in working on an old building. When starting a project, I diligently study all photographs and any existing visual material, scads of descriptive records, and even previous hands-on work with similar building types, and I can still be absolutely stymied. I eagerly spend hours, sometimes days, traveling to the site for that precious time with the building, walking through it and discovering what it is really like. In even a few minutes one can absorb with more than just one's vision, employing all one's senses to understand the genius loci, the spirit of the place. One feels its temperature, rubs its textures, hears its echoes, and senses its personality and its ghosts; only then can one begin to comprehend the place so that the right responses can come tumbling out. No matter how tedious the journey, the memory of that sense of the place's character and reality acquired often in only a brief but intense period remains with me as a reliable guide.

Why do people go to Graceland, Brentwood, or Versace's gate in South Beach? Because they want and need to be where "it" really, authentically happened.

Ask any middle-class American homeowner if he wants his house furnished in genuine antiques or reproductions, and probably the response will be antiques even though they are beyond the budget. Antiques are more expensive, of course, because they are widely thought to have intrinsic value as the real thing. A Chippendale mahogany side chair circa 1760 from the important Philadelphia rococo school was on sale in New York for $450,000; a High Point reproduction of the same chair, no matter how carefully done and employing great workmanship, might cost about $3,000. Authenticity here is valued at more than 150 times the imitation. Too much has been made of museum shop reproductions of ancient artifacts which copy the imperfections of age much as this is attempted in the reproduction of a Chippendale chair. People know and present the museum reproduction as a practical substitute for the deeply illegal and fabulously expensive importation of the true artifact. The extent of extraordinary detective work and forensic analysis that underpins the amazing valuations for real antiques constitutes proof positive of the hunger for the authentic.

The Architecture of the Absurd is a spreading visual illness that in its projection of disorder, degeneration of values, and plain ugliness is both a symptom of and a contributor to the decline of our cities. Its continued unchallenged prevalence provides implicit evidence of the preservation movement's shrinking from involvement in this common abuse of common old buildings. Although not our subject here, the relatively new typical suburban commercial strip, despite some of Robert Venturi's provocative observations, is also a scene of profound disorder, environmental waste, and general unsightliness. Together, these two panoramas constitute America's exposition of some of the most offensive man-made landscapes in history.

In contrast, the underlying strength in themed environments is coherence, safety, and cleanness. In other words, they are places primarily of order and control which gain their popularity as sanctuaries from the surrounding norm of filth, disorder, and chaos. These themed places have two drawbacks, however: They tend to be overcontrolled, and they are obviously false to everyone. The fakery tends to engender a culturewide cynicism which has been shown over time to harden into a contempt for many of society's basic institutions, from government to marriage, that further compounds the velocity of the downward spiral in the quality of urban and suburban life.

For preservationists the wave of newly created historically themed environments presents a second challenge that is sharpened by an extraordinary level of expertise in building replication. Why save the old when you can build the old anywhere? Why save Old Town when you can build an ersatz Old Town with modern conveniences out in the clean and safe suburbs, free of undesirables? This issue is exemplified by the wildly successful, totally new but old-looking town of Celebration in Orlando which, because of the deep pockets and know-how of the Disney Corporation, presents such a wonderfully safe, clean, and orderly alternative to the messiness of preservation in old urban areas. The corporately created traditional design is so convincing that it makes a mockery of the architects' postmodern work; its only failure is that it looks too good because it is too just-done, too freshly unwrapped, too clean. This is where the difficult to reproduce distinctive telltale patina flaws of the genuinely old become incredibly important, perhaps the saving grace for preservation activists.

How can preservation stand up to this new enticement and reach out to the sometimes clear but often latent yearning for the authentic? Preservation does offer an architecturally different environment which could, for the sake of argument, be considered similar to the historically themed (although through real history) so that it could provide some appeal to the vacation part of our lives. However, it will surely lose out to the newness, cleanness, safety, and order of the fake themed without additional help.

We all want to play, to escape to a rule-free paradise, but we also don't want to be phonies; like the movieland Mafia don, we want and need respect. We can take time out to pretend, but we do not want to be considered pretenders. In the intensity of the inner city we see the premium paid for self-esteem and the death penalty paid for dissing. Everyone fears being exposed to ridicule; to be fooled is to be a fool, a direct threat to our egos and self-worth. By preserving historic architecture, adaptive reuse offers some of the appeal of the historically themed environment but grounds a project in a real past with honestly expressed new elements. Therefore, an owner, visitor, or inhabitant is not dissed; he or she is in fact ensured of respect. Preservation is authenticity itself. In this regard, the new-old hybrid of adaptive reuse is superior to restoration, which can superficially be confused with the themed.

Preservation offers two methodologies to the juggernaut of simulation: restoration and adaptive reuse. The very process of careful restoration tends to overemphasize control and squeeze out permissiveness and play. With the process of making the old totally new again, there are restorations that look painfully like reproductions and convey an uncomfortable feeling of resemblance to the too-clean-to-be-real fakery of the themed. It is precisely the removed patinas, largely the product of sun, wind, rain, and airborne particles of dirt, which plainly make the real distinguishable from the fake. We naturally use terms such as *mellowing, aging* and *deep rich coloring* to reflect our positive responses to genuinely older buildings. The effect of long-term weathering, natural oxidation, bleaching, nicks, cracks, and spalling provides a comforting feeling of authenticity. Imagine one's unease on inspecting a series of travel brochures of Europe and seeing all the buildings perfectly cleaned, straightened, and polished as if brand new. Let us all praise nice, old, beautifully dirty by age buildings.

The second preservation response—adaptive reuse—offers in the clear retention and expression of the patina-confirmed old and the incorporation of the undisguised modern some of that sought-after authenticity. At the same time it includes some of the charm and order of the themed, derived from its old parts, and therefore some of the vacation values of play and permissiveness. The flexibility of adaptive reuse combines the permissiveness, order, and charm of the themed with tangible authenticity and excludes the corrosive effects of obvious or mistaken fakery.

In *Travels in Hyperreality* Umberto Eco says that he came to America "in search of instances where the American imagination demands the real thing and, to attain it, must fabricate the absolute fake." Preservationists must show they have the real thing and don't need to go to all that expense and bother to make the perfect fake. Since the opportunity to express a truly original idea is rare, the strategy of the new driving out the old will always be common. In the present proliferation of simulation, however, much of the new, despite being overtly false, will start to drive out the old by means of its superior economic performance. The battle is an intricate moral struggle. Preservationists want to retain old structures not only for their obvious assets of beauty and scale but also because these buildings represent values ingrained in history, such as morality, integrity, and ethics. This practice is now confronted by the threshold issue of truth or falsity in an allegedly historical presentation. Preservation is very much an ethical issue.

The oldest name for truth in western philosophy is *aletheia,* which can be translated as "disclosure, unconcealment, revelation." Preservationists need to practice unconcealing, revealing, and disclosing the falseness of themed environments. Urbanists should fight back against transmography and the real threat of the themed by forming truth squads to expose the incipient faux and simulated places of today; otherwise the fake and transmogrified trashings will win. There is a basic issue of honesty here that needs to be communicated: Preservation has it, and the themed doesn't. If people can be made to understand this, preservation will have a good future.

Mindful of the disheartening fate facing many urban buildings, as I became more involved in preserving downtowns, I set aside a great deal of study time to learn the communication systems and understand the messages of old downtown buildings, as is discussed next.

VISIONS OF THE FUTURE/THE SYNTAX OF THE CITY

TIME PRESENT AND TIME PAST

ARE BOTH PERHAPS PRESENT IN TIME FUTURE,

AND TIME FUTURE CONTAINED IN TIME PAST.

{ T. S. Eliot, *Four Quartets,* "Burnt Norton"}

As reported in the *New York Times Magazine* (December 2, 1956), a group of architects declared that in the future, homes would be "dumbbell-shaped," with the parents on one side and the children on the other. This poignant child isolation vision of the future, presumably including handy tot-sized feeding slots, may be a real dumbbell, but it is part of a long tradition of slightly demented visions of the future on the part of architects. Rather than looking at the usual trotted out collection of futuristic goofy cities on LSD and steroidal organic architectural concoctions, a good opportunity to see quite a few real and intensely serious former visions of the future is as close as a block of old buildings in any downtown area. For me, learning to read these aspirations and evaluate the life stories of these buildings was an extremely helpful teleological instruction in understanding downtowns. Unlike the constant and predictable architectural discussion of space, this is my own unspatial variation on what French theoreticians call *architecture parlante.*

Look at the different stylistic treatment of each individual building's streetfront

It should be obvious that each designer or builder stretched mightily to give some special distinction to his or her specific slice of the block. A typical downtown block usually consists of a number of row structures which are either remodelings or replacements of older buildings that occurred haphazardly over time. Few designers of facades bother to take their neighbors into account other than to be as completely different as possible from them. I know this well because on two occasions, by chance, I found myself working for two developers with projects next to each other. Despite the fact that, or perhaps because, all four developers were of the same genus—white, male, and middle-aged—they nurtured a splendid acrimony toward each other. Excessive time was diverted from meetings hatching schemes to undermine, sometimes quite literally, the neighboring project. I came to be regarded as something of a double agent whose mission was shuttle diplomacy, mostly conveying thunderous phony intimidations which would elicit matching threats of the real estate equivalent of nuclear annihilation such as "Tell him next time," always concluding with the term *caca* and the designation of precise bodily locations. The worst were orders (unexecuted) to insert live rats in the rival's walls or (actually executed) preempting the other's project name by using it first, but at the very least the directive was to be architecturally different (in reality only partially executed).

The traditional and more pacific solution to this problem is to choose stylistic differences which convey more thought, visual separation, and meaning. Since most buildings in a row are similar in size, their semantic and stylistic effects are communicated through details. Details, which we see as ornament, usually are derived from a joint between the parts of a building (a capital on a column is a joint), and this joint-based ornament is the conveyor of style.

In effect, when each of these typical downtown buildings was born (construction was completed), the designer was offering up more than an enthusiastic reflection of the latest fashion; quite often he or she was actually presenting a vision of the future. By opting for a particular style, the architect was proselytizing, consciously or unconsciously, to the client and ultimately to the world the philosophy behind the creation of that style, which customarily would have been tirelessly advocated as a cure-all for humankind's ills of the moment. Styles are at the very least emblematic of the seminal ideas associated with the cultures that have produced them. Looking at the block as an architectural-philosophical lineup, one can appreciate the likelihood that each of the styles represented was once ethusiastically promoted as a kind of architectural messiah.

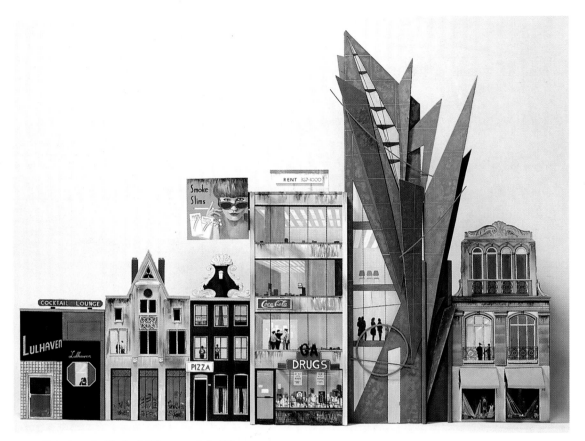

3-14. *Painting of a block of different style buildings.*

John Ruskin, one of the most resonant voices of the Victorian era, put forward God's architecture, Medieval Gothic, as the only salvation of the modern age. William Morris contrasted the ugliness of the machine world with the ritual and architecture of the Middle Ages and maintained that only through such arts and crafts could there be any real saving of humankind. H. H. Richardson saw similar rewards in the Romanesque style. The City Beautiful movement that grew out of the Chicago Columbian Exposition of 1893 held that only through grand classical design could the nation's cities be rescued. The same missionary zeal came with the contemporaneous Viennese Secession, Art Nouveau, and the later Art Deco movement, not to mention all the stylistic revivals. Indeed, Walter Gropius and others of the modern Bauhaus, International Style, felt that only their way—functional architecture based on industrial processes—could alleviate the sufferings of the workers of the world and cure all the planet's ills, the very opposite of Ruskin.

The most recent craze—deconstruction—is inventively promoted to express pluralism and the democratic idea that wholeness, beauty, and coherence do not depend on homogenization. Even the previous antithetical style, postmodernism, was argued for on a similar humanistic basis. In this perspective ordinary, usually ignored city blocks can be read through their styles as unique comparative displays of nineteenth- and twentieth-century philosophies and can even suggest by their condition how these major competing movements and visions have been regarded over the years.

In his book *How Buildings Learn*, Stewart Brand wisely observes, "A building is not something you finish. A building is something you start." This novel shift of focus to the temporal existence of the building and what happens to the structure over its life enriches our observations of a downtown block by looking beyond the styles to the various building conditions, the appliqués and overlays done over time, the palimpsests of the past, and the interaction with today's users. By making a series of readings and interpretations of these row structures, one can get a fairly accurate portrait of our civilization over the past hundred years and some good indications of the future. I stress the notion of accuracy because other forms of communication—whatever is spoken, written, filmed, or sung—is rarely without some slant or bias; protective of our egos, we put a spin on everything. But buildings can't be spun and so remain a truthful passive recording of the strivings, public issues, aspirations, and values of both their time and their heritage and therefore a reliable source of projections. As Lewis Mumford said, "In the city time becomes visible."

Look at the physical condition of each individual building

All buildings, like all bodies, wage a continuous war with nature. The apparent solidity and permanence of metal, stone, and glass over weak flesh is an illusion and, as any physicist will attest, just a bunch of active particles in a constant state of movement and transformation. It is often said that buildings, like some wines, get better as they get older, but only rarely and only if they are lovingly maintained. The patina we admire in an old building may seem to be the mellow aging of a material, but on occasion it may actually represent its metastasized decomposition. We can easily distinguish between a new historicized condominium in Florida and an old palazzo in Italy by the thousands of cracks, dirt discolorations, and moldy encrustations of the Italian stucco. At first glance these imperfections may be romantically charming, but many times they are indicative of the kind of neglect that comes with tough times or grinding poverty. Deterioration often speaks, of the implicit economic balance sheet running like an undercurrent below every building. Expensive to erect and maintain, the majority of buildings were purpose-built commercial vessels that cannot stand empty for long or even survive partially filled.

To quote myself twenty-six years ago, "buildings are destroyed on ledger books" long before the wrecker's ball comes. Bad building maintenance reveals underlying economic difficulties and is a predictor of impending major change, including demolition. An exception

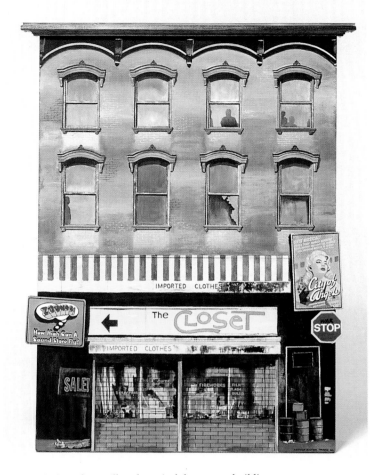

3-15. *Painting of a small-scale typical downtown building.*

would be not poor owners who refuse to paint their own houses and thus are expressing something about the neighbors, their relationship with society, and of course, themselves; another would be buildings in places such as Sarajevo, Belfast, South Central Los Angeles, and a thousand other cities that bear the scars of internecine warfare, a constant reminder to civilization of the violence it so often inflicts on itself. Condition says a lot.

Look at the graphic elements applied to each individual building

Over time most buildings acquire layers of applied messages in the form of signs, symbols, and graphics which have imposed a new language completely ignorant of, or at least totally disinterested in, the visual, philosophic, and stylistic articulations of the original design. These ephemeral but strident message systems represent an instant updating of our current collective concerns, but one needs to dig beneath the durably good news optimism of the advertising to learn that society fears, for example, crime (movies about the bottom 1 percent of society), smelling bad (deodorants), or sexual repression (sports cars). Advertising makes the overlay's contents the reflected counter-image of our obsessions.

There are three types of overlays: street scale, highway scale, and personal scale. Storefronts, street signs, attention-grabbing gimmicks, fads, and fashions at street scale are designed to startle and captivate the strolling pedestrian. Their messages can at times even have some literary content and be consciously or unconsciously funny, reflecting the desirable first step of engaging the peripatetic observer for longer periods. An advertisement for a show called *Moon over Buffalo*, for example, would require some remembrance of the kitschy songs of the past to provoke a smile. Quasi-art forms such as window dressing and poster design have grown up in this service. Street scale has always been easily accommodated within the traditional architectural frame.

3-16. *Painting of roofscape advertisements and palimpsests.*

The newer highway scale overlays climb up on the walls of buildings so that they can be read at a distance from moving cars. To catch bored commuting eyes, these messages must be simpler and much larger, reaching in the process a gigantic facade-killing scale, forming a whole new architecture crowned with fantastic roofscapes. In developed versions such as those in Japan, the basic building has become a purely basic structure. Its architectural design has virtually disappeared, and the building's purpose, beyond keeping the rain off the internal activity, is to support surrealistically inflated images such as a hundred-foot-long bottle of gin, a three-story-high basketball player, and a starlet with a 12-foot-long cleavage. The expansion of scale and size requires the compression of messages, and so even a curt "drink this" gives way to a nonverbal moving image such as an erupting volcano in Las Vegas. In very concentrated renditions such as the Ginza, Times Square, and Piccadilly Circus, a phantasmagorical new world is created, reminding us of G. K. Chesterton's comment on seeing Times Square: "What a glorious garden of wonders this would be to anyone who was lucky enough to be unable to read."

However, when literate people pause to read and ponder highway scale, even in fairly modest versions, they are forced to confront the ubiquitous advance of a global homogenized omniculture which tends to steamroll over local traditions and cultures. Few traditional streetscapes can maintain their dignity and identity when festooned with 15-foot-high letters spelling "SONY," "COCA COLA," or "DRANO." At any scale one remains struck by the world-wide dominance of multinational corporate consumerism, which appears to be the true conqueror after the cold war. Today Rembrandt is a toothpaste.

The third form of overlay—personal scale—is frequently a message of protest with a cover of anonymity. Graffiti now occurs practically everywhere. Some of these urban tattoos are passionately for or against something, many are cries for recognition, and a lot are the childish scribbles of teenage rebellion. In the inner city personal scale overlay has risen to assume the noble mantle of wall-sized memorial murals to popular casualties of gangland warfare. Recently, graffiti has become a form of publishing containing warnings and notices of things about to happen, frequently signed with identifying tags, but in most other areas spray-can art has become an instantly recognized electric symbol of urban ills and decay. The fact that graffiti occurs and that we cannot seem to stop it says more about us than does what the writing actually says. Yet in the many countries under repressive political regimes it is the truest news source, the real voice of the people, and therefore a decipherable prophecy of the future.

Discover the palimpsest of each individual building

A careful examination of a downtown block, particularly focusing on exposed party walls, usually will show the partially erased layers of old images surviving in a faded fragmentary form. These images could include an advertisement for a long-forgotten elixir, the promotion of an unsuccessful candidate for an abolished political office, and a logo with an incredibly cheap bargain price, such as Coca Cola for a nickel. These palimpsests of eroded words and pictures also include those elegiac architectural ghosts, the shapes and impressions of a long-demolished building. Together they become a trail of archaeological clues to the formative concerns and precursor attitudes that have helped shape the present time. These shadows of yesterday illuminate the etiology and evolution of today's urgencies and highlight the differences—what may have been lost or gained. The sense of the passage of time and the nostalgic impression of a simpler, less frenetic society may be provoked by a faded sign for ginger beer. The outline of a demolished apartment building on a party wall memorializes the colors residents used to personalize their flats, the imprints of their dressers and beds, and the solarized shadows of once-hung family pictures, all speaking softly of the lives spent there.

Most of the buildings in these ordinary blocks came about over the span of the last hundred years and so provide both an insight into the nineteenth century and a provocative comparison to the present as we approach the millennium. The discovery of the palimpsest gives us the measure of change.

Observe the present-day users of each individual building

Particularly evident in the downtowns of America's hollowed-out cities is the juxtaposition between the socioeconomic level of the current occupants and that of those for whom the original buildings were designed. Hookers and drug dealers may lounge about the elegant staircases and balustrades of long-gone bankers. The active use by noncommercial occupants illuminates some uncelebrated functions of architecture: Buildings designed to shelter can, in the case of deteriorated crime-infested areas, become a form of entrapment for the vulnerable; buildings designed to protect can shut out the rejected and the homeless. Buildings alone, as Hopper's paintings show us, can

3-17. Painting of public art.

stimulate intense feelings and evoke moods of alienation and desperation. In the process of focusing on a structure, we naturally imagine the daily lives of its inhabitants. An open upper window lit by a television set suggests loneliness and elicits reflections on the state of the extended family, the care of the aged, the degree of compassion in our society, and ultimately our own fate.

THE BLOCK AS AN EVALUATOR OF THE FUTURE

Throughout most of the twentieth century we have seen countless visions of the city of the future in books, movies, and art. People think they know the future and dream of it as a time of innocence where everything will be known and everything will be doable, where everything wrong will be fixed, and where everything will be different from today. Tomorrow, we used to say, everything will be better.

Visions of tomorrow are one of the most durable chimeras of our culture. Yet in the movies and other presentations there is both a sameness and a sense of unreality to all those images. In detail, they seem to ring false in two ways. One is that the physical designs are obvious extrapolations from existing forms and therefore are really not satisfyingly new; this is underscored by the basic contradiction of devising something acceptable in the realm of the unknown. Although this paradox will never be solved, the second way they seem false can be rectified. Subconsciously, we feel when looking at these futuristic images that something is missing; they are not properly grounded, and there is a sense of spurious authenticity. Innately, we know that the world of the future will not be all new; practically, we know that utopia has a past, that an instant, all newly built city with no vestiges of yesterday is rare. This omission of the past is deliberate, and the presence of an existing context is subversive, since it shatters illusions and is therefore a source of revelations.

I realized the weight of this grounding in reality that an ordinary downtown block can provide when I made a series of paintings of blocks, incorporating in one a new, hot-off-the-press, so-called cutting-edge design and in others fictitious buildings derived from today's trends to emphasize how avant-garde buildings and future projections are always presented in isolation as if the earth had been wiped out. In a world scrubbed new, the future is always pictured with no bothersome old things around for comparison. When we put these new wonders into the old context—as in reality they would be—they are instantly cut down to size and demystified and become just another look-at-me stylistic treatment, just another in the row of visions of the future. Placing almost any new proposal, trend, or style in such a context is a fair way of seeing and judging it. These apparently unremarkable blocks can become crucibles for evaluating the proposed future.

As with any text, emphasis shifts in interpreting, but this source—a simple block of downtown buildings—is real, truthful, and articulate. People are always rushing about, preoccupied moving targets, but an obvious fundamental advantage of buildings is that they stand still for analysis. In many ways which our busy eyes do not recognize motion is the enemy of thought. Motion pictures, television, and videos entertain, and their constant movement uses up our concentration, literally consuming our thoughts in anticipation of the next motion. The immobility of buildings forces us to stop and accept their inherent invitation to reflect.

Usually a block or two of the average urban landscape can reveal to a stationary observer a large segment of the gamut of society's concerns. As archaeologists have long known, architecture is the oldest form of written history, and this architectural reading—as opposed to information imparted in print, images, or the spoken word—is always the truth. It is not too much to say that these quotidian streetscapes are each a sort of Rosetta stone of our civilization.

Growing to appreciate downtown blocks by learning to read their substantial depositions makes the learner in the process an aficionado of downtown buildings, just as learning a foreign language makes one inevitably interested in the culture and history of a foreign country. Research into or seminars on what might be called the syntax of the city and the development of this language in depth might have the benefit of recruiting or converting people into urban preservationists. It was for me an essential aid in comprehending the value of preservation and enriching my understanding of cities, a necessity for wrestling with specific downtowns, as described in Chapter 4.

[DOWNTOWNS]

CHARLESTON
South Carolina

"He's coming down the street" someone yelled from downstairs, "and he's wearing a gold suit."

Our star, our developer, the man who was going to save Charleston from massive wanton philistine historic warehouse demolition, was very late for the television broadcast from the council chamber in city hall. All morning I had been gingerly taping my plans and sketches of the waterfront warehouse renewal across the stern and forbidding visages of General Pierre Gustave Toutant Beauregard and other Confederate heroes resplendent in their massive gold frames. Suddenly he was there, dressed not in gold but in a blindingly yellow suit, lemon yellow shirt, and radiation-alert yellow tie, finished off with the de rigueur white belt and white shoes.

"I hear it's in color," he said.

"You're late, the crew is ready, here's your script" said I. The color drained from the face of this brilliantly attired figure. His eyes bulged as if he had just been stabbed in the back at the end of a B movie.

"You mean I have to read something?"

I noticed that his hands holding the papers began to shake. The cameraman said "Ready" and he became a man afflicted with the jerks. After two false starts, hiccups, and some garbled sentences, it was clear to one and all that it was a no go.

John Leroy Baker was a man of such Barrymore daring and Olympian self-confidence that his favorite morning activity was to walk up to an unfamiliar but bosomy woman, shove a hundred-dollar bill down her cleavage, smile, and walk away. Although he hailed from the wet T-shirt section of Myrtle Beach, he had had a career in Hollywood but was vague on why he had traded that for warehouse preservation. The reason became obvious the minute the lights went on and the cameras began to roll: Mr. Baker was handicapped by severe stage fright.

Since my role had momentarily switched from architect to television producer, I dragged the general contractor's representative over to read the proclamation of how we were going to save Charleston. He was a good steady man with all the charm of a lead pipe fitting, but he gamely delivered the address as though reading building specs, a performance which could have put the most agitated and incendiary mob to sleep.

Yet even with this kind of theater we were hot. We were on television. The subject was interesting. The day before, the *Wall Street Journal* had come to town to interview Mayor Palmer Gaillard and had quoted him saying that he was "squarely behind both sides." That hot. Preservation, and therefore architecture, in 1974 was media honey.

Several months earlier a woman named Tunky Somerall had called our office representing Save Our Charleston, a group composed predominantly of the leading ladies of the city. They had gotten organized almost in front of the bulldozer that was about to wreck a series of old warehouses along the waterfront, a collection of random structures involving open spaces such as Lodge Alley, reputedly the site of the first Revolutionary War tea party, predating the one in Boston. These old workaday warehouses were linked by their age and use into what could be loosely called a district which, if saved and rehabilitated, would assuredly influence and even determine the future of large adjacent depressed districts.

4-1. *Lodge Alley in 1974.*

4-2. *Sketch of proposed renovation of adjacent warehouses.*

4-3. *Roofs of threatened warehouses.*

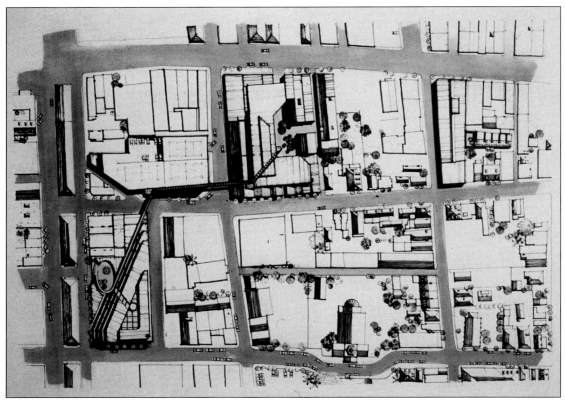

4-4. *Plan of linked reused warehouses and new development.*

4-5. *State Street warehouses.*

4-6. *Restoration of old arches and openings.*

It was then, during the early stages of this venture, that I realized the power of privately developed connective preservation as a renewal strategy for cities: If you work on the neckbone and the legbone, you will affect the headbone and the pelvicbone and eventually the full spine; you will not change the entire body of the city, but you will get some circulation going, and for a lot of downtowns that is a miracle.

If you link pleasurable and nostalgic reuses of key but economically unproductive structures in such a way that they may trigger a different reuse or new infill projects, you will create a district with the appeal and power to influence other districts. The new historic district gains considerable steam from involving cultural facilities and being part of a waterfront, a naturally common occurrence, with all the enjoyable dynamics that involves. I thought of calling this strategy LINRAW (Link Nostalgic Reuse with Arts and Waterfronts), but it sounded too much like a government program.

My approach to downtowns in the early 1970s developed in the context of the emerging failure of the first postwar town-planning panacea—urban renewal—and the suffocating climate of the second wave of heroic skyscrapers and trophy developments but decades before our current urban caricature, which I call the Round Roof Syndrome. It also came after too many chummy conferences full of tweed jackets expostulating on dysfunctional land use, families, and transportation and policy and planning symposia on systemic and regional problems of infrastructure, illegitimacy, pollution, and poverty which seemed to result in little discernible progress. We obviously must continue to deal with the litany of broad urban issues, but we can look at the big picture and simultaneously pursue incremental, linked, doable projects which have a real chance to blossom into tangible results in a few short years or at least within our lifetime. This incremental result-oriented approach seemed particularly apt when there appeared to be disagreement about the long-term problems and goals.

What do cities have at the last resort? They don't usually have oil, diamonds, gold, or manganese deposits or trees to cut down; at the bottom of the barrel their only basic resource is old buildings. Often economically unproductive, derelict, or in the worst case in ruins; old architecture should be seen as the only abundant natural equity left. You work with what you've got. Often, by concentrating on the oldest and worst structures, I would discover a thematic idea that could conceptually tie together a chain of economically born-again buildings, cultural facilities, and carefully shaped public spaces, almost inevitably leading to the source of the original settlement—the waterfront.

Life-supporting even when not commerce-supporting, a waterfront is the single common element in all but the most artificial cities and usually is the site of its most venerable parts. Add to this the subliminal chemistry of the water's edge. The French have long extolled the almost instinctive gastronomic appeal of dining *a bord de l'eau*. In our duty-heavy lives, the waterfront suggests recreation and play, nature at its most elemental, beauty, and Dionysian release; waterfronts are seminal, and we have an innate and intuitive attachment to them as the source of all life-forms.

In contrast to the burgeoning, all-too-new suburbs, I have always exploited these old gray hairs for their nostalgic value, real, created, or imagined. The stronger the linkage between these rejuvenated antiques, the greater the impact of what has been in effect a gerrymandered historic district. The notion of a historic district (legal or implied) is powerful because it establishes a club, and a club by definition has snob appeal. The mere act of definition prompts exclusivity and therefore desirability and class distinction in a mass world. Tom Wolfe has observed that in our affluent egalitarian society, people are looking to separate themselves from the rest of the crowd, and the fastest way is the cultural route. Rich people buy their way onto prestigious museum boards, go to interminable concerts and operas, stand in long lines to see Old Masters, and expend any effort deemed necessary to raise their cultural position in society.

Historic preservation is certifiably U and culturally approved, and property values in a historic district rise as people demand to join the club. Architects wax on about the irreplaceable details and textures of worthy edifices, but the proprietors of most of the stereotypical lead tenants in commercial use buildings, often disparagingly called fern bars, know that nostalgia in the yuppie clubhouse is what their audience wants. Why is all this such a powerful combination? The appeal is to ego, nostalgia, human fellowship, and sex. The problems of American cities are so massive that only an appeal to such an array of basic human desires and needs has a chance of working. It is important to stress that this is only one approach that is not applicable everywhere and that there may be many strategies, but if the right resources and conditions are present, it seems, unlike so many other programs, to work.

Critics will say that the appeal to historic nostalgia is an oversimplification and can lead to the Disneyesque, but this concern has been overemphasized and represents a problem that is far more manageable than the real threat of urban disintegration. Nostalgia for the authentic old is a complex of feelings, but if we can get people to swallow the increasingly bitter medicine of center-city renewal with a heavy honey coating of nostalgia, the achievement will beat endless talkathon conferences and scholarly writing usually addressed not to practical solutions but to other academics. Nostalgia, charm, and the natural attraction of waterfronts are manipulative or, more precisely, seductive devices which should be enlisted in any effort to save our urban areas.

As used here, nostalgia is bait to capture an audience, without which meaningful improvement in our environment is difficult. Nostalgia is in part a fundamental human device to stay the slide towards death. It remains an audience grabber, and without listeners, we are just talking to ourselves.

Since, out of the blue, we got another project in Charleston, the restoration of the Cathedral of St. John the Baptist, I was able to check from time to time on our master plan for redevelopment. At first there was no progress because the main backer of our multiple reuses turned out not to be our friend in the colorful suit, who was—surprise—a front, but the largest general contractor in North Carolina, who had gone belly-up for totally unrelated reasons. Even ten years later, although the realized projects were pathetic, all the threatened structures were at least still standing, waiting to dance. In about the eleventh year, activity began to take off, and when I dropped in a few years later, the hotel we had proposed in Lodge Alley was open; most of the warehouses were busy with restaurant, retail, and office uses; and the adjacent old market buildings and surrounding areas were dangerously veering toward theme park status, although when you've seen as much urban decay as I have, you become much more tolerant of tourist detritus. It may be a lot better to sell computer chips rather than potato chips, but in America's downtowns it is a success when people sell anything other than drugs.

NASHVILLE
Tennessee

The burghers of Nashville knew they had trouble in their old downtown when one of their wives was attacked in that singular nineteenth-century commercial invention, the through-block shopping arcade. The civic leaders thought that what they did—run the insurance companies and the state government—was what Nashville was all about. So dainty and proper were the upper echelons of Nashville society that when a woman started choking on her lunch after one of my presentations (not a direct cause, I believe) and my wife raced across the room to help, the sight of one woman performing the humping procedure of a Heimlich maneuver on another, successfully expelling the gagging meat on the terrifying third try, so mortified the enormous crowd that not a word about it was spoken afterward. This bizarre reaction took place in the basement of William Strickland's appropriately bizarre 1851 Egyptian Revival church on Church Street in the old downtown.

The civic leaders also thought that their Cumberland River was a go-nowhere open sewer (it had been repeatedly dammed by the U.S. Corps of Engineers). Downtown, in short, was dangerous and shabby and counterproductive to their self-image, and so they were promoting new and taller buildings in splendid isolation from it. One such monolith, which was announced as we arrived, was a new performing arts center that was remarkably evocative of a high-rise penitentiary; despite all the tough concrete panels, it had come in embarrassingly over budget. The architect, in a piece of masterfully reverse public relations, said that he could take $10 million out of the lobby alone, but after all, he was only responding to burghers who expected a thoroughly grandiose marbleized foyer for their opera and ballet.

Unlike the city fathers, there was grassroots enthusiasm for preservation around town which focused on the old railroad station, which was only a slightly smaller version of the Old Post Office Building I had been fighting to save in Washington. I spoke at many rallies and speechathons to save the station, and I particularly recall one memorable series. There was a fellow from Texas who scared all of us with an advertisement for a Texas-size demolition company whose motto was "We could wreck the pyramids." He was followed by a speaker who showed slides of cast iron details which seemed to show telltale evidence of termites. I remember musing that there must be a tough breed of termites in the south that could chew on cast iron and wondering how much maturing of their palate would be necessary before they would dine on steel and aluminum and about possible mutations that might prefer concrete: *Termes horribilis*, the preservation equivalent of kudzu. Then I recalled that the majority of old buildings in downtown Nashville had wood joist construction and that I should tell that earnest fellow before his next show that those were wood details.

It was one tough day when I told the city fathers that the world thinks of Nashville as Country Music City, awash in Goo-Goo bars with entertainment by pea-picking folks like Minnie Pearl. This was years before the Branson, Missouri, phenomenon and an unwelcome, very controversial observation. Our master plan celebrated this opinion with the reactivation of the acoustically sensational old wood-framed Ryman Auditorium (abandoned after thirty years by the Grand Ole Opry for a suburban theme park) and the idea of a chain of recording studios and music venues connecting to the old abandoned warehouses lining the Cumberland River, where Nashville began in the 1770s. We walked and talked up our plan of a stepping-stone

4-7. *Aerial view of downtown Nashville.*

4-8. *Model of development linkage.*

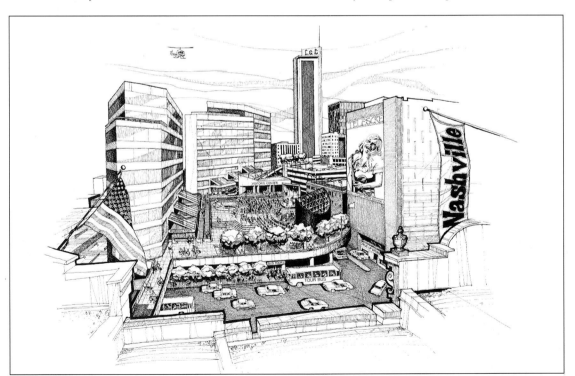

4-9. *Connecting link of music studios.*

4-10. *Old, partly vacant warehouses on Second Avenue.*

4-11. *Section showing new commercial uses.*

4-12. *Closed old Ryman Auditorium.*

4-13. *Proposed restoration of the Ryman.*

series of developments reattaching the downtown to the river, from Printer's Alley and Tootsie's Orchid Lounge down to the old empty concrete terminal building at the water's edge. Focus on the river, I said, reuse those old lofts, and for God's sake don't fall for that urban cliché of malling the main commercial street. Mayor Fulton got up after my presentation and said that these guys from Washington are right; the first thing we have to do is that mall.

I returned many times to push for the plan from 1976 on, and the city continued to say it was working on it. The city did do the mall, and it was almost the coup de grâce for the heart of Nashville. Fifteen years later the allegedly terminally dilapidated buildings on First and Second avenues had become the backbone of a bustling entertainment district, shuttle boats to Opryland and tour boats were on the Cumberland, the Ryman had been restored, and the place was humming. The new life had nothing to do with insurance and government and everything to do with music, preservation, and the river.

It may be apparent by now that one lesson from these two experiences is that like turning a giant supercarrier around, a downtown takes time. Severely aggravating an inherently ponderous process in the best of times is the fact that too many of the core reasons for having a downtown—retailing, manufacturing, and a majority of the business community—are no longer there.

YORK

Pennsylvania

There was a sign in York saying that it was the "Bar Bell Capital of the World" and a museum that went with the sign; although, needless to say, we never found time in our busy schedule to take in the exhibits, it was a good example, like Nashville, of a not-quite-on-target self-image. In 1975 we were invited to York to deal with the "inky stinky Codorus Creek," a waterway dividing the downtown area which had recently flooded a good portion of the poorest neighborhood and was ominously rising again.

People were very restive about this and did not become calmer when I had to inform them that our mandate was to plan for a statistical hundred-year flood and that they had just been visited by a flood that mathematically should come only once every 300 years. Facing the packed, sweaty, and murmuring crowd in city hall that night and knowing that those people might misconstrue the fact that I was from Washington, I felt like a lonely tax collector who had blundered into a convention of the Michigan Militia. Just as I sensed a hint of a groundswell of sympathy for my proposals, a small plump black woman in the first row got up and thundered in a voice that could have come straight from God herself, reverberating off the rafters, "WHAT THE HELL ARE YOU GOING TO DO ABOUT PROSTITUTION?" I explained that I was an architect and urban planner, thanked her for her concern, and said I would look into it.

Following my evolving sensibility in regard to downtowns, the concept for York was beginning to focus on a few key reuse projects, the main one being the Eyster Wyster Foundry right on the creek, an extremely handsome heavy old timber building that was ideal for a range of new uses and a perfect pivot for my design. Planning in York was a matter of deep democracy, since

4-14. *Codorus Creek, old Eyster Wyster Foundry.*

we were continuously explaining and presenting and holding hands with the many constituencies (actually warring factions), up to as many as nine in a day, since they would not sit together.

In retrospect, it was not surprising that an old wood foundry that had survived 125 years of hot blast furnaces, would catch fire and burn completely to the ground while sitting dormant. Someone was paying close attention, because a good deal of our plan went up in smoke with it, leaving the city with only smaller and much less interesting structures. However, there was still the big Codorus Creek.

My idea was to use a novel inflatable version of a bascule dam to create in effect a Lake Codorus as a recreational amenity in the heart of town with the capability of being deflated during floods. The only problem was that the inky stinky Codorus Creek really did stink, and so we hired Dames and Moore, engineering specialists in microbial water analysis, who sampled, tested, analyzed, and reported that the problem was *Actinomycetes,* a microorganism that was feeding off the dark material in the water and then dying and creating the foul smell. In a petri dish the creek water was stinky because it was inky. The dark inky matter came from the Gladfelter Paper Works just outside of town, a heavy contributor to the economy of the region.

4-15. *Old foundry from the bridge over the creek.*

4-16. *Sketch of the redevelopment of the creek.*

4-17. *Foundry on fire.*

4-18. *Model of proposed development.*

This was long before the environmental movement became popular and activist. People took the news very hard and thought I had handed them some kind of scientific mumbo jumbo that was going to kill their jobs. While I was having my muffler repaired one day, the mechanic kept mumbling under his breath about me and my plan, and I became concerned about whether I would see the car or Washington again. As a result of our work, however, the creek was cleaned up, the dam was installed, and the boat basin was built. I look forward to returning as soon as that generation dies off.

York was our first master plan for a central business district that included an implementation strategy: how exactly the community could bring the plan to reality on its own. Using a 15-foot-long progress chart, I showed step by step how all the various factors, constituencies, disciplines, and issues would move through a checking and rechecking process. It included hiring what we called a "public entrepreneur" responsible to a "project action committee" (PAC) representing the full range of active interests downtown. The chart showed comprehensive timetables showing who did what when: when public financial structuring was needed, when developer packages would be put out to the private sector, when public reviews would happen. It covered everything, including the probable left turns required when something would go wrong, all directed toward the reality of construction. (After experience with several more downtowns, I came to believe that the task was too much for a single individual and that three- to four-person teams, as described in Chapter 6, would be more effective.)

We were not naive enough to believe that the chart would be religiously followed, but it did make everyone aware of the hard and soft complexities and the need for a PAC to honcho the process. The toughest part of any plan is the launch, and this gave York a place to start.

ROCKVILLE
Maryland

Rockville was another case of a substantially agitated populace that made for maximum attendance at town meetings. Rockville and Lancaster, Pennsylvania, which we could easily observe while working in York, are textbook examples of the fashion in urban revitalization in the early 1960s. Victor Gruen, then a famous name in shopping center design, proposed a new mall for downtown Lancaster, and Geddes Becher Qualls and Cunningham, a highly regarded Philadelphia firm (Geddes later became dean of Princeton's school of architecture) designed a similar mall for downtown Rockville. Both malls were made of fashionable poured-in-place concrete, both followed the suburban dumbbell formula of department store anchors on both ends, and both had involved the demolition of existing structures and main streets. Both were cosmic disasters.

Lancaster saw it first just at the completion of construction. A sobering experience for me as an urban designer was seeing the not quite dry complex in au courant design being smashed by a wrecking ball, a fate usually reserved for old, tired, and worn-out structures. The never-occupied windowless new anchor department store building was converted into, appropriately, a munitions plant. The Rockville mall received an American Institute of Architects (AIA) award but failed to win the hearts of the citizenry, any shoppers, or any department stores.

In safe suburban Rockville in 1975 a trip to the mall's garage was considered almost suicidal. I used to show slides of the blitzed old Main Street, a thoroughly undistinguished collection of buildings, and could hear the gnashing of teeth in the audience. Unfortunately, we were totally frustrated and hamstrung in Rockville because by the time

4-19. *Rockville in the 1950s.*

4-20. *Rockville in the 1970s.*

we arrived, the mall was locally called the Karen Ann Quinlan project. The city and the principal lender did not want to pull the plug on the thing, because then they would own it. So it remained in limbo, dragging the area down. We put a street back with a bandstand and farmer's market, but it was awkward and crooked because the mall was in the way.

4-21. *Rockville in 1982.*

Following the fad of the day, we engaged in endless community charettes in which any citizen could unburden herself or himself on any subject. They were set up like squishy New Age, twelve-step seminars to focus one's personal energy on uplifting thoughts, but for a change people did not want to talk about themselves; all they wanted to talk about was that damn mall.

The whole 1979 downtown plan, which revolved around the old semi-Victorian court-house, has had only one important recommendation implemented. Across the street, a residential building with streetfront commercial applications that we envisaged had been built, albeit in a style of Victorianesque postmodernism with chickenpox details that forever fixes it as a hangover from the 1980s. Years ago the mall was offered to Hollywood via ads in *Variety* as a building it could blow up for a Schwartzenegger-type action movie, but there were no takers. In

4-22. *Rockville in 1997.*

1995 the mall, along with our urban design improvements, was finally demolished, giving downtown Rockville all the charm and warmth of Dresden after the firebombing in World War II. Like the stigma that attaches to a building where there has been a multiple murder, there is a pall over the cavity remaining from the extracted mall, whose immediate future is to be a parking lot next to the other parking lots. The lesson here is that open space can look pretty awful and that just as progress proceeds at a glacial speed, it takes even longer to correct a badly conceived megastructure in an old downtown.

FORT WAYNE
Indiana

"All politics is local," former Speaker of the House Tip O'Neill wrote. Unfortunately, we found that local politics is often a bit compromised and sometimes is a bottomless cesspool of corruption. Doing a downtown plan immerses one knee-deep in the muck of primal politics, an unwelcome lesson for most urban designers, who prefer to hide behind maps, computers, and theories.

In 1974 the mayor of Fort Wayne, a real pol of the old school, became so entranced by our ideas for the last extant block in the central business district (CBD) not flattened into a

4-23. *Aerial view of the focus block.*

parking lot or converted into whirlwind-creating high-rise office towers where chandeliers constantly sway that he made it the cornerstone of his reelection campaign.

Almost an archaeological find, there sat an entire block of in-use nineteenth-century buildings which had withstood the fiery winds of fashion and the frigid blasts of arctic gusts over the vast prairie of asphalted blocks that made a visit to the center of Fort Wayne such a bracing experience. The very completeness of the block framed our proposed skating rink and plaza sheltered in its backyards and alleys from the terrible gales whipping through the largely deserted downtown. The very ad hoc quality of the leftover spaces was to provide charm as well as protection, while the jet stream winds above drove vertical aerodynamic turbines which would heat and cool the internal plaza.

Unfortunately, the embrace of our plan by the mayor, who with his cigar, walk, and phrasing could have subbed for Groucho Marx but was a lot less amusing because of some allegedly murky liquor business, was fatal. One of the many privileges of living in Washington is that when you call anywhere outside the Beltway and identify your location, people make assumptions and you get the real skinny fast and early, particularly when you call a newspaper on election night; the news was not good for the mayor who had hired us.

Wearing as much thermal underwear as we could fit under our parkas, we resolutely trudged out to visit the new mayor after that fateful November election. A former basketball coach whose main qualification for office seemed to be noninvolvement in the liquor business,

4-24. *Storefronts of the block.*

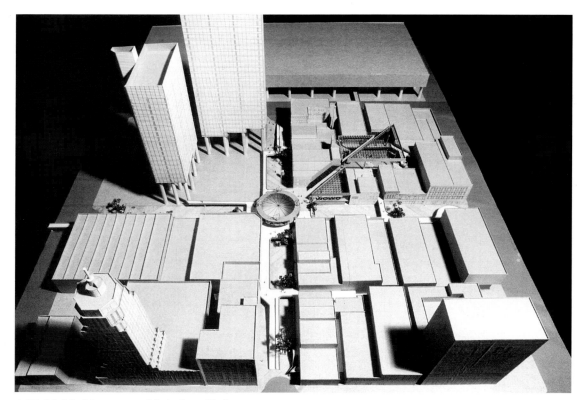

4-25. *Model of downtown with the focus block.*

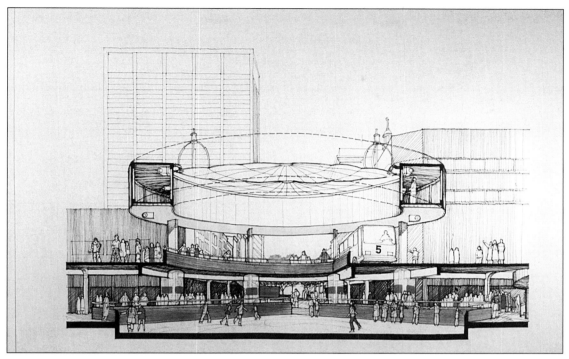

4-26. *Proposed covered skating rink.*

the new mayor, who was known affectionately as Bubblehead, wore a whistle around his neck which he would blow and then yell "Time out" to signal this displeasure. Our plan, which was tied too tightly to his predecessor, had already fouled out in his mind, and he gave it and us the whistle. Today the block is still in full use and includes an apartment building.

PETERSBURG
Virginia

In Petersburg our 1975 plan got caught up in a similar difficulty. Technically, our client was the director of tourism, whose mission was to promote Petersburg's claim to fame as a besieged city at the end of the Civil War whose perimeter of defense had been breached by Pennsylvania coal miners who detonated a massive explosion in a tunnel under the Confederate lines. The resulting crater became the handle for every twentieth-century entity: the Crater Planning District, the Crater Improvement Commission, the Crater Recycling Center, the Crater Proctology Center, Greater Crater Pizza, and so on. A visit to the actual crater was distinctly underwhelming. In 110 years nature had pretty much turned what was still breathlessly described at the Crater Museum as a Krakatoa-like event into a slightly-depressed unremark-

4-27. *Aerial view of downtown Petersburg.*

able patch of woods. I sensed immediately that even further heavy promotion of this hole in the ground was not going to bring in the crowds.

As in our previous project cities, we discovered many benignly neglected buildings, including a remarkable octagonal market which sat facing a hardware store where time had been in such a coma that one did not want to startle the ancient dust on the old nails and tools with even a whisper. I wondered how we could preserve and even embalm for future viewing the tarrying of change embodied in these and other adjacent structures.

Nearby, of course, and cut off by decades of ill-conceived improvements, was Petersburg's source, the Appomattox River, which, along with flood control measures, we would reintroduce into the area to bring it all together in a coherent riverfront project. I invited the entire, by then intrigued town to lunch one day at the octagonal market. It accepted, after which, like a Pied Piper with a bullhorn, I led the wonderfully enthusiastic crowd on a tour of its downtown, describing our proposed changes along the way. It was a great heartwarming and happy success. We were close, but it was not to be.

As I mentioned previously, our client was the director of tourism, not the city, because tourism had the money. Far away from the crater and the downtown, Petersburg had cleverly incorporated an interchange on the heavily used north-south Interstate I-95, where four motels flourished because the spot was ideally located seven to eight hours from New York City on the way to Florida. It was a perfect tourist sleep trap on which the tourism director, like the troll under the bridge, had cannily levied a tourism toll, some of which, it was alleged, had made its way into his private account. Once again political change fueled by a dark discovery doomed our plan.

Years later, when a hurricane flooded and severely damaged the time-warp buildings that had been kept in part because of our efforts, I thought of our little harbor with its built-in flood protection devices and reminded the civic leaders of this once-loved image. Some cities have the energy to fight for survival, and others, like Petersburg, once larger than Richmond but by then a quarter of its size, choose to slide into decline through a kind of common consent.

4-28. *Old warehouses downtown.*

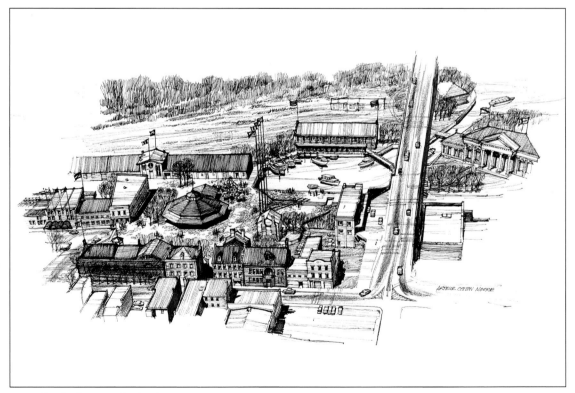

4-29. *Sketch of proposed redevelopment.*

4-30. *Night lighting of the new harbor area.*

4-31. *Town luncheon.*

COLUMBUS
Georgia

When we all sat down for the kickoff lunch in Columbus, I noticed that as the city council members and the downtown boosters took their seats, no one was sitting next to the mayor. After some introductory chitchat, I asked the booster on my right what that meant. "We have a weak mayor system of government, and that is a very weak mayor," he answered laughing. After almost demolishing his glass to get our attention, the mayor struggled to his feet and made some introductory pleasantries that dealt with the issue of why Mr. Moore needed a police helicopter. My response—that I needed to get an overall aerial perspective—may have been all the words I addressed to him in the whole time we were replanning his downtown.

It sounds crass, but like wildly scanning the room at a college mixer, doing a downtown requires finding out lightning fast who the major players are. Columbus in 1975 was a hardscrabble mill town marked by how, when the whistle blew at five o'clock, the burned, baked, cracked ocher ground and the dirty old red brick mills came alive with the change of shifts. It reminded me of old socialist black and white movies featuring the mass of workers, the tough-ass cruel mill foreman, and the unseen but oppressive power of the conglomerate owners. Oppressive too was the summer heat of this frayed industrial setting which predated the Civil War and gained its endurance, strength, and power from the only cool thing in town, the fast-flowing Chattahoochee River. As we walked around, I remember searching desperately for a water fountain in this alleged city of fountains and then scuttling like a crab on hot sand between precious patches of shade.

Although it was not in the downtown area, there was one cultural institution in the city, the Bradley Museum. The Bradleys also owned some of the immense mill complexes along the river; unlike the mayor, Mr. Bradley was definitely a major player. The helicopter photographs we took of those earth-toned mills showed a rare kind of sinewy industrial beauty in which all the parts seemed to have become impeccably consolidated over a very long time; anchoring this venerable mass on the south side were the holdings of Mr. Bradley. In hindsight, one of my minor mistakes was not treating him as the lord of the land he truly was, but as it turned out, he was southern friendly, although he did not really try to help once I devised new uses for some of his empty buildings, such as the Columbus Iron Works, a Confederate gunboat factory which we and a local firm turned into a trade and convention center in 1982 as the south pole of our master plan.

4-32. *Aerial view of downtown.*

I also misjudged the considerable power of single ownership of local newspapers and the intense boredom in the town, which resulted in my being dogged by reporters on every visit as though I were a morphed version of Frank Lloyd Wright and Elvis. Incredibly, and as I look back rather rashly, I sought to confront the real moneymaker for the town: Fort Benning on leave. I had always said that when the boys came to town on Saturday night in 2000 B.C. or yesterday, they did not come for better shopping bargains. Fort Benning was an ocean of fun-loving boys just waiting for Saturday night. Establishments catering to this clientele were popping up like daisies in a wheatfield all over the downtown, and so I boldly proposed an adult entertainment zone as a way of achieving aesthetic and practical control. Oddly, in this deep Bible Belt region in the 1970s, people were far more realistic about this venerable urban function than they would be in today's era of family values. However, since it was not the central focus of our plan and would involve courageous governmental action under the weak mayor, nothing happened except a vastly sharpened interest in our work on the part of the press. I still believe that a return to this idea, perhaps in an altered form, can be a reliable resource for downtowns.

One needs to have almost perfect pitch to hear the nuances while offering up one's ideas to a basically foreign audience. A key element of our scheme was to import into the CBD a waterfront presence, by means of a canal, from the beautiful Chattahoochee, which was walled off from the downtown area by the mills. To someone who lives on and has designed five

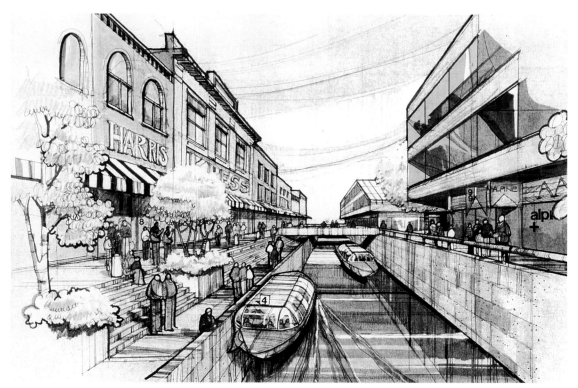

4-33. *Proposed canal for downtown.*

projects along the C&O Canal and who loves Amsterdam, Venice, and Bruges, canals are romantic things and people magnets. But in Columbus it was as though I were talking about root canals, because I heard over and over that canals were those stinky things out at the dump, and despite all our seductive pictures and analogies, canals for Columbians never quite lost that perfume. A wet finger in the wind needs help from the metaphoric equivalent of a wet nose or a wet ear. Our fall-

4-34. *Old Iron Works building.*

back option of a tramway also seemed strange to people who, despite being able to park head in and within spitting distance of any store's cash register, all felt that downtown was going down the commode for lack of parking. The fact that an adjacent parking garage went bankrupt because of a surplus of storefront spaces did not, as they say, matter a hound's tooth.

Despite these missteps, I count Columbus a partial success. New investment came into town, buildings were rehabilitated, new buildings were put up, and most important, a direction which was not a delusion had been set and the town, which before we arrived had been flattened by the usual parade of American urban ills, got some new life. The overwhelming global

4-35. *Old Iron Works converted to a trade and convention center.*

4-36. *Vehicular entrance to the trade and convention center.*

4-37. *End of the main halls of the center.*

4-38. *Auto show in the center.*

4-39. *Decorative use of old manufacturing elements.*

problem of cheap available labor, particularly for textile manufacturing, the raison d'être of Columbus's existence, is bound to take its toll. No amount of creative planning can surmount such a sea change in underlying international economics. But as had occurred in Charleston and Nashville, which had a big lead in established tourist attractions, the alternative nostalgia natural resource linkage seems to have legs, although it takes far longer than most urban designers can abide.

AN ALTERNATIVE TO WASHINGTON'S DOWNTOWN URBAN RENEWAL PLAN

Surely the worst acronym ever was devised when "Businessmen Affected Severely by Yearly Action Plans" was condensed into BASYAP, which inevitably took the plural *basyappers.*

Basyappers were, as the name suggests, a pack of small shop owners selling mostly old books, trinkets, and clothing who were furiously biting and yapping at the heels of the Washington, D.C., Urban Renewal Agency. The lead yapper was a purveyor of uniforms to fire fighters, delivery persons, the clergy, and police officers, giving him a certain air of authority.

The din of yapping arose out of the agency's 1971 decision to demolish the small old shop buildings so that nice new big buildings could be built on their land. Largely through natural ineptitude, the agency was also aimlessly jerking around these small fry with constantly changing projections on when they would be evicted, and the cloud of uncertainty was preventing the basyappers from planning ahead or repairing their gutters, roofs, and facades. All this was accelerating, visually and actually, the deterioration of Washington's old downtown.

I proffered a solution that, in the postmodern mode, was appropriated by others years later in another part of the city and transformed into a true Washington absurdity. I had noticed that there was a great deal of open space for new development on each of the agency's four targeted blocks, but it just wasn't in nice simple rectangular shapes; however, if one applied even a minuscule amount of ingenuity, one could come up with a reasonable structural grid which could be drilled into the existing pattern of open lots, courts, backyards, sideyards, and alleys; with modest cantilevers, a new building could be built which, together with the rehabilitation of the existing buildings, would achieve the urban renewal goal of full density. This idea meant that many of the existing small businesses could stay as the new density was created around them, with no moving or relocation costs and with far lower acquisition expenses for the government. Altogether, this additive renewal approach would cost less and produce a more diverse and interesting downtown. Even after factoring in increased structural

4-40. *Buildings occupied by small shop owners in the downtown area.*

costs, special protection measures, tax implications, and all public expenses, it was far cheaper.

It is fair to say that when the idea was published in the *Washington Post,* it caused an uproar. Committees were formed for and against it, and I was retained by the suddenly revitalized basyappers. Congress held hearings, and I learned that (get a good grip on your chair) government agencies do not always tell the truth or play fair and square and could, with the ease of a raw oyster sliding down a throat, descend to a new shameless level far below even the machinations of the private sector.

Since the National Capital Planning Commission was stacked with representatives from the various government agencies whose backsides showed the tooth marks of the basyappers, it was, to say the least, unreceptive to the proposal. With lobbying by the real estate industry, the conclusion was foregone.

My sketch for the alternative renewal had emphasized the streetfronts of the row of old buildings on the 700 block of F Street, and the large added building behind that row was drawn with deliberate architectural abstractness for clarity of communication of the concept: new being added to old. However, in detailed block-by-block layouts I showed the old buildings fully intact, coexisting with the large new structures, even suggesting some cooperation in their mechanical services.

Years later I saw to my horror that several projects, the best known being Red Lion Row on Pennsylvania Avenue, had been constructed around town and were uncomfortably reminis-

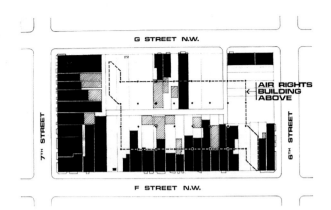

4-41. *Plan of a typical block.*

4-42. *Published sketch of retained buildings.*

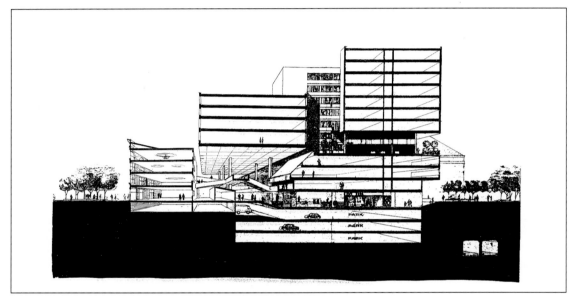

4-43. *Section through old buildings.*

cent of my original diagrammatic sketch for the urban renewal area: small-scale existing and giant new abstractly anonymous buildings. Beyond the absence of not even a feeble attempt to relate the big new thing to the little old buildings, a further conceptual defect had occurred: The old buildings had actually disappeared, with only their front facades remaining. It turned out that a compromise had been struck between the strengthening preservation movement and the developers in which the old row's red brick facades would be propped up by the liberal use of steel struts, while the new unsympathetic pale yellowish concrete megalith would be constructed immediately behind them, with a shallow concealed joining between them to keep the rain out. The combination came to be called by the not totally approving name of *facadomy* and remains one of Washington's few aesthetic contributions to western civilization.

I've learned to be a bit more precise in my delineations, particularly when they're going to be spread over six columns across the front page of a newspaper section.

4-45. *An example of Washington facadomy.*

4-44. *Propped-up old facades.*

WINSTON-SALEM
North Carolina

In Winston-Salem even the weather can be a nicotine delivery system. When the wind shifted from the factories you'd swear that Mother Nature had taken up cigars. This is such deep Philip Morris and R.J. Reynolds country that some people think the town was named after the cigarettes rather than the reverse because there were so many obvious rewards for these products.

We were there because the arts council had decided that downtown Winston was lacking something, specifically, people, charm, interest, and a home for the arts council; it had the usual clutch of high-rise bank buildings, a hotel, and a convention center but remarkably little else. Like so many medium-size American cities, it had an eerie, profoundly disconcerting, quiet empty feeling, as if a neutron bomb had vaporized everyone not protectively encased in automobiles.

The use of cultural and art centers as a revitalization force is a limited but reliable maneuver; it was appropriate in this case since the Winston-Salem Arts Council was one of the oldest of these organizations in the country. Even better, sitting on its board were some well-fixed people from the Hanes family, one of the largest underwear manufacturers in the world, and of course Big Tobacco, which was very lucrative and far less controversial in 1982.

Happily, still remaining next to the almost nonexistent CBD were an old textile mill, a garage, a former Cadillac showroom, a huge empty parking lot, and an old YMCA, all in effect

4-46. *Old textile mill.*   **4-47.** *Mill renovated as an arts center.*

out of service. The mill with its sawtooth roof of north-light monitors was the type of rare industrial building a preservationist dreams about and was perfect for the galleries and studios in the arts council's program. The other two attached buildings—the garage and the Cadillac showroom—were the type of nondescript banal twentieth-century commercial structures that I have always promoted as a valuable equity in our cities. The YMCA had classical pretensions, and the parking lot had no pretensions or utility whatsoever, there being so many adjacent parking lots that a meter maid would have starved to death.

The mill shell was by this time in my practice second nature, particularly with its heavy timber and beautifully structured light-giving forms; its only imperfection was a small but gross exterior alteration that interrupted the basic rhythm of the building. It should have been excised with the original form restored, but the state historic preservation officer ruled against that because this offhand careless change had been done within the first fifteen years of the building's existence, making it as historic as the original. The fact that this noncontributing change triumphed over the basic design system of the building is a good example of the rigid historicism versus design issue that was discussed in Chapter 2.

The connecting garage, which was nearly totally devoid of any quality but the most rudimentary structural frame, became the focus of our most extensive intervention. Its new role became that of the central circulation space containing the then newly required handicap ramps and stairs distributing visitors to the various levels and displaying arts and crafts at the same time. Highly visible through new sloping glass facing the street, the exploded expressionistic elliptical space provided a variety of overlooks designed to intrigue the visitor and double as a venue for small performances and general gatherings.

The purpose of the overall design was to turn the barren parking lot into a central park for the city. The principal donor was a firm woman executive who had inherited a successful

4-48. *Old garage.*

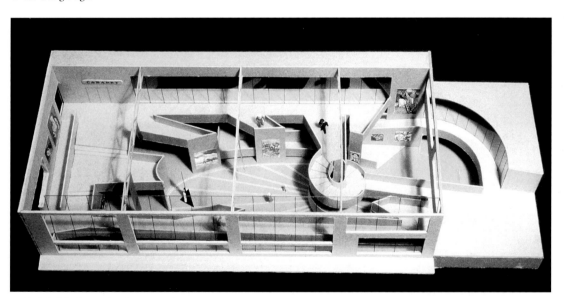

4-49. *Model of a major change to the garage.*

trucking company and was accustomed to dealing with truckers and probably their happy-go-lucky union as well. After she had flat out rejected three schemes, in desperation I flew down and made a model right in front of her; I don't know if it was the attention or the design that won her over.

The new park is subdivided into an upper tree-filled parterre and a large performance amphitheater that takes advantage of the topographic fall and nestles into the slope of the land. A pedestrian bridge links the mill complex to the renovated YMCA and provides the boundary definition of the park; it also acts as a human-made hard-edge foil to the naturalistic, participa-

4-50. *Garage remodeled into a central gallery.*

tory rock garden fountain which forms the backdrop to the stage and contributes a white sound buffer noise that masks the noise of the adjacent main traffic thoroughfare.

The contrasting play of natural stone waterfalls with sweeping concrete geometric forms delivers a focal activity that is visible in all parts of the park. A natural path invites exploring around the fountain and leads over the waterfalls to climb gradually to the bridge level. Immediately, of course, the design was branded in the press as Japanese, and I sensed some disappointment at the public dedication that I was not even remotely what North Carolinians thought a venerable Japanese Zen garden master should look like.

Acceptance by the donor turned out to be only part of the approval process. The board imported William H. Whyte from New York, who had just completed his famous studies on how people interact with public places and the most common design blunders behind the extensive production of dead plazas and lonely parks in most American cities. His review took place in front of a sizable crowd, and I was greatly relieved after my presentation that the sage of public spaces declared that we had done all the right things.

Winston-Salem was one city where we didn't have to invent projects that had to be scraped together from spare change. This was a new experience for me, since I was familiar only

4-51. *Former parking lots.*

4-52. *Winston Square Park.*

with the speculator-client's customary financial fit with accusatory rant or a literal retreat into a womb position on the floor, rolling around with tear-stained cash-flow projections. Whenever there was a change order request, the general contractor would take full responsibility and profusely apologize, and the arts council would graciously take care of it. As the star attraction at the dedication, the council sprang for Zsa Zsa Gabor's considerable cross-country travel expenses and public appearance fee because, as it said, she was the finest example of historic preservation.

CORNING
New York

In 1985 Corning was so exciting in the evening that we took up bowling. However, in the clear light of day the city knew exactly where the real action was. Situated in what was referred to by the locals as Dismal Valley, the town had already transformed its nineteenth-century commercial blocks into a charming, almost precious Market Street devoted adroitly to selling Pyrex and other glassware to tourists driven about in London double-decker buses. We were there to do the Corning Action Plan for a key part of downtown involving a central plaza, a park, and a major parking facility.

The garage, which was built first, dealt with the daunting question of how one quietly inserts a building that can hold 3,000 automobiles into a context of predominantly 20-foot-wide row buildings. The massive scale of such a singularly modern use could easily overwhelm the town's old horse and buggy character. Fortunately, we were able to hide most of the bulk behind existing buildings and covered the exposed side with a sort of market-looking arched facade enriched with many of the nearby Market Street brickwork details. The design had the additional advantage of pointing the way to the old bridge.

State highway engineers had just completed a large, multilane unendearingly functional new bridge across the very shallow, or deeply wet, ditch known as the Chemung River, leaving the old classically styled arched bridge nearby (one source for our garage design) to await demolition. I joined other voices in trying to save the bridge and then had to figure out what to do with it.

There is a unique genre of bridges with buildings on top, such as the original London Bridge, the Ponte Vecchio in Florence, the Rialto in Venice, and the Pulteney Bridge in Bath, which are durably fascinating. So I proposed placing on top of the bridge a museum devoted exclusively to art in glass, a special branch of artistic work, that is both predominantly

4-53. *Aerial view of downtown.*

4-54. *New garage from Market Street.*

4-55. *New garage behind Market Street buildings.*

4-56. *Proposed Museum of Art in Glass on old bridge.*

American and uniquely related to Corning but at that time was ill housed in the Corning Glass Museum. The new world-class museum, shaped into an elongated Crystal Palace, could tie the bifurcated tourist offerings together: the main glass museum (the attraction) on the right bank of the river and the Market Street shops (the revenue) on the left bank. The central glass dome housing the museum café would be covered with Narcissus Quagliata's glass sculpture recalling the ice house in Dr. Zhivago. Designed to be done in Corning-invented polychromic glass (solar self-darkening) and featuring a frieze of stained glass tondos provided by glass artists, the building would shine at night like a colored glass linear lantern, doubled by its reflection in the water. It could become the symbol of this glassmaking town, especially visible to all the traffic crossing the new bridge only a few feet away. Corning is a company town, and unfortunately, back then some Corning products did less well than expected, putting the bridge project on hold. There are performances in the central plaza, a Saturday farmers' market at the garage, and events at Centennial Park, and the old bridge has been reinforced to carry tour buses and pedestrians. I still await the Museum of Art in Glass, however, which was so enthusiastically approved by Corning's board at the time.

BALTIMORE
Maryland

I was just finishing the last slide in my presentation, and as I turned to face the audience, my heart sank when I saw the expression on Mayor Schaefer's face—a contorted scrunched-up prunelike visage, as if he were in terrible pain. As I stammered to an abrupt close, my only thought was that I must really be dead in this town. On the way out I asked the housing and community development director, my nominative client for the new and old wholesale fish market, what I had done wrong. "He loved it; he just hopes that you can pull it off," he replied.

Pulling it off concerned me as well, because the fulcrum for this 1978 leveraged design was tapping into that jealously guarded deep well of resources known as the Highway Trust Fund. The concept arose from the realization that the completion of the Jones Falls Expressway would run through the old fish market building, triggering the funds for a new replacement facility. The space actually needed for the expressway, however, included only the back end of the existing building. Suppose, I thought, the new market was constructed a distance away from the existing old market but precisely equal to its width. Then I could place the rear facade, which had to be moved for the expressway, so that it could join the space between the new building and the old one. In such a pivoted position the old back facade would screen out the new elevated expressway and help form a new square for the city. The old market building, 95 percent still standing, could then be reclaimed as an arts center, a long desired feature for the Inner Harbor area. I had just moved a sizable masonry building twice in the Foundry project, and so I knew firsthand that rotating a major brick facade which would have been demolished otherwise was feasible and not prohibitively expensive. Beyond the special character created by the old wall joining the new and old market buildings in shaping the new square, there was a kind of Calvinistic sense of economy in the maneuver. For reasons buried in the maze of highway bureaucracies, the expressway did not go ahead, and so this urban legerdemain did not happen, although the mayor apparently was impressed.

I was impressed by the mayor when I saw him turn down a $50 million grant from the federal government. As a side task, we had been requested to illustrate the new fad from the Urban Mass Transit Administration: elevated monorails. When Mayor Schaefer saw the frightening image of the monorails above Baltimore streets, he was appalled, said he didn't want those trains going "rattlee rattlee" over his head, and told his salivating minions to forget it.

He must have seen my combative side, because I was named the city's architect, shotgun married to the designer for the Greater Baltimore Committee in a joint Faustian bargain to save the retail district. Essentially, the basic idea was to drop two tomcats into a barrel and watch them fight. Although this might have proved amusing, I later learned that we were just the unknowing surrogates for long-standing grudges and fundamental enmities between the city and the committee that went back to the Charles Center, Baltimore's first great attempt at renewal.

The city's retail district was showing signs of imminent collapse. All three major department stores occupying three corners of the main retail intersection announced that they were leaving. I came up with an idea to join these fading flowers with a lobby spanning the intersection, in effect binding them into one great interconnected superstore. Like a trained cock, our opposite number attacked with fury, and for internal peace I abandoned the idea while it was still in its formative but promising stages. The peace was not to hold, and after many pitched battles we won a

4-57. *Aerial view of the old fish market building.*

4-58. *Rear portion to be destroyed by a freeway.*

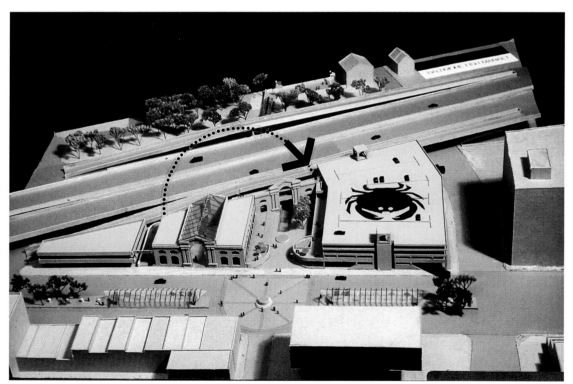

4-59. *Model with rotated facade.*

Pyrrhic victory on the basis of a design recognition of the value of one of the city's oldest institutions (Lexington Market) and its newest (the subway). I realized that the hill supporting the old but still vital Lexington Market was going to be tunneled by the new subway system and that the main retail intersection was at the same elevation as the subterranean subway station platform but was a long block away since the ground sloped steeply. A giant excavation on one side of the subway station would open it up to the sun and provide an opportunity to create a multiterraced sunken garden that would integrate all the sloping sides. The old market and the surrounding area could then be linked to the main retail intersection by a subway station, all communicating through various levels. Of course, the scheme came to be called Baltimore Gardens.

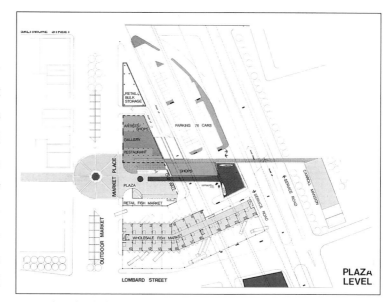

4-60. *Plaza-level plan.*

But the momentum was lost. The future for inner-city retail had further dimmed, and the area could not compete with the simultaneous development of the Inner Harbor; as I have said before, you can't beat a waterfront. Nevertheless, our shifting of the focus to Lexington Market resulted in the city supporting and improving it considerably.

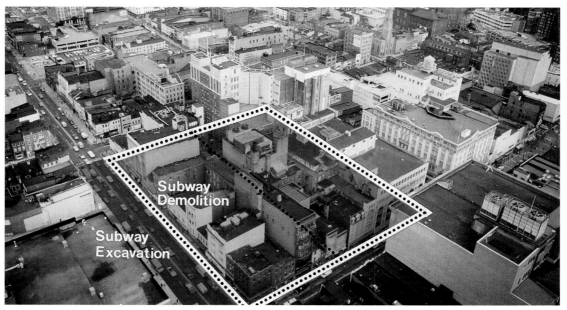

4-61. *Subway work.*

159

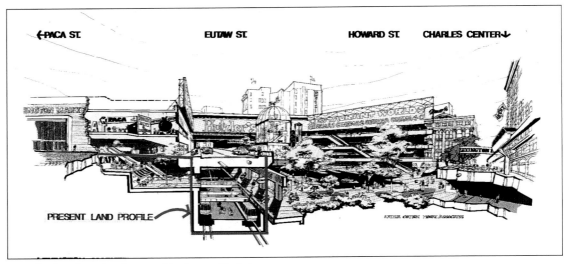

4-62. *Section through subway and Lexington Market.*

4-63. *Model of Baltimore Gardens.*

REFLECTIONS

The urban design–CBD master planning portion of my practice has taken me to thirty-six cities, ranging from Port Mansfield, Texas (where the bizarre task was to raise the population from two to something more commensurate with the bountiful $10 million federal government investment in infrastructure), to Gudrun, Arkansas (location of the world's worst restaurant), to Beaver, Oklahoma (home of the world's only cow chip–throwing contest), to Schenectady, New York (where we were instrumental in creating a performing arts center out of an old vaudeville movie theater and resurrected a block of abused old facades), to St. Petersburg, Florida (where our design solution became the keystone of a court order regarding a crucial landmark).

(The reader may be curious to know exactly how the members of the ladies auxiliary in Beaver made the fresh cow chips suitable for throwing. They dried them out in their ovens.)

As I hope I have shown, the majority of these downtown planning efforts were in some way beneficial, but many also were significantly flawed. Perhaps this was inevitable considering the raft of competing interests, the idiosyncratic and basic problems, the local politics and greed, the sheer overwhelming complexities of any downtown of any size, and my own fumbling for solutions. Nevertheless, they convinced me of the need for multidisciplinary people geared solely for action who can reach out and squeeze the gaps between the overgeneralized and overambitious made-for-speeches policies, the aerial float of academic statistical and design theories, and the hard as cement political and economic realities. Such new generalists, who must be able to provide the follow-through leadership and have the adroitness to put actual recycling and/or renewal into action, are still rare.

4-64. *Typical downtown facades, before.*

4-65. *Typical downtown facades, after.*

At first I thought that these experiences were so varied and polymorphous that they would defy summary or synthesis, but one discouraging trend seems to overshadow all the others: There appears to be a growing lack of interest in the fate of our cities, as if there were a national consensus that their time has passed. Testifying to this distaste has been the spectacular absence of urban affairs in recent political discourse, which we know has been shaped by intensely scrutinized polling data; clearly, any reference to our physical cities is just not popular. The words *urban* and *problem* are Siamese twins in the political code. City ills are so often labeled as intractable that everyone who can seems to have thrown in the towel and headed for the suburbs and beyond. According to Ken Johnson, a demographer at Loyola University, "There's a real growing anti-urbanism out there. People want to be out of the cities, and they are now going further and further past the fringes." It is hard not to see this bailout as part of a larger syndrome discussed in several books in recent years: the notion of growing disengagement in the life of our communities. Sometimes ascribed to the increasing privatization of individual lives produced in part by solitary activities such as extensive television watching, long commuting, and the vast time absorbed by computer attractions, this disengagement certainly plays a strong role in the apparent lack of interest in our cities' fate. Invariably feeding urban disregard and pessimism is skepticism about the notion of progress itself; as has been shown by many others, paradoxically, just as we have achieved the dreams of the nineteenth century, we also have stimulated the rise of further expectations to such a velocity that no real achievement can catch up, and so we have become disappointed and ultimately cynical. As polls consistently show, skepticism hardens into contempt, for all our social and civic institutions, further speeding the downward spiral.

In his excellent book *The Lost City,* Alan Ehrenhalt, writing about the 1950s, says that "stable relationships, civil classrooms, safe streets—the ingredients of what we call community —all come at a price. The price is limits on the choices we can make as individuals." Are today's increased individual choices for freedom and affluence to blame? Is it conceivable that we can put the genie back in the bottle and have good communities again at that price?

Civic disengagement and an antiurban attitude make any reclamation effort much tougher. As an architect and planner, I can only suggest strategies and solutions for the physical side of the city. Obviously, political leadership and a national will are needed to solve the staggering array of problems, from money to sprawl and from crime to illegitimacy. However, in the entropic semiruined city, there exist precisely the sorts of locales where the type of impresario–preservation–urban design with modern updates that I have been describing still—even today—holds promise.

I do not want to seem to denigrate the heuristic academic studies on nodes, paths, patterns, and edges, with their cognitive maps and sociospatial schema; indeed, I have been fascinated by attempts to synthesize urban design issues through photo and computer modeling and by the discovered wisdom of various polling techniques and have incorporated these studies into a general reference background. However, in the action-required-now situations I have confronted, I have yet to find them specifically useful. As may be obvious, my orientation is away from the formal and systemic and more toward Jane Jacobs, Gordon Cullen, and the somewhat anarchistic notions of collage and bricolage.

I wager that most people facing a rough urban high noon showdown, such as Baltimore losing its three department stores at one time, have grown frustrated at finding in their holster resource literature entitled "The City as a Resolution of Design Problems," "Semiotics and

Architecture: Ideological Consumption or Theoretical Work," and "Typological and Morphological Elements of the Concept of Urban Space."

In their book *Concepts of Urban Design,* David Gosling and Barry Maitland refer to a 1983 Regional/Urban Design Assistance Team report on its 1967–1983 community projects which asserts that for urban design to be successful, the following must occur: "The effort is as important as the product" [I have frequently found the effort forgettable and the product all-important]; "it must examine all elements of the community" [too time-consumptive and unfocused in actual experience]; "it must be inter-disciplinary and not the work of a single profession" [I have found that singular authorship after inputs from other disciplines is infinitly more effective than is groupthink]; and "above all there must be citizen participation" [the most overrated pretense of all].

The last point needs elaboration. I have spent my entire life in Washington watching far too much democracy in action close up. One inevitable observation is that we are all too similar to a herd of cloned sheep chasing after whatever was yesterday's feature story in the media. If it is a flat tax, we are all for a flat tax until we learn that our mortgages will no longer be deductible. From the founding fathers to the poor downtown project designer, no one wants every detail to be subject to a plebiscite. That is why we have a representative democracy. Representatives are elected to make decisions which the people can evaluate in a collective way after a period of time. For someone hired to design and/or effectuate urban projects, constant citizen participation is the road to the madhouse. People do not innately know the opportunities or what will work, which is why they hire someone to guide them. After proper polling and investigation of the concerns of the relevant constituencies, architects and urban designers, should think of themselves as surrogates of all the people, including those in the future who will inhabit the downtown and who may have interests quite different from those of the current population. Years ago I was asked to come up with ideas to revitalize a forlorn park in very depressed East St. Louis, where in anticipation of an even more rotten future the only decision that had previously been agreed to was to tear down sequentially every single amenity, literally to demolish every bandshell, swimming pool, comfort station, and shade-giving trellis or tree and metaphorically sow salt. We interviewed everybody, including the toughest gangs decorated with their blood-dripping emblems, and got absolutely nothing but shrugs and blank stares. All too often such citizen participation activities are merely politically correct gestures that are quite lengthy and consume the time needed for thinking. This is a part of ritualistic old planning that we should modify in order to face the next century.

It would be nice if we could revive urban design groups such as the one in John Lindsay's administration in New York. Unlike city planning departments everywhere which simply react (usually negatively) to private sector proposals, his was a proactive group that decided what the city wanted and tried to get it through incentive zoning and other carrot and stick approaches. That brief experiment has not been effectively repeated and is, unfortunately, somewhat unlikely in our increasingly antigovernment political climate.

I have concentrated on finding ways to use single-focus entities (downtown improvement groups, usually crisis-driven), with private professional help, to guide and influence the normal trajectory of private development for the benefit and preservation of downtowns. But on what uses and for what populations should we concentrate our efforts? Instead of our current impasse, it might be helpful to recall the contest between extracting forces which are causing the city to fly apart (centrifugal) and those which have tended or may tend to concentrate the city (centripetal). Some of these factors are old familiar pressures, and some are new factors whose potency has not been assessed.

CENTRIFUGAL FORCES	*CENTRIPETAL FORCES*
OLD	*OLD*
The search for	The place for
Healthy environment/no manufacturing	Manufacturing
Safety/diminished crime	Shopping
Homogeneity/economic and racial similarity	Business
No crowds/more space	Government
Auto-friendly environment	Diversity
Newness/cleanliness/new start	Status/wealthy pockets
Value/low cost	Human contact
Children-friendly/good schools	Mating/dating
Status/landed gentry/poverty concealed	Culture/entertainment/sports adult entertainment
NEW	*NEW*
At-home devices permitting	Travel efficiency to
Shopping	Special events
Business/banking/investing	Oldness/nostalgia
Schools/learning	Tourism/culture/leisure shopping
Work	Interactive entertainment
Information/research	Human contact
New shopping/business environments	Mating/dating

The suburbs were originally promoted as being healthy (no factory smoke), being free of congestion (crowding and the poor), and offering clean new dwellings. But those values were soon buttressed by a rush for safety, better schools, a desire for homogeneity, an auto-friendly environment, and affordability combined with status.

A factor that works both against and in support of cities is diversity. Just as young couples are looking for safe places with good schools, resulting in a comforting uniformity, other population groups are looking for the opposite. The fastest expanding segment of the population is older people, whose main common characteristic is that their children have reached adulthood and left home. This is an unprecedented exploding segment of the population that is blessed by modern medicine and knowledgeable health maintenance and is living a virtually second healthy and sensually aware life; this phenomenon is so recent that most urban prognosticators have not factored it in. Clearly, as this population increases, the prospect for a corresponding second life for urban areas grows. In addition, there is the phenomenon of heterosexual people choosing not to marry, married couples choosing not to procreate, and growth of the gay and lesbian communities; all these groups are child-free and therefore free to discover the diverse charms of the city.

In a speech at the National Press Club, Salmon Rushdie said that "the city is a constant bumping into differences." To the bold, often made so by financial independence, the diversity of different ethnic populations and the nearness of cultural, consumer, people, and medical choices are appealing; to the fearful, controlled-access communities (estimated to reach 225,000 by the year 2000) are a necessity. This is why the human contact factor remains the most reliable positive resource for city centers and an underlying theme in the LINRAW approach. One can't get a facial, a massage, or sex on the Internet. One still has to meet somebody, and that core collective human activity is the bedrock of future downtowns. To see the empathetic affinity between these earthy, nonplastic redone places and the mating and dating game, one has to look at the elaborate attempts to simulate these atmospheres in yuppie restaurants and theme parks. It is easier and obviously more credible with the real thing.

Despite the frequently cited statistics that show how people are working more, there is a growth among some populations of pure leisure time. Demographically, the boomers are moving into the ages where more and more of them will be free or partially free of work and therefore candidates for domestic tourism. In my downtown projects I often set out to create an indigenous new tourist attraction with new-old districts and waterfronts whose locations are almost exotic to a generation reared in the suburbs. Smart cities now promote their new tourist attractions locally and abroad more than they advertise their once-vaunted skylines. Of course, this direction can be overemphasized and there are questionable programs such as heritage tourism in rust bowl cities, but local tourism geared to the alive feeling of human congregation is a repeat business. Preservation has played and can continue to play a role in attracting these markets.

On the old list of urban concentrating factors, there are some, such as business, shopping, and manufacturing, which are in steep decline. Major shopping long ago left most cities for the suburbs, and manufacturing also has decamped for the suburbs or, more often, other countries. Business, however, presents a more mixed picture, even though it is business that is being particularly changed by advances in electronics. We are beginning to be able to get information, go shopping, be entertained, do business, and work at home. This awareness of the freedom to be anywhere and still be completely in touch has spread like wildfire to every suburban and exurban real estate agent. The new freedom clearly has fostered a major new shift away from the city. Indeed, commentators such as George Gilder have observed that urban areas are little more than "leftover baggage from the industrial era."

The only widely accepted functional new factor favoring the city is the stunning realization that as the outward movement has exploded, it is now easier for the majority of people to reach a sports complex or convention center at the hub of the wheel than to travel around the rim to it. It may seem obvious now that the center of a region represents the shortest distance for the maximum number of people, but it took today's rage-inducing commuting gridlock and beltway horrors to make it recognizable.

When all these factors follow their natural course in a time of suburban ascendancy, we end up downtown with the Round Roof Syndrome: a largely abandoned CBD in which the domed courthouse with its new jail wing faces the dome of the old museum and performing arts center and the new domed sports stadium. The new fellow, the sports leviathan, will have little kinetic interaction with the downtown area because it is a destination point to which one goes and then returns directly home. What the new sports palaces, occasionally joined by new convention centers, do provide is extensive demolition to accommodate their vast parking lots, leaving the old cultural facilities trapped in their real estate, standing alone and desperate to become centers of weekend activity and nightlife. This desperation translates out of necessity to involvement with the central city and its conversion into entertainment and party places for the well educated, well protected, and well heeled. To the extent that if it incorporates art and music schools, a surrounding arts community can be a great resource that responds well to recycled old structures. Providence based its downtown renewal on the Rhode Island School of

Design, which draws a spinoff population of artists who have converted empty buildings into galleries and lofts that have attracted tourists and significantly revived the central city.

Cultural constituencies remain one of the few standout resources among the new round roofs and are one reason why I included an arts feature whenever I could in our downtown projects. At the same time, there is an ominous dedensifying of everything else being floated by the paleoplanners who keep pushing for that old bromide, open space despite evidence that in the center of an alarming number of cities, where overcrowding was once the norm, we now see fields of weeds—not even parking lots but areas of total abandonment.

Oddly, there seems to be an argument, principally identified with the architect Rem Koolhaas, which sees elephantine convention centers and sports complexes as a solution for cities simply through their dynamic bigness. Son of megastructure, fad of the mid-1960s, the idea seems even more improbable now because the implicit driving force for the financing and leadership behind megastructures is government and the country is in a period of rapid retreat from government intervention. The best part of the megastructure fad was its silliness. Who can forget the single building stretched like an athletic supporter across the continental United States, the beetlelike walking cities, or the gooey organic urbanoid megathings popping up like mushrooms on speed or bubbling around underwater? Another retreat into Sergeant Pepper's megastructureland may be as useful an urban solution as it was the first time

We have plenty of space for colossal projects in our doughnut downtowns, but in promoting these rare opportunities people feel a need to denigrate the widely applicable incremental interventionist approach simply because they are bored with it. This is just current fashion speaking, but it could help derail a practical method that has been consistently successful in restoring some humanity to our cities since the end of World War II. In some special cases a very big project (usually a romantic architect's dream of the power he or she is customarily denied) may work, but if it fails, the result will be a thermonuclear bomb that will make other disasters, such as the Rockville experience, seem like a hiccup. A distant rosy future for cities was recently projected by an MIT economics professor, Paul Krugman, based on the widely prophesied population boom's ability to soak up available resources such as gasoline, generating Draconian environmental controls so that commuting as we know it will be expensive and difficult. As an extrapolated consequence, people would move back into the city, triggering an urban renaissance. I have three problems with this vision: It is very far off, and our problems are occurring right now; it assumes a straight-line projection into the future, which has almost always proved to be dicey (in the nineteenth century increasing city density was expected to cause an inundation of horse manure, and very recently a hybrid electric-gasoline engine achieved 60 plus miles per gallon, potentially tripling the extent of our resources); and it disregards the future development of electronic business travel, which will make today's systems and teleconferencing look positively medieval.

For anyone interested in our brand of LINRAW, there is diminishing material and opportunity as a result of the new Round Roof Syndrome, but I think that the pleasure-friendly funkiness of the approach (appealing places serving the need for earthy collective human congregation) has staying power and may be one way to soften and modify the desiccated image of American cities. Reusing old waterfronts has proved to be a global success story and, in combination with a preservation linkage, has produced, unlike most other efforts, familiar but generally rewarding results.

Finally, I must be brave enough to comment on the real secret drawing power of the charm factor. Americans returning from Europe frequently are struck by how utterly devoid of delightful and charming places the United States is. Our freeways, skyscrapers, malls, convention centers, and stadiums communicate a mindless mesomorphic truculent strutting power that is harsh, grating, and most certainly not alluring. When Americans think of "God's country," we imagine an all-natural place with no human-made structures, while Europeans feel that nature is best when disciplined to enhance human-made delights. The charm I advocate is not cutesy or contrived picturesque but integral; however, any charm is better than none. American architects are embarrassed to talk about such an apparently superficial quality as charm, yet they are the most reliable European tourists, whose Chianti-stained vacation sketchbooks are like Bibles to Baptists.

Americans have long shown an easy fascination with Belgian villages, often the most popular exhibit at world's fairs, and with historic embalmments such as Mystic Seaport, Williamsburg, and theme parks. From Kennebunkport to Sag Harbor to St. Michaels, the number of small communities that have almost overindulged in charm is remarkable. Oldness welded carefully to charm has created a renaissance in many small towns in America. Such a seductive approach can also work for parts of big cities.

I know this will set some to thumb sucking and muttering darkly about boutiques, chain stores, and fern bars, but it doesn't have to be like that. Charm and appeal can attend a preservationist approach which incorporates any use and activity whatsoever, such as repair workshops, transportation, and light manufacturing. Albert Camus said, "You know what charm is: a way of getting the answer yes without having asked any clear question." Despite many attempts to demystify charm and make it more intellectually respectable with terms such as *appropriate and comfortable scale,* it remains an elusive, undefinable, but organic part of the appeal of a preservationist approach; even more important, it is immediately appreciated by the public and therefore the financial markets. There is no valid reason why design sophistication, even avant-garde work, and charm cannot exist in the same venue.

New-old charm-purveying preservation zones could be complementary to the current governmental initiative of enterprise zones, which try to draw new businesses through tax relief and grants and whose mission is by definition not primarily to increase a city's tax base but to create jobs. In Nietzschean terms, this new governmental initiative is all Apollonian and not a bit Dionysian. Preservation-revived sections of cities with some new jobs and a higher proportion of leisure time charm-rich developments would provide a healthy balance to the enterprise zones' emphasis on no-nonsense work.

For medium-size cities that lack the benefit of the dome of government or the dome of a major sports franchise and are more like pure business enterprises, the future may be a bit more cloudy. Like the Darwinian reduction that occurs after the proliferation of new companies that follows the development of a new industry, many middle-size cities, like their small-town predecessors, could become partial ghost towns without activist intervention. In our age of acceleration where the momentum isn't just the speed of change but the increasing rate of the speed of change, we may see this happen sooner rather than later. It is important to remember that the city, as one look at the massive rusticated fortresslike Strozzi Palace in Florence will tell us, has always been a rough and dangerous place. Evening theater was switched to afternoon matinees in London in the early 1800s because it was too dangerous to go out in the evening. Until a couple of hundred years ago cities did not have a middle class to lose; the population had a few very rich people, and the majority was dangerously poor. Maybe in a way history is repeating itself, and we may take some warning from the fact that our economically polarized situation is not without precedent. Throughout history urban problems of crime, poverty, and the underclass have been endemic. Because of the effort to try to help all parts, we risk having suburban America (where the power is) give up on all city issues, such as the absolutely critical safety net for the poor. The turning away of popular interest from the city leads inexorably to its demise.

In *The New American Ghetto*, Camilo Jose Vergara's proposal that we make the still standing but mostly empty array of predepression skyscrapers in Detroit into a twentieth-century ruin park may be a horror to the urbanist, but the alternative may be demolition. Some will say that such a tour of block after block of emptying skyscrapers, America's optimistic paradigm for civilization, constitutes an obsessive dwelling on an aberration. But some also said that IBM would always be number one, that the communist menace would last forever, and that the United States would never go from being the major lender to the largest debtor nation. Fortunately, a business job revival created by enterprise zones has led to a stay of execution for the skyscrapers, but Detroit is still a long way from being a vacation destination.

I am convinced that one of the greatest evils today is the renewed inclination toward clearance, the deliberate making of empty land in a naive hope of both eliminating problems and attracting departed businesses or industry. Like a wrongdoer trying to eliminate the evidence, we correctly see abandoned areas of cities as accusatory reminders of our failure, but unless there is an actual prospect for development, demolition, which removes forever the last equity of the city, is the wrong response. Bulldozing or burning down crack houses does not deal with the problem of drugs; it just shifts it to the next block. Preservationists should rally to stop the demolition of any consistent collection of recyclable structures and should become a political voice against such disastrous short-term thinking.

Considering the dynamics, it is perfectly possible that the state of American downtowns in twenty years could make the present situation seem positively pleasing. In fact, twenty years ago the National Trust for Historic Preservation's book *America's Forgotten Architecture* made the following assessment: "It is obvious, as one looks at the blight of urban slums, abandoned cities, leveled acres lost to urban renewal or commercial pressures, suburban sprawl, and the dehumanizing new buildings going up around us, that the same right to a decent built environment has hardly even been recognized, much less accepted or implemented."

Some commentators have hailed The Congress for the New Urbanism as the most powerful movement to surface since the decline of communism. This sounds impressive, but it just means that the last seven years and the movement look a lot like past architectural movements which relied on the efficacy of abstract noneconomic and nonutilitarian aesthetics to overcome events, such as the decline of cities, which are the product of infinitively more powerful forces. To commence its New Urbanism Charter with a call to oppose disinvestment in central cities by banks and business interests seems to the real world titanically naive.

There is no better example of the notion of cognitive dissonance—the saying of one thing and the doing of another—than urban investment. I have heard countless hortatory speeches on cities by people who would not invest in an inner-city building if you had their neck in a vise. Investment has been likened to a bird that comes only if all the conditions are just right and, if only one of those vital preconditions isn't perfect, flies away. A deteriorated central-city neighborhood doesn't have any of these preconditions and doesn't attract many birds with money belts. Bankers should suggest that the New Urbanists invest their own life savings, without which they will reside under a bridge, and then banking will listen.

The thinness of the entire neoconservative approach to cities was acutely revealed when Alex Marshall in *Metropolis* magazine pointed out that urban settlements are primarily shaped by their transportation systems and that the nineteenth-century suburbs and towns the New Urbanists want to emulate were shaped by the old system of streetcar lines. Today people commute to work and shop by car usually some distance away, at the Price Club, Home Depot, or the R&D office campus; this means that people will not shop and work primarily in the downtowns of these new towns, making their Main Streets inherently a stage set. The provision for the automobile and the urban shaping it normally provokes has been carefully concealed, adding to the artificiality. Marshall concludes by suggesting that "New Urbanism is just this decade's fashion in suburban design."

The suburbs killed the cities by being more desirable. It may not please neoconservative suburb planners that recent surveys repeatedly show a rejection by a four to one margin of many of their planning ideas in favor of the old suburban designs, except that some people wish that their suburban town centers had a little more of that old-fashioned charm (with acres of free parking) and the mom and pop stores each had the selection of Wal-Mart, the price range of a cut-rate Potomac Mills, and easy access to a golf course. Housing developers have already labeled the New Urbanist suburbs a minor niche market and have invented a hybrid which grafts some of the old-timey look (picket fences, porches) onto the standard suburban model. This betrays the essentially suburban nature of these virtual-reality new-old towns. Paul Goldberger, speaking in a panel discussion, may have spiked New Urbanist pretensions when he said that the real name should be the New Suburbanists.

Almost four decades ago, when I was an employee of Chloethiel Woodard Smith, assigned to a housing development of a couple of thousand units for the Levitt Corporation, I happened to drive through a dying old town that was fairly close to the vast open fields of the site. At a meeting with the Levitt executives, I rhapsodized about the genuine age and rough funkiness of the old town and strongly suggested that instead of trying to create a brand-new, inescapably artificial historical quality for the new Levittown Center, we should wrap our new town around the old town, giving the town life and providing us with a center with a genuine history. I went on to say that those old buildings (one was an old brick Quaker meetinghouse) could lend the new development an authenticity that could not be duplicated at any price. The stunned silence that greeted this proposal convinces me to this day that it was the right course.

The preservationist response to the New Urbanists and to all new town proposals should be to advocate wrapping these new imitation old towns around one of the thousands of existing but shriveling legitimately old towns. Whatever their current economic health, most of these small towns were founded for an organic reason (water source, crossroads, good farming, defensibility). The visible effect of years of natural and gradual adaptation to the specific locale and a residual core sense of community would be a good antidote to the generic coyness, artificiality, and gleaming sentimentality of these new simulated old towns. I welcome the New Urbanists and some of their freshening of principles which have been part of professional practice for decades, but most of all I welcome their clients' very real investments.

I am sad to say that I foresee a more reduced future in town. I still don't see even a glimmer on the horizon of an across-the-board widespread political and economic will to act effectively on the basic inner-city problems of racism, bad schools, poverty, crime, drugs, illegitimacy, and despair and the outer-city problems of disinterest and disengagement. Therefore, I reluctantly return to a few trends.

First, the hollowing out of the central city—the other side of suburban sprawl—will continue largely because of the lack of that aforementioned will and the center's problems, making it simply not a pleasant, family-friendly, appealing, or comfortable place to be. The downsizing will paradoxically be helped by the current fascination with sports arenas and convention centers.

Second, since a credible major mobilization to save the cities is unlikely, the only direction available is a constant unglamorous struggle for new connections, incremental rehabilitation, and financeable small scale-projects marshaled together whenever possible to stem the general slide.

Third, urban centers are multifaceted, and we must accept for now the fact that only selected areas, those with inherent or latent characteristics of diversity, historical interest, and human contact uses, can be acted on.

In the end we have to appeal to the public to save our cities. This appeal should not be based on the usual extraction of monies, utilizing guilt or altruism, that should be saved for the truly needy. This appeal is logically based on the largest and most underutilized urban resource, and therefore the cheapest resource: our old city buildings. These ordinary structures, can be made to contain sufficient charm, practicality, value, and convenience to attract many in the general population, in particular the rapidly expanding and flourishing nonchildbearing part of the population. There is a great but only partially tapped well here. What we need is the development of new activist-generalist teams that can reinvigorate, develop, and transform for the twenty-first century old effective preservationist-based formulas such as LINRAW, which can provide a real alternative to the desiccated Round Roof Syndrome and the abandonment of our central cities.

[CITY PRESERVATION]

NATIONAL AIRPORT

I was sitting on the edge of the couch like a tightly gripped stick. Standing around me like a circular firing squad were the administrator of the Federal Aviation Administration (FAA), a deputy, an assistant, an associate, and probably some acting levels of something, all glaring at me and asking who my source was.

My source, they all rightly suspected, was one of them, but which one? As an accidental journalist, I only knew that I had to fall on my Bic pen rather than reveal my source, which in this case would get one of these fabulous public servants fired. They were incensed because in 1966 I had written an article in the *Washingtonian* magazine that had exposed the carefully concealed plan of the FAA to spend $200 million on rebuilding National Airport; the piece had been picked up by the *Washington Post* and had caused a splendid little flap.

My leak (I like to think of him as the grandfather of Deep Throat), also perspiring, agitated, and threatening, was going a bit overboard, and I was beginning to visualize the fingernail extractor when the administrator suddenly said that he wanted to show me his heliport. On top of the FAA building, an edifice done in the no-pasta Mussolini style, a kind of starved but ominous bureaucratic architecture, the administrator had installed a rooftop heliport that had required reinforcing throughout the building, but unfortunately, this remarkably expensive facility could not be used because of the restricted flight zones newly imposed for security around the White House. Ascribing to me the inflated position of power that bureaucrats believe the fourth estate to have, he must have thought that if I could scuttle his National Airport rebuilding, I could at least land his chopper.

I had pointed out in my article that National Airport was designed for the old, small piston-driven DC-3 and was unsafe for the new generation of large jet aircraft. These new, powerfully, noisy machines not only were making life miserable for all life-forms along the Potomac but were raising an obvious question: If you are going to build a new airport, is that the right place to put it? I wrote that it would be far more prudent to spend a fraction of the $200 million (today, over a billion) on a rail link to the underused Dulles Airport and reclaim the delicious waterfront site of National for a new town almost in town; in fact, we had a huge response from readers wanting to invest in the development. The day President Nixon announced that he wanted to sell National (meaning, of course, to a regional authority or the state of Virginia), we called the White House offering to buy it for that potential new town, and were connected to Charles Colson. Asked if he was the person to speak with about buying National, he said he didn't know what on earth we were talking about. We replied that on the front page of the *Washington Post* that very morning the president had said he wanted to sell it. Shouting that nobody at the White House read the *Washington Post*, Colson slammed down the phone.

There was hard evidence of the safety shortcomings of National's location when an Air Florida jet landed in the Potomac in 1982. However, this is Congress's airport, and the blatantly outrageous congressional parking privileges show plainly who is in charge and who will see that the airport never closes.

My article led to the formation of citizen groups, the first being the Committee against National (CAN), followed by more felicitously named associations, including a splinter group determined to employ replica medieval catapults to hurl doughnuts, matzoh balls, and other assorted baked goods at the airplanes as a nonlethal form of complaint. The image of a sky filled with the flying flak of Danishes, croissants, brioches, and chocolate napoleons seemed to be a real crowd pleaser, and there was talk of international cooperation.

Responding to the tsunamic wave of interest, we made a painfully original protest movie (*Flying Foodstuffs*) which was shown at an SRO rally at Arena Stage. In the packed theater, among our other entertainments, was our lead speaker, the senior senator from Maryland, Daniel Brewster, who arrived dead drunk and delivered a speech in which the only intelligible message was that he didn't have the foggiest notion where he was. Despite this inauspicious start, some watchdog groups remain to this day, making sure that the airport, (now renamed for President Regan) which gained a new terminal building in 1997, does not exceed the flight limits imposed after this peak of resistance. There is also revived talk of a rail or express bus link to Dulles, which is more than doubling the size of its terminal.

One might wonder how this story moves forward our understanding of preservation or even architecture. Well, I was a mite bit short of work at the time, and what little existed was the architectural equivalent of emptying bedpans: doing porches and additions. I longed for those halcyon days in school when we would tackle the entire coast of California, a thirty-room palazzo for an ethereal poet, or a grand new opera house whose main purpose was to frame a classical vista or end an imperial axis. In short, I was looking for a larger scope and thought that at least, without a commission, I could write about the larger issues confronting my hometown. The subject I was dealing with at the airport was not why these government officials were conniving behind everyone's back and plotting huge expenditures of our hard-earned tax money but whether an essentially new airport should be built on National's site. I was learning that skulking, deceptive, furtive, and duplicitous agency heads made good copy and therefore a handy cover for a relatively abstract and unpalatable planning issue.

I was also learning how few people can perceive a city's major physical problems, visualize solutions, and write and draw them for the popular press. As Louis Kahn once advised my Princeton class, "people see with their ears." Our overwhelmingly verbal society, with its emphasis on numerical and language skills, has produced a nonvisual population with collective urban cataracts. You have to write it and speak it and draw it for anyone to pay attention, a not unimportant lesson for a young architect.

In every city there are all too many urban gaps, threats of demolition, prominent eyesores, transportation glitches, unrealized opportunities, and disconnected communities for which architects, preservationists, civic activists, and artists are uniquely qualified to visualize solutions and, in the process, shape the kind of work, reuse, or result they dream about but rarely get.

I have long dreamed of a new and expanded form of creative preservation with the whole city, the whole metropolitan area, as its canvas. After all, preservation and saving cities are really fraternal twins. Sometimes these uncommissioned self-created pro bono projects are just suggestions for creating new access to a pivotal building, bringing street life to a blank wall, or giving civic and popular functions internal uses, and sometimes they are a matter of pointing out new opportunities for residential development or new community access to a park or waterfront. The following examples are from all Americans' second hometown, the nation's capital, but the basic issues they confront can be found in any city. These ideas illustrate areas where there is a void in the general public's approach to city problems which can be filled by engaged or enraged citizens if they see such reconnections as steps in the preservation of the whole city and are prepared to pursue them as political acts.

One caveat needs to be made: None of these proposals has been realized by me or anyone else because of the infamous Washington rule of thirteen, but there has been movement on most of them. When dealing with our nation's capital, one must always keep firmly in mind that when the Founding Fathers set up what is breezily referred to as checks and balances, they were actually creating a political process expressly designed to say no to almost everything. Spastic knee-jerk gridlock extends well beyond the day-to-day well-publicized sparring between the Congress and the executive branch to the supposedly nonpartisan long-term physical development of the monumental city.

Compounding the continuous carnage of democracy is the mother of all American bureaucracies. To the huge cover-your-ass federal bureaucracy must be added the largest number of employees per capita of any city government in the world, all too many of whom are empowered to say no; Washington is a good place to experience what America would be like under communism. Further spicing the capital stew is a scandal-obsessed press corps whose most euphoric fantasies are of an outbreak of mud-slinging hostilities between Congress and the Supreme Court, a president caught with his trousers around his ankles, or a photograph of the entire cabinet at play in a foreign campaign contributor's nudist colony. Getting media attention for anything as unsexy as a building project almost demands that it be discovered as a secret cocaine-processing plant run for profit by the GSA.

The rule of thirteen says that because of all the institutional naysayers, it takes a minimum of thirteen years to get even a beneficial project brought to reality. However, in my experience thirteen may be too optimistic; most of the proposals discussed here are approximately in midcourse. In a normal city a quarter or a tenth of this time should suffice. All these proposals were my inventions and were done strictly pro bono publico with no thought of gain or follow-on work, in my spare time, which, not being infinite, prolonged the process.

THE KENNEDY CENTER STEPS AND PROMENADE

The Kennedy Center often is described by local wags as the box the infamous Watergate building came in. Although others have been far less kind, my complaint with our performing arts center by Edward Durell Stone is that it hovers over the ground like an alien spaceship wary of landing because it has no ostensible connection to the earth or the Potomac, from where it is principally seen. Specifically, it cantilevers its grand terrace two-thirds of the way over an obnoxious highway but remains suspended in the air, suggesting and demonstrating isolation and unattainability; that is not ideal for a civic plaza, presidential memorial, and public theater and entertainment complex.

I devised a set of monumental steps which could be cantilevered up to the terrace, bridging the roadway and connecting the center to the ground and the river. The cantilevered steps would place no pressure on the center's terrace and would be visually buttressed by flanking elevators for the handicapped. The wide steps with multiple landings would become a broad grandstand for gathering, reading, and watching the boat traffic and rowing regattas or the river itself; conceivably, the inclined plaza could become the kind of interactive meeting place that the Spanish Steps are in Rome.

At the river's edge there would be a floating dock for water taxis and ferryboats that would transport patrons from Maryland and Virginia who were sane enough not to fight the bridge traffic, the overcommitted parking garages, and the city's crack force of meter maids. At the bottom of the steps there would be a broad promenade with decorative paving, low and high lighting, benches, trees, and a separated bike path extending around the bend of the river to connect to our Washington Harbour riverside boardwalk. I got the idea by watching how people used the boardwalk over time: They firmly marched in one direction, pivoted on their heels, and marched resolutely back to the other end; they didn't stroll, they paced. People needed a place to go, and the Kennedy Center was both the only other riverfront attraction and the ideal destination. In plain planning sense, the pedestrian linkage of restaurants and theaters is a natural. I presented the idea to the Kennedy Center, which thought it terrific, and together we worked for seven years developing the plan, refining the design, and presenting it for approval to the double file of review agencies and citizen groups. Unknown to me at the time, the center was in possession of a study warning that in the event of an emergency, its exits were inadequate for its theater population; my staircase connection to the riverside park was a solution.

News of the public popularity and review agency approvals reached Capitol Hill, which directed the center not to use any federal money to pay for it. In an effort to keep things moving forward, I found a private donor for $3 million of the $5 million cost, and in a parallel effort a citizen group and I located a foreign government that would consider making

a friendship gesture toward the United States by paying for the whole thing. On the very afternoon the donor package, prepared by the center's development office and us, was to be personally taken by the ambassador to his government the center's president stopped the delivery without an explanation to anyone. The center never even sent a donor package to the wonderfully generous $3 million private donor, much less a thank you card.

5-1. *Cantilevered Kennedy Center terrace.*

5-2. *Aerial view of the Kennedy Center.*

What then happened must have stood in line to happen. Without the courtesy of informing either of the prospective donors, the many enthusiastic support groups, or me, the president decided to do it all himself with a federally funded team hired to do federally funded repairs. He might have succeeded except that the design he and his people came up with showed the intelligence of mud. Basically, they turned a monumental staircase that was appropriate to the center as a presidential memorial, similar in ascendance to the staircases at the Jefferson and Lincoln memorials, into two mean exit stairs that looked inward toward the highway instead of out toward the river, successfully frustrating any linkage to the community.

5-3. *Rendering of proposed steps, boat landing, and promenade.*

What was simply stunning about the center so cavalierly dismissing a sure $3 million and a probable $5 million of private funding was that it was periodically struck by disgruntled musicians seeking more than subsistence pay, the opera company with Plácido Domingo was planning to move out, and it had to repeatedly go around with a tin cup begging for contributions.

The National Capital Planning Commission rejected the center's curious new

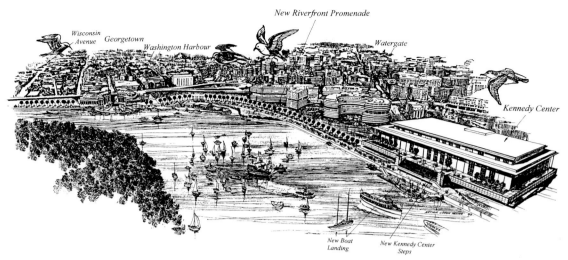

New Riverfront Promenade

Wisconsin Avenue *Georgetown*

Washington Harbour

Watergate

Kennedy Center

New Boat Landing

New Kennedy Center Steps

5-4. *Promenade from the Kennedy Center to the center of Georgetown.*

scheme, saying that it preferred my original design, which it had approved years before.

This story is far from over. Most ideas for urban change, even without such outrageously scandalous behavior, go through a stalled period in which they seem hopeless and then are subsequently revived. I present it here as a prime example of the type of physical misconnection and urban design dysfunction that citizen activists should be looking to find and fix and an example of a level of foolishness that even civically minded efforts can encounter.

THE D.C. TEMPORARY CONTEMPORARY

During his lifetime J. Edgar Hoover was alleged to have had an individual doomsday dossier which he held over the heads of people in Washington to keep them in line. The Hoover spirit prevails with a giant doomsday bunker—the Hoover Building by C. F. Murphy Associates— over Pennsylvania Avenue, seemingly to keep it and the folks at either end of the avenue in line forever. The building has strenuously beaten back all efforts to enliven its blocklong blank penitentiary front with shops or any other evidence of human existence.

In an attempt to enliven the avenue, millions have been lavished on trees, street furniture, and above all paving, but still the FBI's concrete wall, formerly embellished with a few desultory historical decals, has not proved to be a seductive attraction. Recently, granite tiles whose cost far exceeds the total for my modest proposal were glued onto this rampart in a spectacularly unsuccessful attempt to soften the effect of the flinty fortress. A block away are the remnants of the city's attempt at a Soho-like art district, almost terminal but still breathing, and a few blocks to the south, lining the mall, are seven giant government art museums that only show work by dead non-Washingtonians. It is fair to say that the large local artistic community is dying to be shown in either place, or anyplace.

5-5. *Blank wall of FBI building.*

5-6. *Open-air galleries at the blank wall of the FBI building.*

One of the basic characteristics of Paris is that so much happens outside the buildings. Not only are Parisians fanatic about eating and drinking outdoors, but just about everything, including rain-hating objects such as drawings and books, is sold outside as well, as if the French intuitively knew what masters of business administration learn expensively: The fewer steps, doors, and other physical impediments between you and the customer, the better. Outside merchandisers catch even the most casual surfer.

My idea for Mr. Hoover's formidable wall is to line it with art galleries that fold up at night like Parisian bookstalls and are protected from precipitation by retractable awnings. The ever-hungry art community would have a rotating place where still-breathing artists could show and see the latest local stuff, and the enterprise could provide a little playfulness and color on America's Main Street. Even better, America on wheels driving down Main Street could see this open-air art market and might even get out of the car.

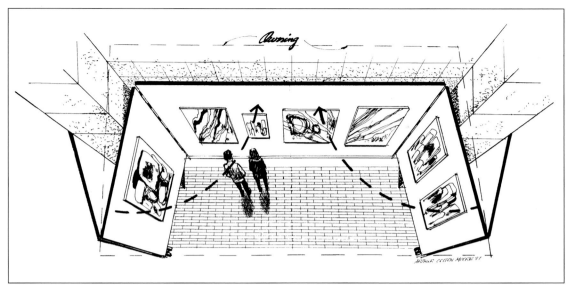

5-7. *Diagram of closeable gallery walls.*

There is an almost complementary, poetic, and American spirit of commingling the nation's sternest and toughest lawmen with the most evanescent nonutilitarian free spirit of art, recalling the endearing image of war protesters putting flowers in soldiers' gun barrels. As I have stressed in the LINRAW approach, the use of art and other cultural amenities for city revitalization is usually fruitful. The smallness and ease of this proposal, light on cost but heavy on visual change, show that new cultural activities do not always entail enormously expensive new museums and opera houses.

MARYLAND AVENUE HOUSING

As in all good Washington testimony, I confess a minor relationship: Senator James McMillan, as in the famous McMillan Plan, was my aunt's grandfather, and in this proposal I blatantly and shamelessly attempt to complete his plan. The McMillan Plan is the three-dimensional conceptualization of L'Enfant's original linear map that grew out of the City Beautiful movement at the turn of the century; it has largely determined the shape of the capital and will continue to do so far into the next century. One of its first achievements was to remove the chaotic collection of rail lines and smoke-belching trains from L'Enfant's grand Mall, but unfortunately they were later plunked down in another key part of the plan.

The best known rendering of the McMillan Plan shows the great swath of the Mall bracketed by two major radiating thoroughfares: Pennsylvania Avenue and Maryland Avenue. Pennsylvania Avenue was well established before the plan, but the highlighted Maryland Avenue was never built. Instead, the space was usurped by the main railroad lines that serve the eastern seaboard. In this proposal I conspired to create the missing Maryland Avenue and

5-8. *Perspective of the 1901 McMillan Plan.*

5-9. *Maryland Avenue right-of-way as railroad tracks.*

insert a twenty-four-hour new housing community right in the thicket of those no-pasta Mussolini government office buildings that become a surreal ghost town after the eight-hour bureaucrats scurry home to the suburbs.

The map of Washington shows radiating diagonal prominent avenues superimposed on a basic grid of streets. In this section of town the GSA, which likes things very big and very square, has built its megaliths religiously on the grid, resulting in a series of triangular leftover unbuilt surplus parcels of land between the giant rectangular buildings and the missing diago-

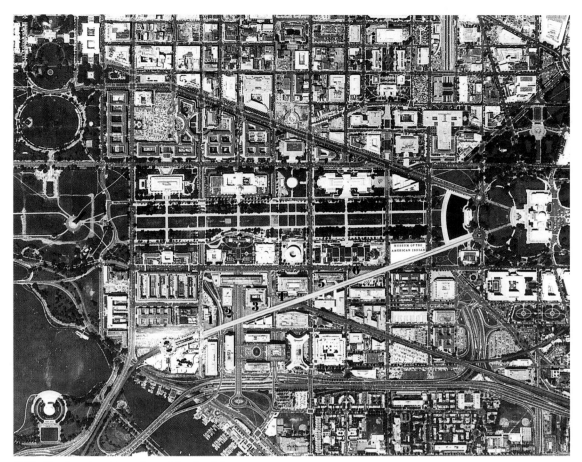

5-10. *New housing sites and new Maryland Avenue.*

nal avenue. The government likes only very large rectangular floor plates, and therefore these little triangles are superfluous to its needs. The leftover land scraps, however, can easily accommodate the typical narrow (55 to 60 feet wide) linear footprints of apartment buildings. Since the rail lines are two to three stories below street level, two-and sometimes three-level parking garages could be built up from that railroad level, the roofs of which would support a new Maryland Avenue lined with apartment buildings. The balance of the avenue's width could be cantilevered over the tracks or could span the tracks, as we did at the nearby Portals Complex. 3,500 apartment units with ground-floor retail could be built on these seven to eight different sites, five times more than the Pennsylvania Avenue Development Commission achieved with thirty years and hundreds of millions of dollars. Unlike that effort, not one resident or business would be displaced.

The Mall is Washington's Central Park, and the modest amount of housing finally built on Pennsylvania Avenue could be like the east side and the Maryland Avenue community could be like Central Park West. This new community would have the not inconsiderable amenity of abundant adjacent parkland in the Mall, the Tidal Basin, and East Potomac Park. There are continuing education facilities in the adjacent Department of Agriculture and the Smithsonian

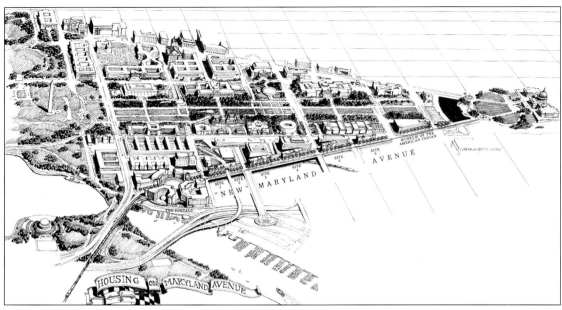

5-11. *Perspective drawing showing the new avenue.*

5-12. *View from the Jefferson Memorial of the new avenue and housing.*

Institution and vast walk-to-work opportunities in the surrounding government offices. Fresh seafood at the Maine Avenue waterfront market is close enough to get but not smell, and the area is embarrassingly well served by two subway lines, various buslines, Amtrak, and northern Virginia commuter rail lines and is spared aircraft noise by the no-fly zone extending from the White House.

L'Enfant saw Maryland Avenue as the link between the Capitol and the waterfront, which in those days provided access to the city's principal highway, the river. That historical connection could now be made, although out of respect for the cherry trees, the last bridge part over Fourteenth Street would be reserved for pedestrians and bicycles. After crossing the traffic, the bridge could broaden into a terraced garden stepping down to the Tidal Basin and the Jefferson Memorial.

Since the land is not needed by the federal government and since Washington is withering for lack of a residential tax base which the 5,000- to 10,000-apartment population would begin to provide, the government should sell the land at a very reduced price and require the developer to build his or her section of the new avenue, normally a public sector obligation. Although this is true elsewhere as well, in Washington the number of beneficial tax paying resi-

184

5-13. *Perspective section through new garages and the new avenue.*   **5-14.** *Terraced garden down to the Tidal Basin.*

dents left in a population mostly on public assistance or too poor to render a significant tax payment had shrunk to about 11 percent in 1997. Is it any wonder the city is strapped?

Before the extensively publicized departure of manufacturing, shopping, and business from the typical center city, the residents moved out as soon as they could afford it. In the end we all know that recapturing some middle-income revenue-positive residents is the key to a real future for our cities.

The District of Columbia government, ever on top of things, sent me a letter saying that when I had personally received title to the land from the feds (a total impossibility) and had paid the D.C. property taxes, it would consider the appropriateness of placing the project on the docket for official D.C. zoning action.

THE ROSSLYN WATERFRONT
Arlington, Virginia

Arlington is known as the final resting place for our nation's heroes, but there are quite a lot of live people there as well. In fact, once part of the national capital district, it forms the left bank of the Potomac as it flows through the original 10-square-mile dedication of land for the capital. When it was returned to Virginia in 1836 because no wild fantasy could imagine Washington ever spreading that far, it was without statutory control of its riverbank. Arlingtonians do not have functional access to the underused beautiful Potomac, which is tenaciously controlled, along with the river's bottom, by the Park Service; together with the Corps

5-15. *Separation of Rosslyn from the Potomac.*

of Engineers and the Environmental Protection Agency, the Park Service also regulates whatever happens on the water. When the live parts of Arlington consisted mostly of pawnshops and poor yokels, nobody seemed to care, but now, with its forest of high-rises such as the Gannett and USA Today towers, it looks, particularly at night, like a miniature version of Manhattan and the true downtown of the region. Rosslyn's 35,000 office workers and 10,000 residents represent merely the tip of a long spine of major development centers which are bound together by the world's most expensive subway system in the most densely populated region in Virginia.

In no other place in the world would a major urban settlement of this dimension not have access to its own riverfront, from which it is walled off by not one but two major limited-access superhighways. No fewer than thirteen lanes full of hell-bent-for-home commuters with pedals pressed firmly to the metal make the barriers far more dangerous than any set of conventional minefields. To make matters wors, the 1950s planner of a grander Rosslyn had opted for one of the greatest urban follies of all time, calling for all new towers to sit on above-grade parking garages joined by sky-bridges. Without dwelling on how block after block of parking garages contribute to the anhedonic absence of street life, the parking podium produces an intermittent ambulatory human plane some six stories above the river. If you stayed up nights diabolically scheming and plotting how to cut people off from their river, you could not have come up with a better configuration than the one that exists in Rosslyn.

I have always been troubled by my daily view of this gigantic nonsense, and in my travels have seen how public elevators and pedestrian bridges are used to negotiate the ups and

186

downs of waterfronts in European capital cities such as Lisbon and Bern; Paris uses pedestrian bridges to access the Seine, and long ago I had seen the bridge and public elevator used to get to Monte Carlo's waterfront before they were replaced by a hotel. I figured we could try to do the same in the new world and proposed extending a weather-protected pedestrian bridge from the human level of Rosslyn's podium over the torrent of traffic on Interstate 66 and the George Washington Parkway to a public elevator that would deliver people to a boathouse, ferry terminal, restaurant, and riverside park. The restaurant and ferry terminal could produce the revenue to pay off the bonds that would raise the $7 million needed for the project. The area would get a boathouse for which the citizens have long been clamoring and direct, easy, and convenient access to its never-visited lovely waterfront park. The bridge would act as an

5-16. *Proposed bridge to the waterfront.*

5-17. *Elevators in tower to parkland.*

umbilical cord, providing services for this new beachhead, not the least of which would be tapping into the area's 20,000 parking spaces, which are mostly empty on evenings and weekends.

But the best part comes out in the macro view. Ferries operating out of this facility could connect the Kennedy Center (the federal city) and Washington Harbour (Georgetown) on the right bank to Rosslyn (northern Virginia) on the left bank. The river would change from a separator of antagonistic battling jurisdictions to a connector of its two banks, flowing through a more interactive region. Virginians could avoid the increasingly clogged bridges, park in the garages of Rosslyn, see a show at the Kennedy Center, and have a drink in Georgetown, all via a short picturesque river cruise. Shades of Hong Kong, Vancouver, Seattle, London, Sydney, and Istanbul.

Expectedly, the Park Service, including some aggrieved public servants checking their wristwatches and retirement calendars and still presumed to be trying to improve the quality of our lives, just hates this idea, but that is my usual starting point. In a frank discussion type of

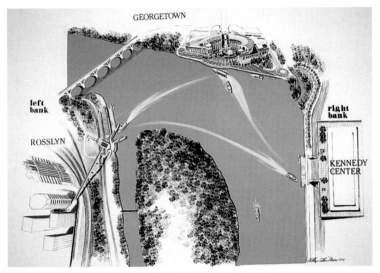

5-18. *Ferryboat between the right and left banks of the Potomac.*

meeting (diplomatese for everything short of landed punches), a Park Service official was given the choice between providing access to parks and waterfront for more than 45,000 Americans and keeping ten choked-on-smoke trees gasping for breath on the polluted shoulder of the freeway. He chose, of course, the trees. Perhaps as a result of some old, misguided, and unhappy experiences with humans, the Park Service appears so shell-shocked by fear of lawsuits in the admittedly litigious climate of Washington that all it wants is to be left alone to mow grass, and analogies to right and left banks in river cities such as London and Paris are like discussing black holes in cyberspace or riverbeds on Mars. Even the historical precedent of public piers in Rosslyn and a federal act referring to re-creating at least one of them cut no ice. There is virtually open admission that the Park Service likes to be reversed by Congress, because then its fanny is not waving in the wind, which of course suggests our next move.

Political lobbying may seem very offputting to people trained in the visual arts, but in city preservation it is where the rubber meets the road.

THE CITY OBSERVATION TOWER/OLD POST OFFICE BUILDING

A lot of planners around the world have presciently built large models of their cities in an effort to get that inestimable urban pattern macro overview. The almost axiomatic and unquestioned assumption is that aerial perspective makes for sage Olympian-like planning decisions. Washington has been short on sage planning for some time, possibly because the city's starved office of planning (which shrank from 84 planners to 10 in 1997) has few computers, although it does have, in compensation, the last complete set of rotary-dial phones outside the Smithsonian. It also does not have a good window view, much less a model view of its subject.

For a city famous for its master plans—L'Enfant and McMillan—and for the degree of heavy breathing on the subject by a whole raft of groups, this is a depressingly sad situation. I thought that since Washington is a low-rise town because of our congressional height limit and since we have the possibility of a great observation perch in the 330-foot-high Old Post Office

5-19. *Old Post Office Tower.*

5-20. *Cutaway section showing elevator to tower.*

Tower (the tallest structure in the district after the Washington Monument), it was a good place to get that macro overview.

The city needs not only the bird's-eye perspective but the perspective of time. Just seeing Washington as it currently exists is only part of the story; what was planned, fought over, sidetracked, and physically there before is very relevant. With this expanded view in mind, I proposed placing the evolution of the scene below, through old photographs and plans which correspond to the actual views, on the massive pillars between the arched openings at the tower's top arcaded level. Since the tower offers a 360-degree view, the entire city could be seen as it is and as it was over its 200 years of existence, a unique opportunity for planner and citizen reflections and a peerless platform for public awareness and discussion of future change. It would also be a great orientation device for the huge number of tourists who seem constantly in a state of befuddlement as they patiently stand in front of the Lafayette Park comfort station hoping for a glimpse of Hillary or Buddy Clinton. It would also make a visit to the tower more of a rich historical and perhaps even educational experience beyond "awesome, what a view, like, where's the Statue of Liberty?"

5-21. *Night view from observation level.*   5-22. *Pier between windows with historical photographs.*

Somewhere deep in the Park Service which runs the tower as a vertical national park, is a mentally retired person who has consistently spiked this plan since 1982, although the rangers who run the tower think it is a great idea. One Smoky the Bear hat said that when one was viewing the Grand Canyon, interpretation was irrelevant and distracting and that this was a similar situation. While the Grand Canyon will change only a very small amount over the next few hundred thousand years, an American city, particularly this city, changes almost day to day.

A coalition of historical and business groups that was formed in 1996 made an unsuccessful attempt to realize this proposal, and will try again.

THE WHITE HOUSE FENCE

As we rounded the corner toward Lafayette Square, we were surprised by the huge size but unfamiliar nature of the crowd in front of the White House. "Nice turnout, but these don't look exactly like our chaps," said one of our group. Hundreds of people, mostly short, white-shirted dark men, roaring, shouting, and screaming, paused for an impressive collective thunderous chant directed at the circling television crews. As we drew closer and could make out a few placards, we learned that these folks were Tamils protesting actions taken by the Sri Lankan government against their people on the other side of the globe. Our protest rally, comfortably distanced from the excited Tamils and huddled under a tree on the east side of the park, included little more than thirty upright souls, including one senator and his large staff attended by two gum-chewing cameramen. Even though the subject of our rally involved a local and national issue—the closing of Pennsylvania Avenue—barely a few feet away, we obviously had not raised the pulse of any news director or our fellow citizens to the extent the Tamils had.

There are really two Washingtons. There is the Washington totally absorbed in daily and now frequently hourly jabbing and counterpunching between the political parties. A megaindustry that supports a huge number of well-fed lobbyists, pundits, consultants, lawyers, and media people sees this political combat as the totality of the city. In a far quieter mode there is the Washington of monuments, museums, parks, cave-dweller residents, and local city businesses, some of which are engaged in the long-term evolution of the physical setting of the nation's capital. Rarely do these two worlds intersect because almost exclusively they work and play in totally separate environments and are complete strangers to each other, but occasionally the two Washingtons bump into each other. This is what happened when the Secret Service persuaded President Clinton to close Pennsylvania Avenue in front of the White House after the Oklahoma City federal building bombing, an idea that was rejected by all presidents over the past thirty years and continues to be opposed by all living former presidents.

It immediately became apparent that closing the avenue had produced not only a never-ending hellish traffic nightmare but, more important, a literal splitting of our nation's capital and a severely negative image for the whole country. I drew cartoons and wrote in the *Washington Post* that "the sense of 'bunkerism'—an ever-expanding protective enclave for the chief executive—reinforces the people's feeling that they are becoming isolated from their president. This is supposed to be an open society, but the closing of Pennsylvania Avenue recalls Franklin D. Roosevelt's famous aphorism that 'the only thing we have to fear is fear itself'. . . France has experienced terrorist explosions throughout its capital city, but the street in front of its presidential palace in Paris has not been closed."

Potential threats to the White House and many other important structures can be met calmly by technological means rather than through the wholesale capitulation represented by tearing up this very historic

5-23. *Plans and old photographs of the Mall.*

avenue. Another approach would be the following: First, restrict truck traffic so that the size of the threat—a truck bomb as was used in Oklahoma City—is eliminated; second, place handsomely designed guardhouses at the corners of 17th and 15th streets as forward observers to monitor the traffic; and third, install a specially designed high-tech clear glass fence behind the current metal fence in front of the White House. The glass fence would be a sandwich of multiple layers of exceptionally strong laminated glass with polyvinylbutyral interlayers—a much thicker and more sophisticated version of what we think of as bulletproof glass—and would be a minimally intrusive element with the virtue of being easily thrown away if we ever reach a more civilized era. Tests and data indicate that such multiple-layer glass panels can be designed to withstand the blast of hundreds of pounds of TNT. Although engineering data on the dynamic loading of glass indicate that a single laminated glass layer could withstand the blast of a car bomb composed of 500 pounds of TNT, a second, somewhat thinner glass fence that was set back would provide additional insurance against an extraordinarily fierce car bomb and other explosive devices or heavy weapons.

Although the fence would be an expensive piece of glazing (estimated at $2 million to $4 million), it would cost less than the three-block-long major demolition, repaving, and relandscaping currently contemplated by the government as an interim solution, not to mention the Park Service's plan for a final solution, estimated at $40 million to $45 million. The general uproar led to a resolution overwhelmingly passed by the Senate to reopen the avenue and to subsequent hearings by the House and the Senate.

A month later I testified at the Senate hearing on reopening the avenue that after a terrorist attack, the Liberty Bell has been protected by an enclosure of similar laminated glass, as have the Uffizi Museum's priceless Botticelli and Michelangelo paintings; that there exists a significant body of experience with using such glass barriers for security; and that there are manufacturers' representatives who can provide test data and actual demonstrations for the Secret Service or any interested party. (At the same time the Park Service was refusing to consider any options for reopening the avenue, the GSA, two blocks away, was conducting seminars on the use of the same laminated glass to protect public buildings.)

Exquisitely bad timing marred the final mass rally that was to put pressure on the White House. The day of the Senate hearing and two days before the rally, a massive bomb in front of Khobar Towers housing American servicemen in Dhahran, Saudi Arabia, exploded. It did not matter that, as in Oklahoma City, the attack was from a truck bomb and that my proposal would eliminate truck traffic; the disaster created an atmosphere that was a collateral fog over any discussion of the real issues.

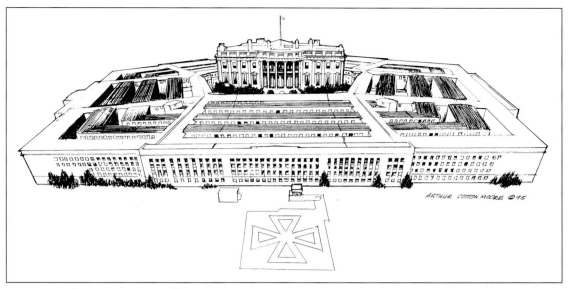

5-24. *White House protected by the Pentagon.*

5-25. *Protective glass fence sketch.*

I ended my testimony before one of the myriad review boards and commissions by reminding my listeners that Thomas Jefferson had ordered that Pennsylvania Avenue run in front of the White House "because kings live in park enclaves, but presidents live on streets." As is typical in Washington, only the negative has been achieved: The permanent landscaping and

5-26. *Bunkerism cartoon.*

5-27. *Cartoon of Pennsylvania Avenue.*

5-28. *Historic Pennsylvania Avenue.*

mauling of the avenue have been blocked by Congress and the review commissions, but the positive protective elements permitting its reopening have been officially ignored.

Immediately thereafter, each end of the once grand avenue was converted into employee parking lots, and the eerily empty center section, surrounded by concrete and steel mechanical barriers, feels uncannily like Checkpoint Charlie at the old Berlin Wall. At least the *Washington Post*, former Presidents Bush, Ford, and Carter, former candidate Dole, and a majority of the senate support reopening the avenue, so we shall see.

D.C. CONVENTION CENTER

I hate board meetings and could feel the pressure beginning to mount. After the meeting I was buttonholed and asked to do something about the city's proposed new convention center.

"C'mon, just pop us a little sketch."

"Arthur, puuuleez!"

The community and several civic groups responded as if they had just swallowed a live bat after seeing a giant Styrofoam box that would blanket six city blocks in the architect's appropriately named massing model showing his design of the convention center.

"It's the box that ate the neighborhood."

"There will be four tractor-trailer trucks in front of my house twenty-four hours a day."

"It makes the Carnegie Library look like a squashed bug."

The 1902 Carnegie Library building directly across the street from the proposed glassy main entrance is an elegant Beaux Arts structure; it was once the city's main library but was abandoned when the new main library was built. It had been prominently sited in its own block, surrounded by a landscaped park, Mt. Vernon Place, to cap the important 8th Street cross-axis from the Mall. The distressed building was already affronted by an adjacent multi-story mirror glass bridge which joined two jumbo chunks of the short-on-tech project called Techworld. The new towering convention center looming just to the north, however, would be ever so much in-its-face closer.

My fax machine hummed as I was graciously included in the protest loop. One and a half blocks to the southwest squatted the existing convention center, a dowdy but industrial-strength concrete box whose singular bow to the Art of Architecture consisted of chamfered corners. Years before I had opposed its location with a proposal to enclose our sleepy football stadium, directly east of the Capitol, and link it to the sparsely used old armory hall, creating the world's biggest convention center. The stadium was feverishly active then for some eight games a year, but now, with the team decamped to Maryland and the armory pressed into service for quadrennial inaugural balls, these two white elephants just sit around on their bond issues.

Competition among convention centers is like world-class sumo wrestling; one can't be too big or too fat. The former championship size of the present center had long been outstripped by fatter facilities in other cities. Apparently conventions, which I have always felt are merely an abundance of boring hot air inhaled by a lot of tax write-off suits playing hooky, continue to inflate, making every city scramble to keep up. Thus the new center with its nine-

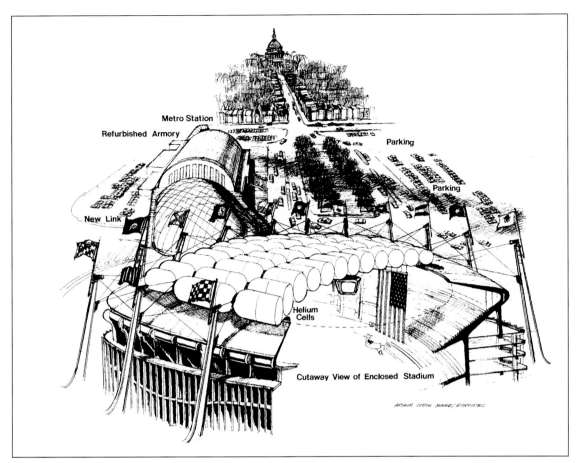

5-29. *Old proposal for a new convention center.*

block-long perimeter was being designed to make the existing center look like a charming miniature that nobody would know was useless and empty.

My sketch in the *Washington Post* offered two suggestions. I learned that the center's south end facing the Carnegie was mostly a large empty interior devoted to some circulation and much airy grandeur, and so I suggested putting its escalators outside in an open-air semi-circular plaza which would give some breathing space to the old library and a better entrance and drop-off point for the center; the second idea was to nurture the surrounding community's retail establishments by incorporating streetfront perimeter shops around the big building. Since an obvious objection could be that this would take away precious convention space, I proposed a trade-off: the three-story building could cantilever its two upper floors 10 feet over the property line provided that a 20-foot-deep space all along the street level was assigned to retail and community uses. The streets around the center would become lively, catering to conventioneers and the neighborhood, and the center would not lose a square foot of space. The cantilever would even provide weather protection for window-shopping. But the main goal was that the community not be suffocated by a sky-consuming towering blank fortress.

5-30. *The threatened old Carnegie Library.*

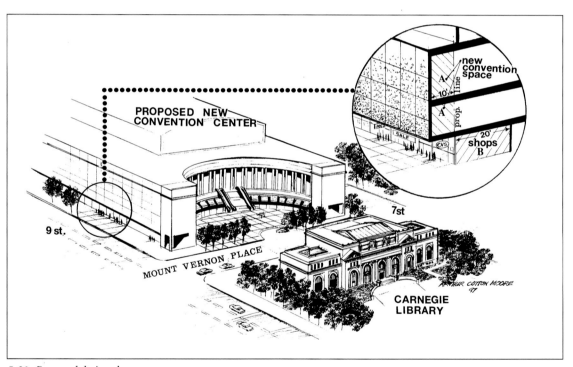

5-31. *Proposed design changes.*

It might have been a coincidence, but a few days after this proposal was published, a community meeting was held with center officials at which the crowd got so agitated that the police had to be called to restore order. Subsequently, a letter to the editor from the convention authority stated curiously that it did not have a design (although people had seen it), but when it got one, whatever it was it would be much better than my suggestions. Of course.

Although the White House fence and the D.C. Convention Center proposals fall into the familiar category of protest, they are included here as examples of not just being negative but offering positive solutions through specific, illustrated constructive ideas.

REFLECTIONS

The lesson of these struggles is not that it is not over until the fat lady sings but that it is never over. Every city is an ongoing organism that constantly coughs up fresh people, fresh problems, and fresh opportunities for provocative projects that address fresh needs. To some this may seem like tilting at the proverbial windmill, but I believe that if one has a genuine solution to a real problem, one has a civic responsibility to act on it. In city preservation, as in all preservation, one has to take the very long view. These pro bono proposals are the sort of positive agitation that recalls Günter Grass's statement that "the job of a [good] citizen is to keep his mouth open." They also suggest the wide range of possible urban interventions. Quite small and inexpensive art-related ideas can add to that slippery but pivotal notion of the quality of life in a city, ambitious sweeps for new housing speak to the basic underlying dynamics of urban reclamation, and responses such as the White House fence confront the contemporary evil novelty of people who see bombs as the answer to their problems.

There will always be something new and something old for which there is a range of corrective or additive solutions that usually baffle our securely uncreative and harassed authorities. It helps very much to be able to diagram the economics behind proposals. Developer experience was useful in conceiving many of these ideas because the first question always asked is, 'How do you pay for it?' The Rosslyn waterfront proposal was helped by experience in municipal bonds, and the Maryland Avenue housing project benefited from having developed, financed, designed, and built an apartment building on a tight site.

For people accustomed to working with feverish developers, it is important to recognize that for the most part in these political planning efforts one is not dealing with individuals whose personal cash is on the green felt and who are pushing like a red-hot piston to get something built. Instead, one quickly learns to appreciate that the world is divided into three groups: doers and owners (the developers), employees, and attendees. The employee world is frustratingly slow, because some employees are just putting in time and are in no hurry to see something get done. But these frustrations pale next to working with the attendees who make up a large portion of the committees, commissions, and civic associations with which a city preservationist must ultimately bargain. Predominantly volunteers, they have nothing at stake—no investment, no job—and therefore little real motivation. So one constantly hears a cry for consensus on some strategized prioritized Statement of Missions and Goals (always the first clue to imminent inaction), when in reality all urban improvements have a downside and therefore some heated opposition which will inevitably surface to preclude the imaginary happy universal consensus. Motivating citizen attendees to take aggressive action on a project is one of the toughest jobs facing city preservationists.

Some of my work started as pro bono civic contributions, such as the Old Post Office, which was a totally altruistic effort for the first six years, until the GSA realized that demolition was not an option and put it out for a design competition; now, seventeen years later, I am back working on its tower pro bono publico. My involvement in the Georgetown Waterfront began solely as one citizen founder of the strictly unofficial Georgetown Planning Council (mostly design professionals). Drawings I did for the council's 1965 report seem to have a life of their own, reappearing on occasions even though the situation on the ground has completely changed.

Architecture, like politics, is really and ideally local, and an architect's involvement in his or her city should be a natural extension of his or her professional and civic interests, whether it be for profit or pro bono. These are instances where native knowledge is a powerful advantage. The far greater importance of these examples, however, is that through their realization or simply through the community awareness provoked by the attendant discussion, one can make a decided difference in helping to preserve a city. I have often heard it said that such civic proposals should not be pursued because it is like throwing a few pearls into a sea of misery, but we must attack the overriding comprehensive issues before treating ourselves to the candy. One fairly overwhelming contradiction to this is the D.C. Office of Planning's effort to get its comprehensive plan approved, which has been going on for thirty years with no end in sight.

Not too long ago I listened to a panel of crotchety tobacco-stained warriors droning on about the need for metropolitanwide planning for infrastructure and how we were all going to hell if we did not confront the problems of poverty, bad SAT scores, the breakup of the family, and sewage treatment in a multijurisdictional comprehensively coherent way. I suggested that we should then proceed directly to Beelzebub, because there was little prospect of a jurisdictional meltdown or of Virginia or Maryland even thinking about getting into bed with each other, much less with Washington's Marion Barry. The troops had been at it so long in so many hazy fly-filled conferences that their routines, designed expressly to swat down each other's positions, sounded like they were coming from some poor bloke who realizes too late that everybody has heard the joke already. All sensible people support regional planning that addresses our large systemic problems, but even the most gung-ho among us must admit that it is a very long process that can look somewhat ineffectual to people who are convinced they are drowning. We can continue long-range planning efforts and simultaneously do incremental, immediately realizable small projects. We all can walk and chew gum at the same time.

Too often a persistent reality-avoiding planning fog is concealed under the hallowed cause of regionalism. In the metropolitan region of Washington the rich suburbs with political power are demonstrably not interested in marrying up with the financial difficulties of the politically impotent district. In constantly chasing only regionalism, veteran planners demonstrate the tendency to maintain ingrained patterns of thought and behavior long after they are no longer appropriate. Each area of the country has its own obstacles to regionalism, making incrementalism of the sort discussed here a more practical option.

It is my impression, formed after visiting sixty-four countries and a lot of cities, that any place which can boast having more than a handful of attractions is doing quite well; these attractions do not stop poverty or illegitimacy, but it takes surprisingly few of them to lift the spirits and make communities more enjoyable and worthy of attention. Most city guides, panting to seduce any visitors, particularly repeat (local) tourists, include their version of the American sideshow, and while they overlook local sights that are idiosyncratically interesting, they generally focus on a town's attractive projects. Paris is the classic example of project objectification; from the Champs Elysee to the Louvre pyramid, the city seems to proceed project by project. Although no American city will ever equal Paris, a few unpretentious attractions are better than none.

We need a test of solvability. All the physical urban problems associated with these proposals, which hopefully will stimulate efforts elsewhere, are solvable. Poverty, the decline of the family, and an agreed on, finite, precise frozen-in-time comprehensive plan for a metropolitan region may not be solvable any time soon. The concept of city preservation renews, through the ancient Greek ideal of the polis—the citizen's proper engagement and identification with the city—the Aristotelian notion of the community of communities.

[EXPANSIONS]

Some of my most memorable experiences over the past thirty-three years have involved projects that didn't happen. One of those projects began with an invitation by the prospective client to visit what he described as a "truly awesome, beautiful" old mill in New Hope, Pennsylvania. I was met at the train station by a very personable young man who showed me an extraordinarily wonderful rambling industrial structure perched dramatically and romantically on a huge rock formation in the Delaware River. It was being used to manufacture cheap vinyl handbags, an employment sadly out of whack with the riverine past of the place. This marginal enterprise had recently gone into bankruptcy, making the site conveniently available. Near a lovely swan-filled canal there was a French restaurant which seemed to have been transported magically from Provence. After a bottle of Pouilly-Fuissé and an elegantly languid lunch of impeccably poached salmon veronique, we strolled back to get more admiring photographs of the mill.

"What do you need to get started?" my gracious host, with whom I had become quite chummy, asked. "Just a letter agreement with authorization to proceed on your company letterhead," I replied.

The would-be developer leaned over and opened the trunk of his car. Arrayed in perfect order were his stationery, envelopes, stamps, blotter and pen set, desktop, Rolodex, staplers, and business cards, along with a folding chair and an old manual typewriter. As he leaned over to type the agreement, I suggested that he send it to me instead, since I had a train to catch.

All the way home I tried to get that fantastic mill out of my mind, but I had been burned often enough by get-rich-quick, suspender-wearing, yellow-tied hotshot MBAs who were, to put it mildly, severely undercapitalized not to stick my head in the noose again. In the beginning of my practice I would have given it a go, and the New Hope mill might have become one more story in this book that would attempt to render the feeling of what the experience was like in the trenches of often underbudgeted developer projects.

Despite these personal experiences of pratfalls and hazards (such as empty pockets, clients in the cooler, and occasional gunfire) along the way, I hope I have shown that adaptive reuse done in an exploratory way, with design latitude, offers a rich array of opportunities for creative work and is ideally suited for all the existing, economically unproductive, ordinary buildings that languish in every city across the country. The preservation community has had too little interest and involvement in them, but perhaps its enthusiasm can be reinvigorated and it can regain its former intensity and fervor. We need to foster education about the language of old downtown buildings because only by being able to read their life stories can the public become engaged enough to value them and act on their behalf. Knowledge of the syntax of the city will underpin and reinforce a preservationist approach to the city.

The uglification of our cities, most plaintively evident in the abject abuse we inflict on our defenseless buildings, should concern all citizens as a clear mirror of society's ills. Compounding this urban disfigurement and as a general reaction to it is the great success of the new simulacra of traditionally themed environments. This rapidly growing trend has challenged the elemental tenet of preservation: Why preserve when we can with our current affluence and expertise build virtually anything in a preferable new location that will function better and be free of undesirable elements? How we respond to that challenge will determine the preservation paradigm for the twenty-first century.

The overwhelmingly exciting explosion of complexities, vicissitudes, and responsibilities inherent in moving from a single building to a whole downtown begs for the medium of film and a sound track or at least better writing than mine to convey the incredible and exhilarating three-dimensional speed of simultaneous problem solving and visual invention required. It means nothing less than harnessing the multidisciplined modalities of architecture, engineering, planning, urban design, risk management, landscape architecture, real estate development economics, financial structuring, land use techniques, lawyering, municipal administration and management, and political strategy into sensible, doable, and coherent physical changes. It demands more skill than I can usually muster at performance, fund-raising, persuasion, entertainment, street smarts, and occasional injections of the purest grade of chutzpah.

Through a new stretching from normal practice to a metropolitan scale, there is much more that preservation can do to improve the quality of city life. Although my proactive pro bono efforts so far have been mixed and are still in progress, I hope that some of my experiences, especially in this time of disillusionment, will stimulate engagement by others in their own hometowns. In contrast to the prevailing emphasis on regional planning, pro bono publico and similar individual efforts show the strength of a modest incremental project-by-project approach with the prospect of timely and tangible results which may ultimately help spur long-range planning. In fact, the ever-elusive grail of regional cooperation probably would come about more easily after the establishment of confidence achieved through working experiences on mutually beneficial cross-jurisdictional incremental projects similar to that proposed for the Rosslyn waterfront. The concept of city preservation with political-economic involvement on a large scale could turn out to be one of the most effective avenues for fighting the decline of our cities.

Tying together adaptively reused ordinary buildings, as in LINRAW, with individual pro bono activism is a reasonable method to revitalize at least some parts of our cities and stimulate thinking about other approaches. I am not suggesting solutions to the great socioeconomic problems of cities, such as an inner-city underclass with no jobs. Rather, these ideas represent a recognition that cities consist of a plurality of different areas with quite different prospects. Some of these areas probably will respond to preservationist approaches, and a city with attractive projects and revitalized areas is not a dead city. This may be the best we can do when faced with the real possibility of largely dead or deadly cities and a good strategy for rescuing the immediate future while we wait for the political will to deal with major systemic urban problems. In the meantime, I would like to offer a few stretchings in areas that are not often discussed.

PERMISSIVE DISCONTINUITY

"I have good vision and good eyes, and I didn't see any naked women there," said Washington's playful mayor, Marion Barry, when asked by a reporter what he was doing at a Christmas party hosted by an establishment named "This Is It" whose unsubtle facade incorporated unambiguous photographs and a declaration that the most beautiful all-nude dancing girls in D.C. were available for viewing inside. The explanation was tendered that the ladies might have had the night off, since it was holiday time.

Mr. Barry neglected to mention that "This Is It" was bracketed by establishments named "Adam & Eve" and "Paradise," and that just on the other side of an embarrassed branch post office was "Benny's Home of the Porno Stars," "The Cocoon," "Butterfly," and the "Gold Rush."

As the architect of and a development partner in a new office building across the street in 1980, I knew that 'This Is It' and the row of other similar businesses did not take any nights off and seemed to be relentlessly blasting away twenty-four hours a day, seven days a week. They were not helping leasing, particularly when one of our first tenants, a woman lawyer who came to her office directly from a Saturday morning riding lesson, still in jodhpurs and boots with crop in hand, was offered a cash inducement to give some of the inebriated customers of those all too close neighbors a personal ride.

Despite persistent harassment by very muscular bouncers, pimps, and hooks, I spent some time trying to get this block to clean up its act. In an effort to persuade, I designed a

6-1. *Fourteenth Street adult entertainment district, 1980.*

scheme to unify and tone down its graphics through a series of canopies, knowing that the process of upgrading would strip off (sorry) the usual transmographic overlays and reveal an intriguing row of buildings which included Neoclassical, Second Empire, Victorian, and Art Deco facades. But other people with immeasurably more resources tied up in real estate in the surrounding area were considerably less tolerant, and eventually these buildings and their activities were blitzed and replaced by a staid and plodding office building and a parking lot. The result was the destruction of an irreplaceable block of buildings with an average age close to 100 years which had, to say the least, an enthusiastic and thriving clientele. The owners of these places never went to meetings, as I did, to discuss vacancy rates. After demolition, like crabgrass in a manicured lawn, the same emporiums began sprouting up in residential neighborhoods all over the city, causing endless local firefights.

There are functions of a city which rarely make it inside the covers of city planning treatises. These functions have two characteristics: They gain their appeal from being sharply different from (discontinuous) and more permissive than the general ethos and morality of the surrounding area, and they are elemental, genetic, and as old as the first human settlement.

In Chapter 4 I suggested that among all the centripetal city uses and trends, human contact is the most powerful and represents the last basic advantage of the city in an antiurban, electronically equipped fearful world. Clearly, the most common manifestation of human contact is represented by perfectly respectable theaters, nightclubs, bars, dance halls, and restaurants where the mating and dating rituals of relationships can take place.

People want to go on dates "where it's happening," and that still is somewhere in the city. This suggests that in this population the underlying driving force for coming to the city is a sexual force, whether heterosexual, bisexual, or homosexual, whether flirting with it, being around it, or having it. As Henry Miller put it, "sex is one of the nine reasons for reincarnation. The other eight are unimportant." Certainly there is room here for simple companionship and

6-2. *Proposed renovation of old facades.*

fellowship, although this can happen in the suburbs just as easily and therefore cannot be counted on as a motive to help save a city. There are other, non-sex-related permissive discontinuity uses, such as gambling, but they have no particular need for human contact and therefore no fundamental need for the city and can be found wherever they are permitted, be it an Indian reservation, phone booth, riverboat, uninhabitable desert, or church basement.

The need for people to congregate in groups to meet, date, and mate represents the numerically largest human contact market. In this majority is a major subgroup, the gay and lesbian community, which is intensely urban-oriented and culturally sophisticated. In many communities historic preservation is even considered a targeted gay political issue. The widespread development of establishments specifically catering to the gay community has greatly enriched our cities. (In researching historic preservation constituents on the World Wide Web, I found there was a page for a gay and lesbian preservation organization in Los Angeles; however, on visiting the page, I discovered that the preservation pursued by this group involved historic dildos, venerable forms of rubber goods, and other legendary erotically useful equipment. Despite the nonarchitectural focus of these collections, there is still an easily observable city-loving proarchitectural constituency in the gay community which should be a reliable resource for city renewal.)

It is important to state that I am not talking about pornography; that $8 billion market is primarily a movie, video rental, mail order, or Internet-provided product which clearly represents a booming business of vicarious experiences conveyed through printed and recorded

6-3. *All that remains is a palimpsest.*

matter consumed by people in their homes, requiring no real collective human contact, visual or tactile. Pornography can be obtained everywhere, as easily in the suburbs as in the city; therefore, like gambling, it is a permissive activity that is not discontinuous and offers no real strength for the central city. What a city has is not fiction or pictures but real bodies in real places. It is also important to keep in mind that what is acceptable now was not so before, and what is not respectable now will be respectable immediately or in the near future. Lord Shawcross correctly noted over thirty years ago that "the so-called new morality is too often the old immorality condoned." The progression on this front is somewhat like the stock market: Just as it seems to go forward, there is a retreat, yet when we step back and look at a significantly longer time period, there is real change which is widely acknowledged even when it is sometimes deplored. I noted with amusement that the mutual stock fund SinShares was so successful that it changed its portfolio name to FunShares to broaden its holdings without divesting any of the old sin-money-making companies.

Society has, with considerable hypocrisy, assigned this general subject to a taboo area, while at the same time our popular entertainment and a large portion of our mainstream media not only constantly assault the bounds of propriety but seek desperately to punch through those bounds to shock an increasingly jaded audience. Therefore, we have a whole range of human contact activities in whose midst there is a constantly moving blue line between respectability and nonrespectability. Our policy for these activities is "ignore it," and we see its effects when almost daily conflicts between sexually oriented enterprises and neighborhood groups break out all over the country. These predictable battles are dependably greeted with great surprise by officials who inevitably buck the problem to the courts, where the familiar constitutional issues are raised, essentially beginning the cycle all over again. These are uses for which an enforced location is easier to implement because of society's censure. Done with care, they can be of economic benefit for a city.

Although this is still primarily a male-oriented industry, there are clubs catering to women, such as Chippendale's in Manhattan and New Ai (new love) in Japan. A more recent market, however, are the 2,500 upscale "gentlemen's clubs" around the country, among which are growing numbers that actively try to attract couples as well as individual women.

Since this is a book about the physical environment as opposed to the purely physical, I also want to remind that this subject includes suppressed urban economic resources that are partially controlled by and beneficial to the criminal world. This black market often requires expensive public services such as police, health, and substance control yet is almost totally unproductive of tax revenues. In the new desperation of our cities we should look at this difficult issue again. Politically, it should be easier now that most of the middle class has left the city and the few remaining pockets are the most likely to be afflicted by the random proliferation of hookers and table-dance bars or whatever the current craze is. Each locality could begin at zero and determine exactly what absolutely will not be permitted, after which freedom should reign. It seems unbelievably quaint now, but in my father's southern hometown, playing canasta on Sunday in mixed company was forbidden.

It continues to make sense to concentrate a permissive industry in nonresidential districts where it can be easily policed, health-controlled, and taxed; separation and buffering from other districts are pivotal. The devil is in the details, and they have to be tailored precisely to a specific urban area. Even public health booths offering condoms were attacked when they were located in an old Catholic working-class neighborhood in Bedford, Massachusetts. This is still new regulatory territory, and there are no formulas. In Washington, for example, there is a zoning ordinance mandating that no sexually oriented business be located within 300 feet of another one, frustrating any districting for surveillance and control.

Informally, permissive districting has evolved over time in places such as "the Block" in Baltimore, which does have, although this is not publicly asserted, an advantageous affect on the city's drawing power for conventions. There are many places in Europe where it has been successfully done, such as Hamburg and Amsterdam. One of the few examples of a planned attempt to recognize this function in the United States is the Combat Zone in Boston, but rather than a trailblazing attempt, the efforts of the Boston Redevelopment Authority have mostly entailed a recognition of rights and problems with few positive actions. The fact that some of the pioneer efforts in any controversial endeavor have not been successful is a fairly common experience and should not deter other cities from experimentation.

My idea is to use permissive activity as one more arrow in the badly depleted quiver of the dedicated preservationist and urbanist. Especially for those areas of the city which are unlikely to see major new redevelopment and have, as most do, rows of nineteenth- and twentieth-century buildings, we should consider a mapped zone that would permit permissive discontinuity uses and would require the owners to rehabilitate the structures in accordance with design guidelines and a review process. Historically, such areas were offensively dirty, tawdry, and seamy, but as the French Quarter in New Orleans and Key West demonstrate, as they get more clean and charming, somehow they become more acceptable. Housed in restored buildings, safely controlled by the authorities, and appropriately distanced and buffered from schools, churches, homes, and other sensitive areas, such districts could make a major economic contribution to the city. I have seen many almost comatose old retail districts where these powerful permissive economics could provide a second life with aesthetically pleasing preservation.

Despite all urban logic and historical precedent, such businesses are locating in the suburbs, including those of sun belt cities such as Atlanta and Jacksonville. Meanwhile, downtown, with a Scott Joplin look-alike on the piano in a carved mahogany Victorian paneled interior with ormolu details fit for Rhett Butler and tasseled lamps splashing light on women straight out of Toulouse-Lautrec drawings, one might be able to raise money for charity with spring house tours. Speaking of Lautrec, many great cultural figures did their most creative work in areas of high permissiveness. William Faulkner once declared that "the perfect home for a writer is a brothel—because in the morning hours it's always calm and in contrast at night there's always a party atmosphere."

One of the sidelights of the Dick Morris (former adviser to President Clinton) affair was that prostitution is not illegal in Washington, only solicitation for prostitution; call girls are called and don't have to ask. If this absurdity does not reveal the legal foolishness and duplicity in this area, I don't know what does. Mr. Morris later was rewarded with a $2.5 million book contract for his indiscretions.

A noticeable number of young women—single, married, and single mothers—are preferring to jump around with less than usual on, for very good pay, to taking conventional jobs, and the number is growing, according to Dr. Judith Lynne Hanna, an anthropologist who studies this area and who estimates that a third of the dancers in many clubs are stripping to pay for college and graduate school, making for much academic discussion on how sex work empowers women. Dr. Hanna, who also testifies in First Amendment cases, has written that "some dancers believe they pay homage to the gods of love, Eros and Venus, and celebrate female beauty and fecundity in their performances." As a lover of cities I simply would ask, How many tourists and conventioneers would visit New Orleans if there was not a French Quarter?

This of course is the real point. The preservation of old buildings and sexually permissive activities have a scenographic affinity which can be exploited so that together they become another reliable economic rehabilitation resource for the city of the future.

These human contact activities catering to predominantly sexually motivated young people and the comparatively smaller adult entertainment market cause the city to contain exciting and permissive facilities ranging from nightclubs and restaurants to experimental over-the-edge-of-propriety theater. This frisson makes the city appealing to a nonsexually driven market called "empty nesters" by realtors. This mostly older and affluent population, attracted by the full range of urban conveniences, is covertly drawn by the excitement and edginess spun off from the aforementioned groups and together with them forms a durable and sizable market for the city that has yet to be maximized. It is a way for older people to feel young again by proximity and not be left on the suburban shelf. Demographers have pointed out that people over age sixty-five are the fastest growing segment of the population and that their numbers will explode in the twenty-first century. Moreover, as the health and vigor of the formerly sidelined elderly medically improve, these people will increasingly enjoy a second childproof sexual life, and this sea change will result in sexually oriented businesses (perhaps pickup bars for seventy-year-olds) specifically catering to both them and their natural predisposition to the concept of preservation. Future permissive districts will include the postparental (popies), who may become more important than the yuppie market, and that could be good news for cities. The key to this economic market is that cities retain their racy advantage.

PRESERVATION IN THE AVANT-GARDE

In these new stretchings, I don't want to be too prescriptive and lose sight of the fact that preservation is architecture and must always be primarily an artistic effort.

Although preservation is associated more often with the rear guard, there is an opening in the idea of creative preservation for some avant-gardeness in the concept of the audience frame, since one of the benefits preservation brings to the table is an audience. Most artistic and architectural cutting-edge discourse can be characterized as running away from an audience because an audience usually is seen as the great unwashed general public, intellectually speaking.

But there are different types of audiences that architects, like all artists, must address, including those considered to be in the avant-garde—the form givers—whom I will simply call the creators of newness. In devising a new form and/or idea, the creators of newness want above all recognition for their work. The avant-garde's celebrated rejection of or antagonism to society (épater le bourgeois) is first a tactic to obtain notice, which is the first step in achieving the desired recognition. In seeking recognition, the creators of newness are fundamentally appealing to an audience—the germinal audience—composed of the critics and receptive intellectuals who are pivotal in granting that first recognition. In the normal process of dissemination of newness, particularly for playwrights and architects who are involved in very public arts, the originators of that newness must continue to seek recognition from the intelligentsia—the contributing audience—who will be the prime consumers of the newness and will provide feedback similar to the response one gets in a theater.

In the further dissemination and, some would say, the inevitable watering down and aging of the newness, the original vanguard is replaced or augmented by people also promoting and practicing what by then has become a style, which they offer to the wider aware public, who keep it going by being the sustaining audience. Finally, there is a trickling down to the general audience, which is where the newness invariably becomes a hackneyed trite idea, now contaminated for all previous audiences, who identify its atrophy and death and begin the search for a new newness.

In attempting to communicate, the creators of newness need to refine and recapitulate their new forms or ideas in a way that connects to a specific audience. One effective way to make such a bridge, particularly in architecture, is to establish a frame of reference, experience, or understanding around the new idea. One of the premises of this discussion is recognition of the need for such an audience-engaging frame and acknowledgment that it facilitates freer experimentation and more rapid acceptance of radical new ideas. Society wants new forms and ideas and recognizes that they may come in outrageous shapes; the bridge to recognition is made easier by the audience frame.

Arthur Miller used the frame of a very conventional setting for *Death of a Salesman* inside which he could communicate the idea of the hollowness of existence. Roy Lichtenstein has used the familiar frame of the comic strip to produce an original and avant-garde art, and the artist Mike Kelley has used the familiar frame of rag dolls to explore the ravages of society. Jean-Paul Sartre's frame was the storytelling novel used to communicate existential philosophy.

An architect can use the literal frame of the retained shell of an old building to engage an audience, freely experiment with design inside, and find greater acceptance of newness because of the frame. The Viennese group Coop Himmelblau's first major published work in the United States was the remodeling of a small rooftop space in a traditional building. The force and power of the design rests largely on its contrast and opposition to its traditional but still dominant frame. In the Star Carpet Works the frame of the old factory made the unconventional forms inside acceptable to the client and the conservative neighborhood. In a totally new waterfront project such as Washington Harbour I used the frame of an overall forceful urban design that clearly facilitated access to the water's edge to experiment with architectural design. The preserved architectural frame as utilized in much freestyle preservation both builds a bridge to the audience and provides an opportunity for avant-garde experimentation.

NEW LEADERSHIP

In stark contrast to the activism suggested in Chapter 5 are the endless symposia where everyone seems to agree that the words *cities* and *intractable problems* are increasingly synonymous, yet with all the public hand-wringing, the downward slide persists. We all have attended numerous bone-dry conferences and panels where there is interminable talk about either statistical urban trends or personal experiences that show how local neighborhood groups can advantageously work together. Most of these presentations have two factors in common: They are overly generalized or too acutely personal and therefore are practically inapplicable, and they are nonvisual. The two go hand in hand. Visuals provide an inescapable razor-sharp focus to specific issues such as graffiti, housing, economic disconnects, and development opportunities out of which the possibility of pragmatic action grows. We need to recognize that subsequent effective steps are a combination of political, economic, and visual work efforts which too often are undertaken separately.

How can we get more effective leadership (clearly needed) and a fresh perspective on city preservation? What organizational vehicle might coordinate a convergence of specialized thinking among people involved in the political and economic realms of urban affairs, with a visual focus on practical options? One unexplored venue for this new focus is the reflective, nonmembership arena of the think tank. These institutions are staffed by academic, semiacademic, and out-of-office politically savvy people as well as former publicists, legislators, political science professors, and political consultants who in an off election year might hanker for reinvolvement in that most local of front lines, city politics. In the same institutions there are people who have both academic and practical training in economics and probably a few who may be closet financiers and wannabe developers who itch to deal with the real world. The idea is to try a new approach to city problems by creating new investigative alliances composed of visual people (urban designers) and political and economic people. This three-sided conflated focus approach could draw as needed from sociologists, statisticians, and members of other disciplines but would focus on actual doable projects to improve specific target cities. If this coalition turns out to be productive, it could spawn working joint ventures which could actually start real projects. Whatever the result, it would be a worthwhile attempt to counterbalance the pervasive and so far ineffective theoretical socioeconomic approach to cities.

The benefit to the think tank is a fresh breeze of practicality and a new perspective on urban affairs. In effect, it would provide the incubation for the new hybrid teams and would bask in their success. For the political types the benefits would be a focused immersion in city politics, the toughest classroom of all; for economists it could be a grounding in practicalities and the opening of new careers with substantial economic rewards; for architects and urban designers it would be an exposure to the workings of the power bases in the real world. The benefit to our urban environment might be the best result of all.

THE NEW PRESERVATION

EXPANSIONS

There are five ways in which preservation can become more elastic to reach its critical audiences for its own benefit and for the benefit of our cities. They are synopsized here from the preceding chapters.

1. Expand the scope to ordinary buildings

We are running out or have run out of landmark buildings to be saved. Unlike Europe, America is sufficiently young that its reservoir of grand structures that survived the 1950s and 1960s urban renewal massacres have almost all been preserved, restored, or adapted. But the remaining large inventory in the more ordinary late nineteenth- and twentieth-century building stock has been largely overlooked. Saving and adapting this substantial equity not only will keep us busy for years but also will significantly help keep our cities breathing. This is not a new observation, but it is one that particularly needs to be vigorously promoted. The preservation movement will have to endure some mockery as the focus shifts to what the public may see as humble and dismissable and discardable in the glorious cause of progress, but the movement suffered similar scornful attacks twenty-five years ago by people who wanted to remove major old buildings such as the Old Post Office in the name of progress.

2. Open up design to greater experimentation

We should permit greater latitude in adaptation and call for more of a design emphasis, particularly in the introduction of new elements in the treatment of old buildings. Preservationists need to be more tolerant of experimental design, particularly when such design still serves to highlight and celebrate the old fabric and when the old part is a useful mediator between the new interventions and the existing neighborhood. But even beyond the benefits of transition, creative juxtapositions and even startling combinations should be given much more room for creative design, particularly when a project involves less than landmark structures. The notion of design experimentation within preservation may seem strange, but changes can be made as long as the original host still exists. At the same time, preservation in a free hybrid form could actually become part of the vanguard.

3. Expand permissiveness in use

Although there are reuses that may seem jarring and inappropriate—for example, the conversion of churches into warehouses and discotheques—there needs to be far greater tolerance for uses which may simply act as a holding action to forestall demolition. Moreover, in the honorable effort to give life back to our cities, we should become more accepting of uses from the permissive discontinuity menu. Human contact uses should be accepted for their viability as an economic reality responding to a real market and a part of cities since time immemorial. Their acceptability will be vastly increased if they are properly districted and contribute to the cause of preservation.

4. Stretch the notion of a past worth saving

The last stylistic period which seems to have developed a secure following is Art Deco, which might have seemed peculiar to people back in the 1930s when they looked at the new Art Moderne. Now we have to move the interest line forward to embrace modern buildings of the 1940s and 1950s. Not only are they more than a half century old, we do not want to repeat the fallacy of the modernists, the fantasy that the past is not part of the present and therefore is discardable. It was, after all, modern building projects that caused the destruction of the older buildings which spurred the preservation movement. Early modern and International Style buildings should now be candidates for preservation. Today's popular excuse for demolition is that the 1950s curtain wall does not meet energy criteria and therefore the glass facades must be thrown away so that the frame can be reskinned. Restorers and adaptive reusers confronted a similar problem in the past in the form of acres of leaky single-pane glazing in nineteenth-century buildings and can be inventive again with the curtain wall of the International Style.

Of course, only a portion of what has been built should be a candidate for some form of preservation. There are clear and obvious and great modern buildings that we all could agree ought to be kept, and there is a vast dross of banal and insignificant work that could be discarded. The worrisome issue is the questionables. Without the real test of judgments made over time, we really cannot be sure of many in this gray area. Here is where the heterodic new-old adaptation can be most useful. I can see a process whereby highly debatable architectures could be retained in a partial or fragmentary form, in new compositions of predominantly contemporary design. We could thereby develop a new category between save and demolish—the hybrid, quasi-preservation that permits major adaptation to future needs for those questionables. In essence, free adaptive new-old combinations could be a hedge against the snap determinations that have previously removed so many wonderful but temporarily out-of-fashion buildings.

5. Enlarge the realm of preservation

To borrow an expression from the GOP, preservation should be a big tent that places followers of restoration, adaptive remodelers, civic activists, and even city agitators under the same roof. Preservation should extend to the entire city and embrace the thought that whereas the quality of life in the city would be greatly enhanced by the saving of some fine old edifices, it also would be enhanced by a brand-new element that makes needed connections or provides access to existing places, energizes populations in a symbolic fashion, or in some intangible way adds to the patrimony of a city. City preservation, the proponent position, unlike the negative stance of old, may be the grandest role of all.

NEW ACTIVISM

Along with perpetual fighting over the demolition of worthy structures and the noble struggle against the installation of insensitive horrors and destructive new elements, we should take a leaf from the highly competitive activities of the national political parties and issue politics. Political recruiting and propaganda programs forged through the intense heat of campaigns should be studied for effective ideas that produce actual results. For example, the issuing of positions that weigh on urban issues, a natural progression, must be communicated immediately (faxed, telephoned, and E-mailed) to the media and power centers. As the Clinton election machine and its "war room" have taught us, timing is everything because the world in general and the media in particular have the attention span of a puppy. Too often I have seen worthwhile groups dither and delay and become totally irrelevant.

Following political education, I would urge a new approach to public relations so that protest efforts, such as our rally on Pennsylvania Avenue in Lafayette Park, do not wind up under a tree, in the obituaries, or on the television station's cutting room floor. Stunts and witty outrageousness make good copy, but nothing succeeds in our regrettably celebrity-obsessed culture like the use of celebrities. Look how People for the Ethical Treatment of Animals used celebrity models to fight the fur industry; it got a lot more ink and goodwill with supermodel

Christy Turlington in the buff than it did by throwing red paint at fur coats. The National Endowment for the Arts moves above the newspaper fold when its spokesperson turns out to be a movie star like Alec Baldwin. Winston-Salem got a lot of mileage and contributions from hiring Zsa Zsa Gabor for one evening. I don't say that this subservience to the star fixation of the press is edifying, but it is a reliable avenue to good coverage, without which the message is simply unheard and useless. Most preservation battles in the future will be fought and won in the fourth estate.

Obtaining good preservation results has always relied too much on a stick or carrot process: the denial of permits by review boards and preservation officials or the giving of tax benefits. To these raw coercive approaches we should add public relations methods of exposure to preservation issues. Specifically, we have to find ways to get regular engaging reviews for the public on topical present and future proposals for our cities. All other art and craft forms, such as books, paintings, television shows, plays, and movies, are exhaustively reviewed, and the result of such attention has led to better quality. Critical judgments have shaped popular demand, and the producers of these works have responded. But considering the volume of construction, the many issues that concern the preservationist, planner, and civic activist are too rarely publicly reviewed by a knowledgeable critic, with the exception of a few large cities. There is no difference between a person who wants you to come to his movie and a person who wants you to come to her shopping center, except that the former is subject to a gauntlet of critical opinion and the latter is not. Both want to make sales, but to the latter there is no impetus for quality. Often no one is pointing out that in the newly proposed or built center there has been a failure to preserve an important piece of history or the fact that the developer is presenting a simulated historical architectural impression. People have many options, and with information they will vote with their feet for quality.

To these positive expansions of the notions and means of preservation I would like to add one negative activity. It seems to me that some of the energy of preservationists could be reignited to condemn, shame, ridicule, and stomp on the mindless uglifications and the new bogus historically themed environments discussed in Chapter 3. An old-fashioned truth and beauty squad or tribunal of authenticity might seem positively refreshing in our cynical times. Proclamations trumpeting the comical thinness and exposing the artificiality of the new fake environments would implicitly underscore the honesty of preservation. The challenge to ridicule the ridiculous may seem unnecessary until we remember that most people are in an environmental stupor, barely conscious of their surroundings. Waking them up with humor and derision could be another original way of building a greater constituency for our old cities.

6-4. *Painting of the bittersweetness of tourism.*

Finally, to all the cautionary examples in Chapter 3 I would like to add the following concerns. Some minor problems for American preservation could be characterized as too much Euro, too much treacle, and too little accommodation for the automobile.

We should not just be re-creating European places. While Europe contains inspiration for the urban revitalizer, it also has areas which are as bad as the worst of America. We don't want to simply copy those old famous parts of great cities which frequently gained their strength through the rigid geometry imposed by authoritarian or aristocratic regimes, because they are not flexible contemporary democratic paradigms and we do not want to be a warmed-over Europe. Our need is to transform these examples into a contemporary American architecture that incorporates preservation but also reflects the fact that the United States is a more populist, multicultural, nonaristocratic individualistic society. I believe we can do this without being overly politically correct and while continuing to emphasize quality.

We have to fight against excessive sentimentality, cutsiness, and cartoonish treacle. Although this is not a disaster that sends critics into spasms, there is a strong tendency for any attraction involving tourism to become cloyingly overcute. This treacle factor is often a matter of too much success rather than too little and is therefore basically not a cosmically unmanageable problem. More frequently the issue is too little attraction. Nevertheless, we do not want the necessary vacation-oriented economic reuse to make preservation corny.

Architects, preservationists, and planners who follow their European predilections love public transit for good and practical reasons. But even constant pressure for public transit is not going to change auto-dependent America in the near future, especially if the preserved projects emphasize leisure time activities which we know result in private automobile use. The car is fundamentally a foreign element unknown by the creators of many old buildings, but an accommodation for private vehicles is essential to today's economic success of reuse. We therefore need to devise new solutions to this dilemma which may require major accommodations for the car and stimulate explorations of the new-old hybrids I have been emphasizing.

In sum, I am maintaining not only that freestyle adaptive reuse is often functionally preferable and far more widely applicable than restoration but also that a new-old hybrid has the capacity to renew architecture and form the basis for whole new directions in design. I say this because some people regard the new work spreading out from California as modern design in a seizure, virtually in the last gasping throes of expiration. In the hands of Frank Gehry this work is wonderful, but as it gets into less sure hands, it will be increasingly questionable. At the end of its century, in order to titillate, modernism seems to have gone into a final chaotic and spasmodic period. On a recent project I counted seven different facade materials in seven separate convulsive forms, each in effect playing its own tune, like the Spike Jones orchestra without Spike. It is exhausting to look at these paroxysms of design, and it is inconceivable that this is a viable model for a new urbanism. How could an all-deconstructivist community be livable? It appears to be a form of decadent rococo modernism with zaps replacing the curves. But my main complaint is that this work is so self-referential that it is blind to any civic duty. In this climate, the new-old hybrid of reinvigorated permissive adaptive reuse preservation has the capacity to lead us to a new aesthetic with the not inconsiderable civic utility of being a very appropriate and useful tool in the continuous struggle to save our endangered cities.

This may be a good time to rethink our approach to cities precisely because this is still a down time for the central city. Unlike the rampant speculation of the 1980s, the unattractive financial situation of our downtowns means that there is not constant pressure for every old building to be demolished because it did not attain the full floor area ratio (density) on the site. When the economy is hot, every old building has a negative value in preventing that dreamed-of high-rise cash cow from happening. In a down market, city people are often forced to stay because they cannot sell and therefore turn their attention to improving their neighborhoods. Commercial interests in that depressed market, also out of desperation, are more receptive to nonstandard ideas. At this time a low-cost regenerative incremental application of the freestyle permissive adaptive reuse, LINRAW-type approach has a better chance of being heard, being implemented, and succeeding.

Civic activists, planners, and preservationists are not much bogged down by theorizing, but architects are always knee deep in theory. After the postmodern critique of the exaggerated claims of modernism's ability to change society, most new architectural theorizing retreated from any action that would engage the public realm and therefore any practical involvement in the city or the neighborhood. This book is intended to offer evidence that there are ways for all concerned citizens and professionals to be effective and that the preservation of our heritage and our cities can be achieved only by contemplation followed by action.

THE POWERS OF PRESERVATION

In several parts of this book I have shown places where preservation efforts have failed. No realistic movement believes that it has limitless capabilities. It is the continual comprehension of these failures which galvanizes collective action informed by the recognition of real limits into an effective urban force.

As the most politically aware of all architectural movements, preservation has been by far the most powerful. Its powers, derived largely from its multifaceted charms and attractions, will only be multiplied by the expansion of its scope, range, and purpose, making it inevitably a major player in determining the future of the American landscape.

Barry, Marion. 1983. *Washington Post*. March 17, p. A1.

Baudrillard, Jean. 1988. *America*. Translated by Chris Turner. London: Verso.

Baudrillard, Jean. 1994. *The Illusion of the End*. Translated by Chris Turner. Stanford: Stanford,CA: University Press.

Brand, Stewart. 1994. *How Buildings Learn: What Happens after They're Built*. New York: Viking Penguin.

Braque, George. 1982. *New York Times*. October 10, Section 2, Arts and Leisure.

Bryan, John Morill. 1976. *Robert Mills Architect 1781–1855: An Unpublished Diary and Early Drawings, the Results of Recent Research*. Columbia, SC: Columbia Museum of Art.

Camus, Albert. 1991. *The Fall*. Translated by Justin O'Brien. New York: Vintage.

Chesterton, G. K. 1968. *What I Saw in America*, 2d ed. London: DaCapo Press.

Clapp, James A. 1984. *The City: A Dictionary of Quotable Thought on Cities and Urban Life*. New Brunswick, NJ: Rutgers University Press.

Cullen, Gordon. 1961. *Townscape*. London: Architectural Press.

Eco, Umberto. 1986. *Travels in Hyperreality*. Translated by William Weaver. San Diego, New York, London: Harcourt Brace & Company.

Ehrenhalt, Alan. 1995. *The Lost City*. New York: Basic Books.

Giedion, Sigfried. 1967. *Space, Time and Architecture: The Growth of a New Tradition*, 5th ed. Cambridge, MA: Harvard University Press.

Gosling, David, and Barry Maitland. 1984. *Concepts of Urban Design*. London: Academy Editions, and New York: St. Martin's Press.

Hale, Jonathan. 1994. *The Old Way of Seeing*. Boston, New York: Houghton Mifflin.

Hanna, Judith Lynne. Stripping the First Amendment and Corsetting the Striptease Dancer. forthcoming. *The Drama Review*.

Hughes, Robert. 1996. *The Shock of the New*. New York: Knopf.

Jacoby, Mary Moore, ed. 1994. *The Churches of Charleston and the Lowcountry*. Columbia: Preservation Society of Charleston, University of South Carolina Press.

Jencks, Charles. 1973. *Modern Movements in Architecture*. Garden City, NY: Anchor.

Kotkin, Joel. *Washington Post*. March 10, 1996. Outlook.

Kousoulas, Claudia D., and George W. Kousoulas 1995. *Contemporary Architecture in Washington, D.C.* New York: Preservation Press, Wiley.

Krier, Rob. 1979. *Urban Space*. New York: Rizzoli, and London: Academy Editions.

Krugman, Paul. 1996. White collars turn blue. *New York Times Magazine*. September 29.

Leiby, Richard. 1996. *Washington Post*. June 30, p. G1.

Maddex, Diane. 1973. Foreword to *Historic Buildings of Washington, D.C.,* by Arthur Cotton Moore. Pittsburgh: Ober Park Associates.

Maddex, Diane, ed. 1985. *Master Builders.* Washington, DC: Preservation Press, National Trust for Historic Preservation.

Marshall, Alex. 1996. Suburb in Disguise. *Metropolis,* July–August, p. 70.

McKenzie, Evan. 1994. *Privatopia: Homeowner Associations and the Rise of Residential Private Government.* New Haven, CT: Yale University Press.

Moore, Arthur Cotton. 1979. Adaptive Abuse. *Journal of the American Institute of Architects,* August.

Moore, Arthur Cotton. 1996. *Washington Post.* February 4, p. C8. Outlook.

Moore, Arthur Cotton. 1966. The Washington National Airport Boondoggle. *Washingtonian,* December.

Nagel, Thomas. 1979. *Mortal Questions.* Cambridge, UK: Cambridge University Press.

Nesbitt, Kate, ed. 1996. *Theorizing a New Agenda for Architecture: An Anthology of Architectural Theory, 1965–1995.* New York: Princeton Architectural Press.

O'Neill, Tip, and Gary Hymel. 1994. *All Politics Is Local and Other Rules of the Game.* New York: Times Books.

Peterson, Anne E. 1978. *Hornblower and Marshall Architects.* Washington, DC: Preservation Press, National Trust for Historic Preservation.

Petras, Ross, and Kathryn Petras. 1993. *The 776 Stupidest Things Ever Said.* New York: Doubleday.

Placzek, Adolf K., ed. 1982. *Macmillan Encyclopedia of Architects.* London: Free Press, Collier Macmillan.

Rogers, M. ed. *Contradictory Quotations.* Gunter Grass. From *The Penquin Dictionary of Twentieth Century Quotations,* 1993, Harmondsworth, England.

Roosevelt, Franklin D. 1933. *First Inaugural Address.* March 4.

Schlosser, Eric. 1997. The Business of Pornography. *U.S. News and World Report,* February 10.

Scott, Pamela, and Antoinette J. Lee. 1993. *Buildings of the District of Columbia.* New York: Oxford University Press.

Shawcross, Lord Hartley. 1963. "Sayings of the Week." *Observer.* November 17.

Smith, D. Mullett. 1990. *A. B. Mullett, His Relevance in American Architecture and Historic Preservation.* Washington, DC: Mullett-Smith Press.

Taylor, Gary. 1996. *Cultural Selection.* New York: Basic Books.

Venturi, Robert. 1977. *Complexity and Contradiction in Architecture.* New York: Museum of Modern Art.

Vergara, Camilo José. 1995. *The New American Ghetto.* New Brunswick, NJ: Rutgers University Press.

Wallace, Sarah L. 1972. *The Quarterly Journal of the Library of Congress,* 29(4).

Weeks, Christopher. 1994. *Guide to the Architecture of Washington, D.C.* Baltimore: Johns Hopkins University Press.

Wrenn, Tony P., and Elizabeth D. Mulloy. 1976. Foreword to *America's Forgotten Architecture* by James Biddle. New York: Pantheon, Toronto: Random House of Canada, National Trust for Historic Preservation.

Arthur Cotton Moore, FAIA is an national award-winning, internationally recognized architect and planner. Since 1965, he has practiced in 36 cities across the United States, and received over 70 Design Awards, including the AIA National Honor Award. His projects have been published in over 1,900 articles in magazines and newspapers throughout the world, and included in many books. He has traveled to, studied, and photographed architecture in 64 countries, and has lectured extensively at universities throughout the United States, including giving the 1982 Henry Hornbostel Lecture at Carnegie-Mellon University; in 1985, he gave a retrospective lecture on his work at the Hirshhorn Museum, marking the twentieth anniversary of his practice. Mr. Moore has served on design award juries throughout the country, including regional and state AIA programs, the AIA National Honor Award Program, and the Progressive Architecture Magazine Design Award Jury. He is one of 600 architects in the world (113 in America) included in *Contemporary Architects* which recognizes twentieth century architects on an international level. Mr. Moore had a solo gallery exhibition of paintings and furniture in New York in 1990, and subsequent solo exhibitions in Washington, Chicago, and Paris; he has participated in group painting shows in New York, Washington, and Cologne, Germany. His 1995 travelling museum exhibition, "Visions of the Future," was shown in museums in Prague and Poland. Mr. Moore is a sixth generation Washingtonian, a graduate of St. Albans School, Princeton University, and Princeton University School of Architecture. He lives with his wife, Patricia, in Washington, D.C. where he practices architecture, paints, and writes.